A PLUME BOOK

W9-BRM-510

YOU DESERVE A DRINK

Eric Michael Pearson

Modeling is tough.
To get ready for this shoot,
I didn't eat for, like, *two and
a half* hours.

MAMRIE HART grew up in the middle of nowhere North Carolina. She then hightailed it to New York to become a serious actress. Upon realizing that her face is made of rubber, she got into comedy. After years of bartending and performing live in New York basement theaters, she eventually found her own true home, the Internet, where she now resides. With that said, you can literally google anything about her. She also hates writing bios.

Praise for *You Deserve a Drink*

"I loved this book. Mamrie Hart is hilariously brilliant, and really puts things in perspective with *You Deserve a Drink*. Specifically that I do deserve a drink. And the only person I feel like having one with right now is her."
  —Judy Greer, actress and author of *I Don't Know What You Know Me From*

"You know that voice you have inside that tells you not to do certain things because they are reckless, embarrassing, or socially unacceptable? Mamrie

Hart does not have that voice. She does it all and tells it all in *You Deserve a Drink*."   —Rachel Dratch, SNL alum and author of *Girl Walks into a Bar*

"*You Deserve a Drink* is like a night out with Mamrie Hart: charmingly weird and hilariously memorable. All that's missing is the hangover."
                                        —Tyler Oakley, YouTube star

You Deserve a Drink

Boozy Misadventures and
Tales of Debauchery

MAMRIE HART

A PLUME BOOK

PLUME
An imprint of Penguin Random House LLC
375 Hudson Street
New York, New York 10014
penguin.com

LIBRARY OF CONGRESS CATALOGING-IN-PUBLICATION DATA
  Hart, Mamrie, 1983–
  You deserve a drink : boozy misadventures and tales of debauchery / Mamrie Hart.
    pages cm
    ISBN 978-0-14-218167-6
  1. Hart, Mamrie, 1983– 2. Actors—United States—Biography. 3. Entertainers—United States—Biography. 4. Drinking of alcoholic beverages—United States. I. Title.
  PN2287.H27A3 2015
  791.4302'8092—dc23   2015004927

Printed in the United States of America
10 9 8 7 6 5 4 3 2

Set in IT Esprit Book

Penguin is committed to publishing works of quality and integrity. In that spirit, we are proud to offer this book to our readers; however, the story, the experiences, and the words are the author's alone.

The recipes contained in this book are to be followed exactly as written. The Publisher is not responsible for your specific health or allergy needs that may require medical supervision. The Publisher is not responsible for any adverse reactions to the recipes contained in this book.

CONTENTS

FOREWORD

One humid summer night in Austin, Texas, Mamrie Hart and I spent an hour drunkenly arguing and openly crying on the street while wearing David Bowie– and Tina Turner–inspired wigs, butterfly eyelashes, and KEEP AUSTIN WEIRD tie-dyed T-shirts. Yes, we had been out at a bar dressed like that. Yes, the bartender bought us two-too-many shots. Yes, the jury's still out on whether that bartender thought we were reject prostitutes having an existential crisis. And yes, what we were actually arguing about was complete nonsense. But man did those giant orange butterfly wings superglued to Mamrie's eyelids hold up. The next morning we dragged our haggard bodies into our production van (we had been in the middle of filming a travel web series). When the crew left to get some coffee, we finally looked at each other and had this conversation:

"We cool?"

"Yeah, we're just idiots."

"Bloody Mary?"

"Dear God, *yes*."

And that was that. We were back.

That day it really hit me: A friendship with Mamrie Hart is a truly special thing. It's a friendship that, even in the seemingly difficult times, is abso-fucking-lutely ridiculous, in the best way possible. And that, plain and simple, is Mamrie's life.

We've been friends since 2007, where we met on our first sketch comedy team, Finger (pronounced Fing-uh, because we were *clearly hilarious*). One of the first sketches we performed was called "Party Starters," about two girls who start parties everywhere they go, even in inappropriate places (again, *hilarious*). But the core of that sketch has carried through to our friendship. Together we've been globe-trotters, meeting Mexican and American wrestlers, professional bull riders, spiritual healers, one-eyed mini ponies, a woman watching a Britney Spears concert through opera glasses . . . the list goes on. She's pushed a person out of a cab, screaming, "That's Brooklyn, bitch," at the end of a drunken night. She's shown me her blackjack skills while wearing a Snoop Dogg sweatshirt, sloshing a Lemon Drop martini, and flirting with a man to get a free electronic cigarette. She's made me a bra with removable airplane bottles. She's gotten me a green screen as a birthday present and wrapped it with DENTAL DAM written in huge letters across the outside. She's crashed on my couch and farted herself awake in the middle of the night. She's given me a handmade trophy to commemorate my excellent repression skills. She's voluntarily bought swamp suits, a blow-up doll, karate gis, pizza costumes, and an electronic inflatable penis costume for other live shows we've done. She's a special breed.

Needless to say I couldn't be more thankful to have this absurdly sweet, reincarnated-vaudevillian-entertainer-meets-DIY-driven-hillbilly-sass-factory in my life. And now she's created a book that lets you into hers. THANK GOD. Take it from someone who has watched her scoop room service lasagna off a carpeted hotel-room floor and eat it: None of what you're about to read is exaggerated, fabricated, or G-rated. But it is, like her, special.

—Grace Helbig, #1 *New York Times*
bestselling author of *Grace's Guide*

INTRODUCTION

I wrote a book, you guys. This is big. Anyone who knows me at all (and you certainly will by the end of this thing) knows that I don't even *read* books, let alone write them. Sure, I'll occasionally find myself perusing *Us Weekly*, or a lengthy takeout menu, or an ex-boyfriend's Facebook post about his new perfect family, but that's about it.

For those of you who randomly picked this up at Barnes & Noble,* allow me to tell you a little bit about myself. My name is Mamrie Hart and I wanted to write this paperweight to combine my two favorite things: delicious cocktails and embarrassing myself. 'Cause nothing goes together better than dirty martinis and queef stories. A duo for the ages.

In 2011, I created a show called *You Deserve a Drink*, which lives on the Internet.† Every week I make a custom cocktail in honor of whoever in pop culture I think needs one the most. After sitting down and putting these stories on paper, I realized the person who

---

*If you are just pretending to be interested in it so you can eventually drop a deuce in their bathroom, you're not fooling anyone!

†Did you know that spell-check makes you capitalize the word *Internet*? I'm sorry, Sir Internet, I didn't realize how formal we needed to be. I've surfed you while using my bare chest as a burrito plate, but I'll respect your new status position.

most deserves a drink in this book is *you*, the reader! It's gonna be a doozy, dudes. Why, you ask? Because . . . drumroll, please . . .

This book has a built-in drinking game!

Drinking games are a great way to rationalize excessive drinking, plus I selfishly want everyone to have a buzz so they think I'm a better writer than I actually am. The rules on my show are simple—drink every time I make a terrible pun—but that won't work here. I can't be responsible for alcohol poisoning of the literally *dozens* of people who will read this book. Instead, I came up with these rules.

Drink every time I . . .

1. reference an old television show;
2. talk about a food product that could be purchased at 7-Eleven;
3. use a slang term for a reproductive organ.

Turns out, you learn a lot about yourself when you write a book; and turns out, I talk about these three things incessantly. I don't think there's been a day in my adult life when I haven't discussed *Boy Meets World* (why did they make Eric so dumb in the last few seasons?) or at least mentioned nachos.

Another detail you will see scattered among these pages is the word *rutabaga*. No, you are not about to embark on a bio bender about root vegetables. *Rutabaga* is my safe word. Normally safe words are codes used during BDSM (hard-core sex stuff) that the submissive person can use when he/she isn't comfortable. Well, my safe word will be written every time I want my parents to stop reading that chapter. Part of me wishes I had said it before even writing the definition of *safe word*. I know my parents and other family members are going to read this book. It's inevitable. And they will be super proud. I'll be the goddamn Lady Gaga of this year's Thanksgiving!

Sorry, Aunt Debbie, I cannot take the stuffing out of the oven. I can't risk a thumb burn when I have to autograph books next month.

But there are a few tales that my relatives might not want burned into their brains. I figured a safe word would be a good way to prevent future therapy costs, and so they don't "turnip" their noses at me come Turkey Day . . . 'cause rutabagas are turnips (more highbrow classic jokes like that in the pages ahead).

Now that all the rules are in play, let's do this thing. Let's read a fucking book, you guys! You could be reading this on the beach and quietly wondering how, exactly, to get that sand out of *there*, or be by yourself at a bar while you wait for a blind date and want to avoid having conversation with the people around you.* Whatever the circumstances, I hope you have a good time reading it. I had a great time writing it. And with that . . .

Full House, Flamin' Hot Cheetos, and *Chubby Cubbies*. Drink, mothafuckas!

---

*Or still casually trying to take that shit in the bookstore. Honestly, buddy, just go. No one is paying that much attention to you. Drop the ego.

Bad Apple

1½ oz Calvados or other apple brandy
1½ oz vodka
2 oz fresh apple cider
½ oz ginger liqueur

Put everything in a shaker of ice and go to town. Strain into a martini glass. Garnish with a slice of apple, or if you want to be really bad, dip the rim in that delicious caramel dip they stock in the produce department.

I need everyone to sit down right now, because what I am about to say might shock you to the core. Although I am one of the most elegant, refined women you will ever have the pleasure of meeting, truth be told, I have had some pretty ridiculous hangovers in my day. If I had a nickel for every time I've had a hangover, I would've already paid a group of top scientists to find a cure.

The worst hangover I've ever experienced came the morning after my first night living in New York City. The year was 2005. By some grace of God, I had actually graduated from college, and rather than use my diploma for rolling papers (which I'd threatened to do on many occasions), I was going to use that theater degree for good. I was going to be a serious actress.

I won't lie to you. I was nervous. But to have a career in acting, it would have to be either L.A. or NYC. Moving to L.A. would've been easier for me because I had the built-in safety net of my dad and stepmom living there. In L.A., the crime was lower and the

Yes, this girl right here was going to be serious. Mind you, this is my official graduation photo. Everyone else looks poised and ready to take on adulthood. (I, on the other hand, had slept thirty minutes and had cran-grape and vodka in my purse.)

~~tits~~ temps were higher. But if I was going to be the next Meryl Streep, I needed to toughen up. I needed to dig deep and experience *struggle*. The most I struggled in college was when the Papa John's delivery guy would forget the garlic sauce.

I got off my flight from North Carolina, full of hope and a twelve-dollar bag of Chex Mix.* I was ready to take the city by storm, and also mace anyone who came near me. This was 2005, people. Sure, it wasn't 1980s "let's all pretend there isn't a corpse in our subway car" Brooklyn, but it also wasn't the Brooklyn that shows like *Girls* have depicted. Nowadays if you live in Brooklyn,

---

*"What's the deal with airplane snack prices? I know we are twenty thousand feet in the air, but does that mean the prices have to skyrocket?"
—my Jerry Seinfeld impression

your biggest danger is a rent hike when a specialty pickle shop opens next door.

I came prepared to take down anyone who walked too close behind me. I didn't care if you were benignly looking at my purse because you noticed the tag read CUCCI instead of GUCCI; I'd already have one hand on my mace, the other hand on my scarf to choke you out if I needed to. And I wasn't just prepared for an attack on the streets. I was always conjuring up new scenarios to protect myself in my apartment too. Every night before tucking myself into sleepy time, I would make a game plan in case someone broke in. Bubble Wrap right inside the door will sound like gunshots when they step on it! My landlord probably wouldn't be stoked if I spread tar all over my stairs, but maybe I could get away with wads of gum. I was apparently banking on these intruders being the "Wet Bandits" from *Home Alone*.

Luckily, I didn't have to face the Big Bad Apple by myself. I was moving into an apartment with my friend Kat, whom I had been a camp counselor with a year before. I knew from our summer together that if Kat was one thing, it was fun! No chance of a boring roommate there. But to be honest, I was a little anxious about the whole living-with-each-other scenario. Being roommates with someone in a new city is a lot different from being pals in the carefree world of swimming and s'mores. We had hung out on days off, getting ridiculously drunk together and acting like fools, but this was the *real* world. Was Kat going to stop being polite and start getting real?

Truth be told, the only time we'd ever gotten together during the off-season, she ended up wrecking my car. But she paid for it without question! And, sure, there was talk that she didn't actually leave camp of her own accord but was fired for bringing weed on a campout. But I had no confirmation if that rumor was truemor, and surely someone wouldn't be *that* stupid! So I suppressed my nerves and told myself that my new roommate situation was going to be ideal.

I got off the subway at Prospect Avenue in Brooklyn, fully expecting the streets to be covered in chalk outlines and to see rats building nests out of used syringes. Turns out, my street looked like an establishing shot from *The Cosby Show*. The streets had rows and rows of brownstones with big stoops and flower boxes under windows. The only chalk on the sidewalks was for hopscotch. And if there were rats, they were probably the cute puppet ones from *The Muppet Show*. I loosened my grip on my mace as Kat ran up to me, waving.

"Welcome to New York!" she said, wrapping me in a big hug and helping me with my duffel bag. Kat was classically beautiful. She had jet-black hair and fair skin, very 1940s glamour. She was twenty-seven to my twenty-two *and* she wore a leather jacket, so I inevitably felt like a fetus with eyeliner in comparison.

"Kat! Thank God! I was so worried, but this neighborhood is straight out of a magazine! I can't wait to see our place."

She breathed in sharply. "So, there's been a *little* change of plans."

Oh Jesus, I thought to myself. *We're going to be homeless. I am going to have to sell my body on the streets, and I'm so out of shape right now that to make any money I'll have to do a BOGO deal. Or maybe a punch card system . . .*

"They have to fix a couple more things in our place, so it won't be ready for a few days."

A few days?! I didn't have any money for a hotel. Kat found a place that was eight hundred dollars each a month, and after the security deposit and insane broker fee, I was moving to New York with three hundred bucks to my name. I imagined myself staying in a shelter, finally breaking out all the knowledge I had held on to from the film *Curly Sue*. Before I could ask Kat how smooth her sleight of hand was, she eased my worries.

"I already told my friend Maegan that you were coming. I've been staying with her the past month. It's right up this block." I followed Kat, a little nervous about invading a complete stranger's place.

"Relax, we've been best friends since we were five. She's totally cool with you crashing in the living room with me," Kat said, trying to reassure me. *Sure*, I thought to myself. *Having someone you've known since kindergarten stay with you is one thing, but some rando with her cherry-print duffel bag and three-days-without-a-shower greasy head is another.*

"Honey, we're home!" Kat called as we walked up the stairs. Maegan appeared at the front door wearing a 1982 Van Halen Hide Your Sheep Tour T-shirt and cutoff jean shorts, and she had on the exact knee-high gladiator sandals that I had been coveting all summer but had worried would make my calves look like a tray of yeast rolls at Golden Corral. She had wild, curly red hair that stuck out everywhere, kind of like Dana at the end of *Ghostbusters*, when you can't tell if she's about to fuck Bill Murray or wear him as a skin suit. Simply put, Maegan's look was on point.

"It's so nice to meet you! Welcome!" she said as she ushered us into her apartment. It was decked out in the raddest vintage shit I'd ever seen. There was a light-up sign that read DISCO hanging above her bed, and the headboard was made out of a refurbished dashboard, complete with an 8-track player. Maegan grabbed me a Corona while Kat was fixing herself a tequila and orange juice.

"Starting early on the tequila, I see," Maegan called to Kat in the kitchen, then turned to me. "I have that shirt!"

I looked down at my 1983 Kenny Rogers Jovan Musk Tour tee. While I was in shock from the coincidence, she kept going like she had just pointed out a mass-produced tunic we'd both gotten from Target.

"Are you coming to the show with us?" she asked.

"What show?"

"I wanted it to be a surprise!" Kat said, pouring more tequila into her cup. The tequila looked like one of those optical illusion faucet fountains you buy from SkyMall that never stop pouring. "We're seeing the Pixies at Coney Island tonight!"

"Seriously?!" I jumped up, spilling a little Corona on Maegan's pristine midcentury modern couch.

"Oh my god, I'm so sorry," I apologized. Great. First ten minutes at this girl's place and I was already wrecking the joint.

She walked over and wiped it with her hand. "Don't worry about it. Kat spilled an entire bowl of beans and rice on it two nights ago."

Look at me, I thought. *One hour in New York and I've already got these hip-ass adult friends and am going to a show?* Granted, the only song I could name of the Pixies was the one that went, "Uh-huh . . . I got a broken face," but I knew it was going to be fun. I also knew they had an album called *Surfer Rosa,* because I pointed out the cassette tape in a boy's car in high school once and he said, "You like the Pixies?" and I was all like, "Yeah, I love them" (totally lying), and he was all like, "What's your favorite album?" and I was all like, "I think I just started my period. Please take me home."*

The rest of the afternoon was spent drinking Coronas on the stoop with Maegan and her boyfriend, Doug. Maegan had already been living in New York for a year and was armed with loads of advice. I was relieved. I was worried that everyone was going to be too cool for school, but she was so nice. I could already see us becoming good friends.

A few hours later, the four of us crammed into a beat-up gypsy cab and rode down to Coney. I had never used a car service before and felt so fancy! Sure, the guy had twelve tiny pine tree air fresheners hanging from his rearview, and I was sitting on someone's leftover pizza crust, but it wasn't a boring old yellow taxi. After twenty minutes in the car, we were dropped off in front of a Nathan's hot dogs. Stepping out of that old Crown Victoria, I (naturally) immediately stepped in dog shit, but I felt like ScarJo being dropped off at the Oscars.

We got to the venue just as the sun was setting. With the pink sky, ocean, and old amusement park rides behind the stage, I

---

*Don't you miss the days when you could get out of anything by mentioning your period? It's like boys in high school confuse the menstrual cycle with leprosy.

couldn't believe I was finally here. It was the perfect backdrop to start this new chapter of my life. I felt like this moment called for a cheers.

"I'm gonna go grab a drink—you want anything?" I asked Kat as she puffed on a one hitter painted to look like a cigarette.

"Beers are going to be, like, twenty bucks. I came prepared." She reached into her huge purse and pulled out, no lie, an entire carton of orange juice. "It's half OJ, half tequila." How she got that past security, I have no idea. Her bag was like Mary Poppins's for hot messes. Mary Pill Poppins.*

I started to tell her that I'm just one of those people who can't drink tequila, but I stopped myself. I had three hundred dollars to my name and no job. If someone was offering me a way to get drunk, I needed to take it.

I took a big gulp from the carton, already planning a lie about having diabetes if a security guard approached us. I had no problem breaking out the fake seizure from my high school production of *Steel Magnolias*. It always worked when I wanted to get a free glass of juice at brunch. Once the OJ-tequila combo hit my lips, I realized Kat was terrible at ratios.

"Jesus, I know he got away with murdering his wife and all, but what's your problem with OJ?" I asked.

Before Kat could ~~judge~~ laugh at my hilarious joke, the music started and the massive crowd went nuts. Well, as nuts as you can for a group of thirty-five-year-olds about to listen to alternative noise rock.

For the next two hours, I helped Kat finish that carton. The sun set and we lost track of Maegan and her boyfriend, but Kat didn't seem to be worried. The Pixies played songs about everything from Salvador Dalí to scuba diving. I mouthed along to the lyrics I didn't know, Oprah-style. Seriously, if you never noticed this while Oprah

---

*If this is not already a drag queen's name, you guys need to step up your game.

was still on the air, do yourself a favor and find some old episodes. Lady Winfrey never knew the damn words to any of her guests' songs. And I'm not just talking about when a new artist would come on who Oprah had to pretend to give a shit about. I'm talking when she would introduce Tina Turner singing "Proud Mary." Tina would be tearing it up to this classic tune, and then when the camera panned to O, she would be mouthing, "Loud Harry keeps on yearning . . . and we're bowling, bowling!" Oprah had her favorite things, and, well, that was my favorite thing of Oprah's.

I got drunk enough to stop even trying to be into it and instead spied on all the thirtysomething hipsters trying to get fucked up while also balancing their new responsibilities. I took in a lot of conversations that went something like this:

Hey babe, if I take half of another Ecstasy, will I be normal around the sitter in three hours?

Yeah, babe. But just remember tomorrow morning we have Daphne's couples baby yoga graduation and then Conner's prohibition BBQ.

When the concert wrapped up, we found Maegan and Doug. I was pretty drunk at this point, but I could tell that Maegan wasn't in the great mood that she'd been in on the ride here. Kat didn't seem to care, though.

"We should all go into the city and do karaoke!" Kat said, pumping her fist.

I full-on squealed at this idea. I love—I love, love, *love* karaoke. I don't care if I'm staying by myself in a Holiday Inn; if the hotel bar has karaoke, I'm there. I will shamelessly sing "It's Raining Men," complete with jazz runs through the crowd to a roomful of strangers. If this was what life in New York was going to be like, I was going to be kara-okay with it.

"I think we are going to sit this one out," Maegan said. "But y'all have fun."

I was sad she wasn't coming, but I could tell something was off. Maybe she and her boyfriend were fighting. I gave her a big hug.

"Thank you for being hospitable," I slurred in her face, literally spitting on the *spit* part of the word.

And with that, Kat and I started our vocal warm-ups and headed to the train. Now, a train all the way from Coney Island to the East Village can take anywhere from forty-five minutes to seven days. To pass the time, I pretended to pole dance on the train poles, which is a total rookie move. You can always tell tourists in New York by three things: (1) they are standing in front of the Empire State Building trying to decide if Earlybird or Valencia is a better filter for their Instagram; (2) they think it's worth it to wait in an hour-long line for Magnolia Bakery cupcakes; and (3) they think they are the first people to pretend the poles on subway trains are stripper poles. Kat beatboxed as I put on my best sultry face and swung around, completely falling on my ass.

Later that year I would try pole dancing again, and the results would be even more embarrassing. I know we have karaoke to get to, but this is worth a tangent, trust me.

A friend of mine from college, Sean, had taken a job producing one of those terrible "We've Got Three Dozen Kids" shows as soon as we'd graduated. Although being surrounded by an army of Christian values and perms left over from '94 sounded like hell, he was making a serious paycheck nine months out of college, while I still considered a fine meal wandering around Whole Foods stuffing my face with free samples. He came to visit New York one night and was ready to spend some of that hard-earned Christian scrilla. He had been kind of a nerd in college, so I knew he was going to be peacocking.

I met a very drunk Sean at a bar in the East Village, along with a few of his friends whom I didn't know, but they seemed nice. We drank a ridiculous amount of champagne, vodka, and whatever else we could form the words to order. After several hours of imbibing, Sean got an idea to keep the party moving.

"Let's go to the strip club. I'll buy everyone lap dances."

Brilliant idea! *Look at me, chugging champagne and getting lap dances paid for on a random Monday night. I am the white female P. Diddy!* I thought to myself. I was two seconds from starting my own clothing line (instead of Sean John, it would be called On the John), feeling completely pimp. Until then, I'd only "made it rain" with IOU slips. I felt like my baller status was at an all-time high— that is, until we arrived at the *actual* strip club around three a.m.

Sapphire, conveniently located under the Queensboro Bridge, was the saddest thing I had seen since I caught my high school history teacher crying by himself during *Titanic* as I waited to sweep the theater. I had expected to roll into a place with crazy lights and lots of bass pumping through the speakers—basically, I was expecting a live Rihanna video. Instead, we walked into a room where one dude was getting a subpar lap dance as eight other strippers counted down the minutes until they could go home. It was clear to me why they had named this place Sapphire, because it was making me blue.

We took our seats in this den of sadness, and you could almost hear the collective groan from the strippers in the back. I couldn't blame them. I myself have never worked as an exotic dancer, but I have worked in many restaurants; and when you are just about to close and a party of ten rolls in, it fuckin' sucks. That leftover pizza in your fridge and DVR'd *Say Yes to the Dress* are gonna have to wait, because you're stuck for another two hours. I think I even mouthed, "I'm sorry," to the really tired-looking ones as we walked to find a table. It wasn't so much finding a table as deciding which one to take in this completely empty strip club.

I went to the bathroom to give myself a wasted-face pep talk. This usually involved a lot of slurring, "You got dis, bitch," into the mirror and a lot of emphatic hand gestures. (Note to self: Always check to make sure someone isn't trying to take a dump in one of the stalls as you are screaming, "Shut up, you're beautiful!" to yourself.)

I had gotten to the point in my pep talk where I almost aggressively fist-bumped my reflection (before remembering it was a mirror and that would severely hurt me) when one of the exhausted strippers walked in. I curtsied and went back to the table. When I got there, I found the only other girl in the group sitting by herself.

"Where is everybody?"

"They ditched us girls to go get private dances. Sean left us his credit card to get drinks, though."

The music must've been super loud, because all I heard was, "Sean said to do a bunch of Patrón shots and pop a bottle of Moët and Chandon," which is exactly what we did. Just two women who had never met, sitting in a flypaper of a strip club at closing time on a Monday, taking shots and putting money in thongs as we talked to the strippers. And not to knock these ladies, but they really weren't working it. This wasn't the type of place where someone could argue, "She holds up her own body weight upside down, then does eight spins. This isn't just stripping; it's athleticism!" Or a place like the one in *Flashdance*, where your artistic expression is just as valued as your ta-tas. The closest these women came to artistic expression was the "in memory of" tattoos on their shoulder blades.* Their dance moves made them look like C-3PO in drag.

The few times I've been to strip clubs, I've sat there and tried to enjoy myself even though I really would rather have asked the strippers about their young sons' reading levels or told them why they should go back to cosmetology school. But I couldn't just sit back and watch this sad display at Sapphire. I was the white female P. Diddy, after all! I wasn't going to have my ticket punched on the lame train. It was time to board the Hot Mess Express. So, I took matters into my own hands.

Before you could say "terrible decision," I climbed up onstage and was knocking on the window of the DJ booth. I slurred to the DJ to play "Poison," by Bell Biv DeVoe, one of the all-time greatest songs in history.

The beat dropped and so did all of my inhibitions. I started *own-*

---

*You know the ones. They're meant to honor late cousin Melody, but poor Melody ends up looking like Steve Buscemi.

ing that stage. I'm talking medium-level kicks, almost-splits—all of my signature moves. At this point the strippers had sat down and were watching *me*. The poor girl I was there with appeared to be awkwardly clapping, though she might've just been trying to swat gnats away from our Moët. I waited for the chorus to kick in as I slowly sauntered to the pole.

At the sound of "That girl is poisooooon," I started spinning on the pole. And as soon as I did, my right contact lens went flying out of my eye. Mind you, I am legally blind, so I can't see *shit* without contacts, let alone spin around and do tricks. So there I was, on all fours on Sapphire's stage, looking for a contact. Just as I found the thing and held it up in triumph, one of the dancers grabbed the contact and threw it as hard as she could,* like a grenade about to detonate. She looked me square in the good eye and said, "Honey, unless you want some random coochie juice in your eyeball, you gotta let that thing go." I can't thank you enough for that advice, Cinnamon. I really hope she went back and got her final perm credits.

Worth the diversion, right? Okay, back to the scene with Kat! There I was, lying on the floor of a subway car in the same spot a homeless man had probably masturbated to an Archie comic. But at least I had both contacts in. My vision was only obscured by that half bottle of tequila. My eyesight was 20/90-proof.

During our trip, Kat and I reminisced about our summer at camp together.

"Remember that time you drank absinthe at Chrissie's lake house and refused to take off that bonnet all night?"

"Oh God," I slurred, "don't remind me. I have so many pictures of me looking like Little House on the Scary. Change of subject. What the *hell* have you been up to since you got here?"

---

*Which wasn't very far, because it's a contact lens; it weighs nothing. But in my drunken mind, she threw it so hard that it blew the toupee off the bartender.

Turns out that despite her current habit of drinking tequila out of a Tropicana carton, Kat seemed to have her shit together. Her friend had gotten her a job at a recording studio, and she was full of weird celebrity-interaction stories.* Once we hit our stop, we chucked the empty OJ carton in the trash and stumbled into the karaoke bar. Kat beelined to the bar and gave the bartender a smooch on the cheek. She waved to a few other people in the bar and headed back our way with martinis. "These were on the house," she said, winking. *Dayum!* I thought to myself. Kat had covered some ground in the past month.

As they usually do after half a fifth of tequila and martinis, the night got blurry from there. I remember a lot of sweaty dancing, doing sake bombs with some Japanese businessmen, and telling a guy he was attractive in a Bob Ross kind of way.

One thing I do remember perfectly clear is when I finally got my name called to sing. Well, not *my* name, exactly. They called out the name Chauncy, which is my karaoke stage name. Look, when you rock the mic as hard as I do, you need a little obscurity.

I chose the song "Kiss," by Prince, and went full-force with it, telling the group of sake bombers that they didn't need to be beautiful to turn me on. I pointed at Bob Ross to let him know there wasn't a particular sign I was more compatible with. When the last lyric flashed across the screen, I sold it. "I just want your extra time and your"—I shook my ass so hard on that guitar riff, then jumped up and landed in a split—"*kiss!*"

I assumed it was followed by a WELCOME TO NYC, MAMRIE! banner dropping from the rafters and the businessmen hoisting me up on their shoulders as people clamored to shake my hand, but I can't be too sure. Why, you ask? Because I blacked da fuck out.

To this day, I have no idea how we got back to Maegan's place.

---

*I would later work at the same place and witness Stevie Wonder dominating at air hockey, if that gives you any indication of the awesomeness of these stories.

All I know is that I woke up with Andy Capp's Hot Fries in my hair, and it felt like there was a Vine of Mariah Carey hitting her highest note on a loop in my brain. I thought I was alone, but then I heard Maegan and Kat in the bedroom talking tensely. I could tell they were trying to keep it down, but French doors don't really lock in sound like they used to. After I unsuccessfully tried to eavesdrop, Maegan came out, looking totally put together. She had on another awesome vintage rocker tee covered with a blazer. I was still in my Kenny Rogers shirt and . . . yep, no pants.

"Sounds like you guys had fun last night!" she said, smiling. Kat, not saying anything, walked to the bathroom and started the shower. As awkward as I felt about the situation, I had just spent thousands on a theater degree and I was going to act cool about it, dammit. My first NYC acting gig!

"Totally! Thanks for—" I stopped myself, slapping my hand over my mouth. Something felt different. I swirled my tongue around my mouth faster than Joey Newman did at the Christmas dance in seventh grade. It was then that I realized what had happened.

"Holy. Shit."

"What's wrong?"

"No, no, no, no, no." I grabbed a compact out of my purse and smiled into my reflection. "I chipped my front tooth last night! I fucking chipped my tooth."

I must've hit myself with the mic when I went for the split. To be honest, it wasn't that noticeable to the eye, but it felt like such a difference in my mouth. I couldn't stop running my tongue over it. It was like when you finally get your braces off and your teeth feel like glass, or like a hockey rink freshly slicked by a Zamboni.

Maegan went in close to my mouth to check out the damage, which was a risky move considering the rogue Hot Fries. She shook her head, laughing. "I did keep hearing you drunk singing, 'Uh-huh! I got a broken face!' over and over again when you came in."

I cleared my throat. "Hey, I'm really sorry if we were loud coming in last night." I could tell by Maegan's expression that this apology was warranted. "I swear I'm not normally a huge tequila mess. Just, first night and all . . ." My voice trailed off. I was nervous. Here was this girl I could see myself being really good friends with, and I'd given her the worst first impression. This wasn't how I was picturing the adult version of me to be. If I was Maegan, I don't know if I'd even be speaking to this slug of human pantslessness.

"Totally get it," she said as she stood up. "Do me a favor, though, and make sure Kat actually comes into work today. She wants to call out sick, but we are really busy and I know she's just hungover, ya know?"

"Sure thing," I said, the reality hitting me square in the face. Not only were they coworkers; I realized that this Maegan was the same *Maegan who was Kat's boss.*

"Oh, and tell her to not roll in wearing sunglasses." Maegan smiled and left for the day.

Just when I'd recovered from the first slap of reality, the other hand bitch-slapped me into clarity. Maegan hadn't gotten into a fight with her boyfriend. After a month of Kat staying in the living room, Maegan was ready for Kat to move out so she could actually have some time to herself in her own apartment. Our apartment not being ready was the worst for Maegan, and I would soon see why.

While that first night was one for the books (literally; I am writing about it in a book right now), I knew I had to get my shit together. Kat? Not so much. She wanted a Dewey Decimal System of blackout nights. She bounced from job to job. She rarely came home, and when she did, she was never alone. She didn't bat an eye leaving a random one-night stand in our apartment while I was still sleeping, only to have said dude walk in on me eating Froot Loops topless 'cause I thought I was home alone.*

I lived with Kat for five months. I remember one night Kat and

---

*It happened. It was the beginning of the end.

I got into an argument, maybe a week before I told her I was moving out. During it, she said, "You were fun at camp. Why are you so boring now?" That's when I was officially over it.

I was busting my ass, working fifty to sixty hours a week just to make rent, going on any terrible audition that would see me. I didn't need to be around someone who only wanted me to be the most irresponsible version of myself. I didn't need someone encouraging me to be a total wastoid so they'd feel better about their mistakes. I can be a total wastoid of my own accord, thank you very much! Speaking of my own accord, she had crashed my Honda Accord a year before and brushed it off! Why hadn't I trusted my intuition?

If I was going to be an actual functioning adult,* I knew I needed to surround myself with supportive friends. Friends should be like a good bra, lifting you up. Bad friends are like sports bras. They can do wonders when you go out dancing or during high-energy times, but on a day-to-day basis they really just smush down some of your greatest assets.

Side note: If Cracker Barrel is hiring a woman to create phrases for its new apron line, get in touch.

There is one awesome thing that came out of that awkward first roommate situation: the beginning of a long friendship with Maegan. Little did I know I'd end up living in the apartment where I discovered my chipped tooth for five years. Nine years later, I slept on her couch in New York for a week as I tried to convince someone to publish this book. One of these days, I'll stop crashing on her couch . . . or at least quit spilling things on it. #sorryaboutthe lasagna

As for Kat? Well, Kat's time in New York ended shortly after I moved out.

She realized the city was a bit much for her and got the hell out.

---

*One who drinks too much, and gets around, and makes mistakes . . . but an adult nonetheless!

I found out via Facebook stalking that she went to nursing school and is working as a nurse, with an adorable little boy and a husband.

Here's what I learned about living in the Big Apple. (And don't worry—this book isn't all life lessons and hidden meanings. I just had to kick it off with a little credibility before I throw in the naked pudding-wrestling story. . . . Kidding! Or am I?) You can carry a pony keg of pepper spray with you at all times; put as many thumbtacks on your doorbell as you see fit. But at the end of the day, sometimes the person you've got to protect yourself from the most is *yourself.*

Oh, and for the love of God, avoid having roommates at all costs.

Here's us, years later, at Maegan's birthday. I had come a long way since that first night. Put together, no tooth chipping, and I only drank half a bottle of tequila that night. #growingup

Key Lime Crime

2 oz vanilla vodka
Juice of 3 key limes (or 1 big juicy lime if you
can't find key limes)
2 oz pineapple juice
Splash cream (or nondairy equivalent)
Crushed graham crackers for the rim
Simple syrup for the graham crackers to stick to
the rim

Combine all but the last two ingredients in a shaker with ice, shake them up, and strain into a martini glass. If you are feeling crazy, substitute a scoop of ice cream and some ice for the cream and blend dat shit! For the rim job (first rim job joke of the book!) wet the rim of your glass with the simple syrup, then dip it in the crushed graham crackers. A drink and a snack!

You can sub any type of milk for the cream for a lighter result. I prefer to use soy creamer because I am lactose intolerant; my "lighter result" would be me lighting farts on fire if I used real cream.

Hold on to your titties, gals, 'cause this chapter is about spring break! Ah yes, spring break. The annual gathering in warm climates where college students come together to bump *their* warm climates. The breaking of the (cheap motel bed) springs. It is depicted in movies and on TV as a raucous free-for-all of SPF and STDs. But speaking from my own experience, IT IS ALL OF THOSE THINGS.

Spring break is designed to let college students blow off some steam after a few stressful weeks of cramming for midterms. Or at least that's what I hear. Fact is, I spent most of my senior year sitting in my front yard with a cooler of beer and a sign that read YOU HONK, WE DRINK. If you've never tried it before, you should. It's one of my top ten ways to get day-drunk. The rules are pretty self-explanatory: Someone honks, you drink. And if you get a cop to honk or light up their siren, you shotgun a beer.

During most of my college career, my blood alcohol level was higher than my GPA. I am not proud of this fact. Sure, I ended up graduating with a double major, but Lord knows the knowledge retained from those four years is sparse. If I could do it all over again, would I have gone to class more? You're damn right, I (*probably*) would have. The fact is, I am writing this book right now because of the career I have built on drinking. . . . So . . . eat shit, student-loan debt!

Anyway, back to le break. My three friends and I decided that we would be super classy and head to Key West that year. We were all finally twenty-one at that point and didn't have to go all the way to the Bahamas or international waters to drink legally. So, we headed south. We decided to take my friend Melissa's car because, duh, she had a convertible. But convertibles don't have a hell of a lot of trunk space. Try cramming it full of four girls' duffel bags, each overstuffed with bikinis and condoms, and your roommate Erika's "just in case" chocolate fondue fountain, and shit gets real.

I decide to take one for the team by packing light. This meant a small backpack filled with one pair of jean shorts, one jean skirt (it was 2005, don't judge me), and five white ribbed Hanes His Way tank tops. Or wifebeaters, as we so eloquently call them in the South. I went to a craft store earlier that week, bought iron-on letters, and decked each tank out with "Day One," "Day Two," right through to "Day Five." I figured it would save me the trouble of having to decide what to wear every night after a long day of drinking in the sun. And—I'd be able to see the slow deterioration of my condition throughout the week. For example:

FRIEND
(looking at my spring break pics)
Why are you covered in scratches, with a Corona bucket on
your head, French-kissing a stray cat?

ME
(points to chest)
It was Day Four.

FRIEND
Yeah, but that still doesn't—

ME
I said, *Day Four*!

See? Brilliant.

*Censor bar added because apparently Day 3 is when I
decided that bras were unnecessary. And if you've ever
worn a Hanes wifebeater, you know they're as thin as
Prince William's hair.*

With the car packed up, all we had to do was just get there. The drive from Chapel Hill, North Carolina, to Key West, Florida, is about twenty hours. This meant someone was going to be stuck with the dreaded two a.m. to nine a.m. shift of driving. Because I am an insomniac, I was given the honor. Let me paint a picture for you. There's a purple Volvo convertible speeding down I-95. Inside are three sleeping girls, as a fourth chain-smokes with a two-liter of Mountain Dew between her legs, singing every word of Nelly Furtado's first album.

But having the dreaded shift allowed me to wake up my friends in style. As soon as I saw the WELCOME TO THE FLORIDA KEYS sign, I cranked up the song "Kokomo" and opened up the convertible. The sun was rising over the crystal-blue water, and we sang along with the Beach Boys. Everything was majestic . . . until we realized we were still three hours away and were at a traffic standstill. The lyrics "We'll get there fast and then we'll take it slow" had never rung truer.

Now, you would think four girls ready to party would book a room right in the center of town, hoping for their hotel to be packed full of hotties with bodies. Cuties with booties. Wrecks with pecks. One-night flings with ding-a-lings. Menaces with penises? Ok, I'm out.

Regardless, that was not our style. We booked a room at the Atlantic Shores, the clothing-optional gay resort on the edge of town. This might seem like a strange choice, but let me break it down for you.

Q: What looks tacky when you're rocking a mid-2000s bandeau top (besides said mid-2000s bandeau top)?
A: Tan lines. Can't get tan lines if you don't have to wear a bathing suit.

Q: What is the last thing you feel like doing when you are hungover as fuck?
A: Sucking in your stomach. No need to hold in the Corn Nuts gut you acquired on your twenty-hour drive. Those old gay

men weren't going to do a double take on your body unless
you had a birthmark that was the spitting image of
Streisand.

We took a spin around the grounds, which looked like any average roadside beach motel. Honestly, besides the dicks, it could've
been a Motel 6. It made me wonder how many unassuming couples checked in to this hotel not knowing what they were getting
themselves into. I could just picture it:

*Barbara, start the Volvo. This place is a sin inferno . . . a sinferno!
Barb, did you hear that? I made a pun!*

(Cut to Barb with her jaw on the floor as a naked man walks by.)

Despite its family-friendly facade, the real action happened at
the infamous pool. Ah, the pool.

The best part about staying at the Atlantic Shores, besides the
lack of shame, was the pool—specifically, the pool bar. The angel
on the snack bar microphone would call out people's orders in his
best Kathleen Turner impression. You'd hear, "Jeff? I have one big,
juicy sausage ready for Jeff at the snack bar. Jeff, this wiener is
getting cold. Get your ass down here, Jeff."

We ate the hell out of that snack bar. I distinctly remember
dropping ketchup on my bare chest, using a fry to wipe it off, then
eating that fry. And no one batted an eyelash. The only time our
naked existence was even acknowledged was when one old bear
came up to my friend Kirby and said, "Damn, girl, you are whiter
than a refrigerator." To be fair, Kirby makes *me* look tan, and I
look like I was raised in a cave.

The Shores was built on a rocky edge of the water, so there was
no beach. The pool was actually built on a dock, with a fence to
protect it from peepers. However, the fence wasn't *that* tall. Occasionally, you'd stand up to stretch your back and hear cheering,
only to see a wall of dude bros at the neighboring hotel. They literally would just be waiting, beers in hand, like they were tailgating
at a NASCAR race. This doesn't seem that weird until you remem-

ber that we were the only girls there. Surely they weren't constantly hawking that fence on the chance of seeing, at most, eight pale boobs. These frat bros were peeping at a nudist gay resort. Fraternity homoeroticism at its finest.

While the days were spent poolside, the nights were out on the town on the main drag of Duval Street. It's what you would expect from the Florida Keys. Everything is low-key and people crack open their first beer way before noon. It's basically the incarnation of a Jimmy Buffett song, which makes sense because he lived there for many years, and it's where he opened his first Margaritaville restaurant.*

Now, I can totally handle a place having a Jimmy Buffett vibe to it, but I can't really handle the amount of *actual* Jimmy Buffett they play in the bars. I sincerely believe that is why everyone drinks so much there—to deal with the constant parrot-head soundtrack.

Side note: I dated a baseball player for most of high school, and one year he had a superstition that before every game he had to eat grilled salmon and listen to Buffett's entire *Son of a Son of a Sailor* album. This was a very difficult spring. Although, it could've been worse. He could've had one of those superstitions about wearing the same gross-ass pair of underwear all season. But, I'm not judging. I have my own superstition. It's simple. In order to have a happy life, all I've got to do is *not date athletes.*

The day came to finally put on my "Day Five" shirt. Here it is, the finale of spring break, and I haven't so much as made out with anything. I know this is shocking considering the accommodations I chose, but still. I couldn't go back to North Carolina with my only mistake being that knee-length jean skirt (again, 2005, people).

We each shelled out twenty dollars to go to a foam party. How my friends dragged me into it, I'll never know (but Jägermeister might). I don't like being in things I can't see the bottom of. I don't

---

*The fact that Jimmy Buffett doesn't have a restaurant named "Jimmy Buffett's Buffet" is one of the world's greatest pun travesties.

swim in water that isn't completely clear. This foam party was the adult version of those circumstances. And no amount of soap bubbles can clean what I imagine was on the bottom of that club floor. I lasted five minutes in that bubble bath of bodily fluids.

We left and went to a bar on Duval. It was then that I fell in love . . . with the fabulous, gay bartender. You would've thought he was John Waters seeing Divine for the first time. He bought my girls and me two too many shots, and even sent us up to the private roof bar. He might have vaguely looked like Freddie Mercury, but that night, I was his Queen. I was his Fat Bottomed Girl. I was not telling these types of bad jokes.

So far our last hurrah in the Keys was going *gangbusters*. My girls and I danced, and took shots, and we even got our chests painted. I went for a psychedelic theme, complete with tons of glitter. It took us a few minutes of walking around with our glittered-out versions of *Starry Night* on our bare chests to realize no one was looking. Once again we were surrounded only by gay men. I refused to have gone to spring break without so much as kissing someone, so I threw on my Day Five tank (carefully, because of the paint), said good-bye to my mustachioed new BFF, and left to hit up one more bar, making sure there were obviously straight college guys there before entering.

And as if on cue, a cute man appeared! And he was *super* cute. That, or I was *super* drunk—I didn't care which one was the truth. We talked for a bit and I thought to myself, *I will put my mouth on that mouth*. I told him about the Shores, and he told me that he and his friends were staying at a weird bed-and-breakfast that had rabbits running loose on the grounds. I assumed this was either the weirdest or the most brilliant way to get a girl to come home with you, because I was definitely going to have to see.

Now, hold up, I didn't go with him alone. Mama didn't raise no fool. Well, technically she did, but it was my brother. (Hey, Dave!) I brought my three girls with me for safety. And sure enough, that place had bunnies running all over the place. Key West is fucking weird, you guys.

So, we all hung by the pool and played with bunnies and continued drinking. Finally "dude" and I took a walk and actually had a deep conversation. If I remember correctly, I believe it went "Blah, blah, blah, put your tongue deep in my throat."

(RUTABAGA! I repeat, RUTABAGA!)

Finally! I am getting a little action! I thought to myself. We started making out and, I gotta admit, he was a great kisser. But apparently, so was I. Because after about three minutes of making out, just when I thought he was gonna go for a boob grab, it happened. It came out of nowhere. Seriously, it *came* out of nowhere. That's right. He full-on jizzed in his pants. Even worse, he sounded like a goat while doing it. Not like a cute little goat you'd find at a petting zoo. More like one of those screaming goats that geniuses remix on YouTube.

In the immortal words of the Beach Boys, we got there fast and then we took it slow. And by that I mean I froze. My tongue was still in his mouth, and I froze like a statue. How do you react to something like this? If this were someone I was dating, I would've comforted him and said, "It's totally fine, babe. Don't be embarrassed!" Later, at our friends' dinner parties, we would regale them with the story of our "first kiss," all while laughing and passing the haricots verts.

But this wasn't a guy I liked. This was essentially a stranger. One I would probably never see again. So, what did I do? I remembered what to do if you run into a bear in the woods. I put my hands above my head and slowly walked away, still facing him but avoiding eye contact. I even hummed to break the silence. I full-on hummed "Don't Cha," by the Pussycat Dolls, because that shit was the *theme* of spring break.

I quickly went and found my friends, who at this point were way too drunk to be handling small mammals. If I remember correctly, they were reenacting the rabbit scene from *Fatal Attraction*.

"We gotta go."

"What's the matter?"

"We came. We saw. He came. I saw."

We got the hell out of there and promptly passed out in the comfort of our own weird hotel. Sure, there were penises at every turn at our place, but at least they weren't spitting at us. I guess with every experience like this, at least you come away learning from it. So, what did I learn that night?

I learned that you can't just go out looking for someone. It needs to happen naturally, or you're gonna end up going home with someone who probably isn't *that* cute in the light of sobriety, based on him orgasming by a mini make-out session. But the most important thing I learned that trip: *Never* go to sleep with your chest shellacked with glitter. The next morning you have to peel that shit off and it feels like . . . Well, have you ever accidentally gotten superglue on your fingers and they get all dry and you have to rip off your skin to make it go away? This felt like that. Except on your whole chest. Your *whole* chest. If homeboy hadn't creamed his pants and actually had tried to feel me up, my boobs would've felt like a gladiator chest plate. I could've deflected a bullet like Superman.

I also learned to lay off Jimmy Buffett a little. Even though I'd rather put a foot-long Q-tip in my ear than listen to *Son of a Son of a Sailor* again, some of his song titles are a different story. I hopped on the old Wikipedia to look some up, and it turns out they perfectly describe certain times in my life. For example:

"I Wish Lunch Could Last Forever"
—*This is how I feel every day at lunch.*

"Why Don't We Get Drunk (and Screw)"
—*This is how I feel after three shots of tequila.*

"My Head Hurts, My Feet Stink, and I Don't Love Jesus"
—*This is how I feel after eight shots of tequila.*

"You'll Never Work in Dis Bidness Again"
—*This is how my book agent will feel when I turn in this chapter.*

I got a little nostalgic for the Shores a few years back and thought about doing a girls' trip, only to find that it had closed back in 2007. What a shame. The room was so-so, but lying out by that pool with no tan lines or inhibitions was a thing of beauty. Turns out that tanning buck naked in your front yard while eating nachos just doesn't feel the same, no matter how disinterested the men driving by are. Rest in peace, Atlantic Shores.

Topless Tuesday

3 oz gin
1 oz dry vermouth
1 oz pickling liquid
3 dashes Tabasco
3 pickled okras

Combine all ingredients, except for the okras, into a shaker with ice. Swirl vigorously. Strain and garnish with one of the okras. The other two are to eat while you make your drink.

When I was little I was absolutely obsessed with the idea of clubs. I wanted secret handshakes, and special badges, and meetings in a tree house. I imagined myself calling the meetings to order with a hammer for a gavel and everyone cheering when I proclaimed that we would be spending our dues on a pizza party. Despite my visions of grandeur (and breadsticks), my attempts to organize clubs never really panned out.

Okay, fine. They were a disaster. I started a cooking club, Club Sandwich, but it went up in flames when the members said they didn't want to do the dishes. Next, I started a fashion club, the Sew Cool Club. One puffy-paint sweatshirt in and that was kaput. I then started a mystery-solving club, but there was a severe shortage of mysteries around town. By week three, I had to fake that my mom's expensive necklace had gone missing and that we'd been chosen to crack the case. While I dusted the banister for fingerprints with baby powder, the two other members of the Miss-tery

Club played *Sonic the Hedgehog* on my Sega. Later that day my mom found her necklace in a laundry basket and was *pissed*. In my defense, I *was* able to crack the case. It was me.

The closest I ever got to being part of an organized club was being a card-carrying member of Pizza Hut's Book It! program, in which kids got free pizzas for reading books. The greatest part about this reward system was that there was no way for them to regulate it. Technically you could walk in there, point to the teenage cook, and be like, "Reggie, why don't you take five and ice that wrist, 'cause I read eight hundred books this week and plan on treating my entire town to personal pans, buddy." Not that I would ever have had the balls to do that! I was a total Goody Two-shoes, and I wouldn't have wanted to lie to get free personal pans. I could have single-handedly shut down the Hut with the amount of books I was reading.

There was one book series in particular that I was crazy about: *The Baby-sitters Club*.* As someone who now skips parties to stay in and watch *Shark Tank*, I can tell you that the concept of a club that also generated profit made little Mamrie's mind go nuts. But my dreams of running my own BSC (and getting a private landline in my room for meetings) were squashed instantly when I didn't get a single call my first week. In the South, people don't really call "sitters"; they just drop their kids off at their closest relatives' (closest being distance-wise, not relationship-wise). There wasn't any of this "pay someone eight bucks an hour" mumbo jumbo. It was just . . .

Drop her off at Granny Bo's house.

Granny's so senile, she thought kitty litter was Grape-Nuts last week.

She'll be fine for a few hours.

By the end of fifth grade, I had more failed clubs than Miami in

---

*Claudia Kishi would have joined my Sew Cool Club. Why couldn't I have grown up in Stoneybrook?

the late '90s. Little did I know that it wouldn't be till a decade later that I would finally found a club that would not only succeed—nay, it would flourish. And like most things in college, it involved the two Bs: boobs and booze.

It began as a normal Tuesday in the fall of my senior year. This particular day, my friend Melissa and I were drinking bourbon on the rocks and smoking cognac-dipped cigarillos. Melissa and I didn't consider ourselves best friends so much as hetero life partners, or HLPs. Allow me to explain. It's a proven fact that women live longer than men. So we promised that when our significant others died we would move in with each other our last few years, Golden Girls–style, and really whoop it up. Anyway! Melissa, who is now a successful costume designer and is still my HLP, was teaching me how to silk-screen. Sounds like a pretty normal Tuesday, right? The only difference is that we were doing all of this topless.

Why topless, you ask? I *think* it started because we were working with paint and didn't want to stain our shirts. I am the *queen* of staining shirts. If I could legally be topless whenever I wanted, it would save dozens and dozens of Forever 21 blouse casualties every year. But the real reason we were topless was because Melissa is the least modest person I know. She makes Miley Cyrus look like an Amish girl who's not interested in Rumspringa. And with good reason. I'm almost certain the song "Defying Gravity," from *Wicked*, was inspired by her tits. And while I don't go around topless at the drop of a hat, I'm not self-conscious, either. Growing up doing dance competitions and recitals, you had to change costumes in front of a roomful of other girls. I'm not saying that I would go spread-eagle in a tutu or anything. But we were a couple of friends with our shirts off. It wasn't sexual. It was convenient!

The next day, I felt like an Acme anvil had landed on my brain, but I also felt rather accomplished. That was the most fun I'd had in a long time, and I came away with a new skill set. Not to mention I felt super liberated having done it all without a shirt on. I started to understand why guys take off their shirts when they do yard work or other tasks. Yes, it's probably to keep cool, but there is something about going bare chested that makes you feel like a *boss*.

The next Tuesday, Melissa called me up (this was before texting was a thing, and I actually would answer my phone). "Want to come over and drink whiskey and make dream catchers topless?" Fuck yes, I did. I wanted to make that dream catcher and catch my dream of these Tuesdays becoming a regular thing.

Melissa and I kept up this routine for the next month. We started telling our other girlfriends about our Tuesday tradition, and we always got one of two reactions:

Oh, you two! You guys are the craziest. Gotta go. I have a proctology appointment to get an even bigger stick put up my ass. Ta-ta!

Or:

I. WANT. IN.

Slowly but surely, we started inviting people to join us in our new Tuesday ritual. Of course, we were very select about it.* First, it was my roommates. It wasn't awkward because we had already seen each other's boobs a gazillion times. In fact, I could've described their boobs to a police sketch artist and had a perfect rendering. One Topless Tuesday in and they were hooked. We let my gay best friend, Jacob, in on the action, then my roommates' closest friends, until we had a solid dozen girls (plus Jacob) who came every Tuesday.

Each Tuesday was assigned to a different person, meaning that person would be responsible for our activity that week. This could be anything from learning to change a tire to making pillbox hats to learning to give yourself a breast examination. Whatever we did, it was always complete with a ton of laughs, a lot of bourbon, and a lack of shirts. It was the perfect combination of a craft night and a raging party, without ever having to worry about what to wear.

---

*Luckily, this was still the glorious time before phones had HD video and cameras. Back then, if your flip phone did have a camera, every pic ended up looking like a blurry photo of Bigfoot.

Word about our club started spreading fast. I got stopped in the quad by people asking if they could join. Friends of friends of friends wanted in. Melissa and I would be introduced at parties as "Those girls with the Topless Tuesdays that I was telling you about." But the moment I really knew my club was becoming a campus legend was when I was asked about it by my French professor.

Here's my history with this French class. When I was in college, students were required to take three semesters of a foreign language. I had been dreading it and, naturally, waited until the last three semesters of school to sign up for one. The obvious choice was to take Spanish, since I had taken it in high school and remembered *un poco* of the language. But when I signed on to my dial-up Internet to get my courses for that year, the only Spanish class left was at eight a.m. I would be rolling into class still drunk from the night before if I went in that early—so a two p.m. French class it was!

Some people in this world can take a three-day trip to Paris and come back speaking perfect French. I, however, am terrible at learning foreign languages. I can tell you every word to No Doubt's "Just a Girl" even though I haven't listened to it in a good six years, but ask me to count to ten in French and it ain't happening. Luckily, I had a supercool, young teacher (let's call him Jacques) who understood my plight. Jacques was always joking around in class and would allow us to do video assignments or other creative projects in lieu of papers. He had longish curly hair and an air of gay to him, and he always lit up a smoke right after class, which I think is required when you teach French.

One day at the beginning of the semester, when I could see that the struggle was real, I timed my exit from class perfectly to bum a smoke off my teach. I continued to time our exits so that we would sit and have a cigarette together for the next few weeks. He'd give me one on Tuesday; I'd give him one on Thursday. It was probably the longest relationship I had with a man in college.

After a particularly tough day of studying gender in nouns,* I just laid it all out there.

"Look, you know I'm terrible at French, right?"

"*Oui.* You are what we call in French, *le dumbass.*"

"I can respect that. Anyway! I need these credits to graduate. I'm never going to be good at French. Can we strike up a deal?"

He took a big drag off his Parliament Light.

"You teach levels one through three. I need one through three to graduate. I'll take your classes, try my best, make really fun projects, and always have cigarettes waiting. Just don't fail me. Please?"

With that Jacques took another long drag on his cig (the French are *so* dramatic), put his backpack on, and said, "See you on Thursday," and walked away. Just like that.

Cut to later in the semester. Jacques was writing some shit I didn't understand on the board, while I was in a different world tallying what ingredients I needed to pick up for the aphrodisiac Chinese cooking class at Topless Tuesday that afternoon. We were three months into the club, and it had circled back to being my day to lead the activity. There were about twenty people coming that day, so that would mean . . . three gallons of lychee martini? Do lychees make you want to hump stuff? I was snapped out of my thoughts by Jacques' voice.

"Again, next Thursday, please come in with a two-hundred-word paper, in French, telling me the plot of your favorite movie."

A two-hundred-word paper *in French*? I didn't know two hundred words total, let alone how to put them together in some semblance of order. Walking outside, I let him know that I probably would be cranking out some sort of video or other alternative project because this assignment wasn't going to happen. That's when he said it:

"Mamrie, I'm still surprised you're so bad at French. After all, you

---

*The French word for balls is *les couilles*. It's a feminine noun. That makes zero sense. Don't you dare tell me French isn't hard as *les couilles*!

have so much in common with the culture. You love to smoke, you're always eating cheese in class, clearly hygiene isn't a huge priority." I nodded. "And from what I hear, you have no problem with nudity."

Fuck a duck, he knew.

I stared at him in disbelief, cheese tumbling out of my mouth and hitting the brick walkway.

"It's a small campus, Mamrie. Word spreads." Then he casually put out his smoke and walked away.

Wait a sec. Small campus? *Small campus?* University of North Carolina–Chapel Hill had thirty thousand undergrads alone. Talk of Topless Tuesday was making its way around campus quicker than herpes in the southwest dorms.

I decided we needed to institute some professionalism in this club. We couldn't have randoms showing up and storming our meetings, or have professors gossiping about it. Yes, I understand *professionalism* is a strange word to hear from someone who at the previous Topless Tuesday wore unicorn stickers as pasties while singing Fleetwood Mac's "The Chain" on the karaoke machine. That isn't the point. The point is this was my moment. The club I dreamed of having for all those years was finally happening—and I wanted to make sure it was the best ever.

Melissa and I got down to business. We usually had around fifteen regular attendees at our TTs (which sounds like "titties" when you say it, and although I would like to claim that brilliance, I am just now realizing it ten years later). First, we needed to make their membership more official.

I knew that when the sororities on our campus invited new members to join, it would take place on Bid Day. As soon as pledges got their bouquet of balloons or Tri-Delt monogrammed hoodie left on their dorm-room door, they would run screaming to the quad like they'd just taken down a pony keg of Red Bull and vodka.* But we weren't a sorority! We were the antisorority, in a way. I

---

*'Cause they probably had.

know this isn't the case with all of them, but you so often hear those horror stories of sororities that openly discuss girls' looks when choosing whom to let in.*

> *I know Kelsey H. isn't the smartest—I've actually seen her eat a fake apple—but have you seen her abs? They are amaze. She's in!*

> *Mary Catherine is seriously at least four pounds overweight, but her dad does own the largest Sea-Doo company in the Southeast. She's in!*

Topless Tuesday, on the other hand, celebrated all looks and body types. The only mixer we needed was ginger ale for our bourbon. So on our "bid day," we decided to take a classier approach. Melissa and I dressed up in our nicest silk robes (yes, there was more than one silky robe option) and had my roommate drive us around to each new member's house. There, on their doorstep, we would hand them a formal, handwritten invitation (with a personalized poem inside) and a glass of champagne to toast their membership. The whole thing was risqué and ridiculous, but there was an air of elegance to it. Well, until we got to about the eighth or ninth house, and then we were just drunk girls in robes, cheersing *way* too loud. I might've puked in a yard—who's to say?

The following Tuesday, we invited the newbies to the first-ever Topless Tuesday Welcome Potluck Dinner. We were throwing it at Melissa's house, and because it was only a minute's drive away, I wore jean shorts, a silk robe, and nothing else. However, I did have my deep fryer and ingredients for fried okra.†

---

*Obviously this is a huge generalization. I was friends with lots of incredible sorority girls in my day, so don't get your Tri-Delt panties in a wad, ladies.

†Some people might say it's way too risky to fry okra topless, what with the four-hundred-degree splatters of oil flying out. But I think life is no fun unless you take risks. Also, my chest is covered in oil-burn scars.

I parked my Honda behind Melissa's house in the yard. I knew a lot of people were coming and there was limited parking, but we were close enough for me to park in her grass (a true sign of friendship in the South). As I rounded the house to her front yard, I saw a few new members headed inside and decided they needed a proper welcome. I put down my FryDaddy full of grease, opened up my robe, and shook my goods while singing out, "Welllllcome to Topless Tuesday, bitches!"

Just as I was about to ask them to help me carry my shit, one of them turned around and spoke.

"There's a For Rent sign in the yard. We were just hoping to see the house. . . ."

Standing there, robe open, ta-tas to the moon, you could've heard a cricket blink. It was a silent standoff. They looked shocked. I looked naked. They looked at my boobs. I still looked naked.

We stood there, not knowing what to do for what felt like an eternity but was probably ten seconds. I had to make a move.

I could've apologized, could've told them that now probably wasn't a great time to see the place. I could've. But where's the fun in that?

"You wanna see the house? Sure! Come on in. Just a heads-up, though, we are having a party. So you'll have to stay for a drink."

I led them right into the pandemonium. Talking Heads played on a record player in the corner, and twenty girls in their bras or nahs happily did their thing like it was no big deal. There was a topless gal organizing her cheese tray, another one pulling a slow-roasted pork shoulder out of the oven. It was like a twelve-year-old Mario Batali's wet dream.

Just as I was about to completely lie about the square footage of the place, Melissa rounded the corner with a tray full of cocktails. She handed the tray to one of the shocked guests and said, "Two questions. Would you like a Singapore Sling? And who the hell are you?"

"They saw the For Rent sign and wanted to take a look at the place."

"New friends! Let me show you around." With that she whisked them away for the grand tour as I called out after her, "I'll try to keep you *abreast* of any more visitors!" followed by a wink and pointing of a finger gun at myself in the hallway mirror.

The rest of the night was a total success, bewildered guests and all. We stuffed our faces and even organized a calendar designating each member a Tuesday to lead the lesson or activity. It was the perfect kickoff for what ended up being a solid year of Topless Tuesdays.

Here's where I want to take a moment and tell you why I loved this club so much. I'm sure a lot of you read this and wonder, *Why no shirt? Couldn't you have learned to knit and get drunk while also keeping the girls under wraps?* Of course we could've. But here's why I think it was important.

I want to tell you about a certain TT member. Let's say her name was Claire. Claire came to her first Tuesday not knowing what to expect. She had heard us talk about our club before but didn't know if the toplessness was just something we talked about for shock value.

When Claire came to that initiation potluck, I saw her act shy for the first time since I'd known her. She had a great time socializing and drunkenly dished out her cobbler, but she left her shirt on the whole time. About two Tuesdays later, I walked in and saw that Claire was in her bra. A month later she was in tassels. Three months later and the girl was teaching me how to play Chinese checkers butt-ass naked.

You see, the club was never about the nudity. It was about creating a space, a day, a group of people you didn't need to impress with your body. Girls spend so much time trying to look good in front of each other, and for what? Do I really care if my friend has a muffin top? Do I give a shit if another friend has weird nipples? FUCK NO. Topless Tuesday was a judgment-free zone. And becoming that comfortable without clothes around my friends actually made me more comfortable *in* my clothes all the other days of the week. Topless Tuesdays was a place to go, *Ah, nobody is perfect. Literally, no* body *is perfect.* So, why do I stress about mine?

Fast-forward to present day. My friends Hannah, Grace, and I do a live show called the #NoFilterShow, which we tour around from time to time. We do a lot of audience participation, I do a live *You Deserve a Drink* segment onstage, and it always derails into ridiculousness.

Don't mind us. Just three adult women in pencil costumes orchestrating an entire stage show around fart sound effects.

During one of our recent shows, while doing an old-school dating game bit, I was dressed as an ice-cream sundae and Grace was dressed as a wedge of cheese, with Hannah serving as our host. It's a silly audience-participation bit that involves (naturally) a lot of puns about whatever costumes we're wearing. Grace and I usually delve into terrible, self-involved characters who are more concerned with creating the weird story line than actually talking to the audience members who are trying to date us.

Anyway, as I was sitting there laughing onstage, having fun with my friends, an audience member took it upon himself to scream out "saggy tits" at me. Yes. Go ahead and reread that sentence; take it all in. Saggy tits.

I was flabbergasted. Normally I would've shot back a super-clever response in my character's voice, but I was so caught off guard, I actually kind of blacked out. I only realized from GIFs on Tumblr the next day that I made the guy stand up and told him I was going to murder him. But, like, in a "fun murder" way.

I should've told him that if I have saggy tits I can at least get a breast lift, but there is no operation or amount of money that can ever lift his saggy-ass personality. But I didn't, and I hate that I didn't. Luckily, Grace, in her cheese-wedge glory, backed me up and told everyone to subscribe to his YouTube channel, youtube .com/imadick. (Which is probably an actual channel at this point, so I'm sorry–slash–you're welcome to whoever owns it.)

All comebacks aside, here is why that arsehole threw me off so bad. I read all kinds of insanely rude comments on my videos. On the Internet, people have the protection of anonymity and say things to you that they would never say to your face. While I hate that aspect of YouTube, it comes with the territory, and I chose to make myself vulnerable to it. But this wasn't YouTube. This wasn't a comments section.

This jackass took a moment when everyone was having fun and decided to be rude about my body. This makes zero sense, and for a variety of reasons:

A. I was dressed as an ice-cream sundae—the least boob-flaunting outfit of all time!

B.   This wasn't a high school improv assembly you are forced to go to because it's also chock-full of latent anti-drug messaging. This was a show that everyone in the audience (this guy included) paid twenty-five euros for.

C.   I am the most self-deprecating person I know. I've probably made a joke about tucking my tits into my shoes before, because that's what I think is funny. It's funny because it's *self*-deprecation—not someone else making a dig about my body to my face.

My ego wasn't hurt; I was just mad. And here's why. I am totally comfortable in my body, despite whether I happen to be taking care of it or whether I'm carrying some extra weight. But that might not be the case for everyone who was in that audience. I have no doubt that a good majority of the girls there were super uncomfortable with that statement. If this guy could say rude things to the person onstage, what kind of shit would he say to the girls at the table beside him?

I wish I'd had my Topless Tuesday crew to march onstage in their various shapes and sizes and give him a dose of reality, to show him what actual women look like. They aren't just the waifish models in his mom's L.L.Bean catalog that he steals to jerk off to in his bedroom. I'm sure Melissa would've promptly asked him to pull his balls out so we could judge the sag level of those bad boys.*

That is why I think my club was important. No, we didn't solve mysteries or get our own landline. But we did, for a magical moment in time, have women feeling a little more comfortable about their bodies, throwing caution (and Spanx) to the wind. If that arsehole had yelled "saggy tits" at Claire on week one, she would've shown up to week two wearing a turtleneck over a snowsuit. But

---

*But he probably would've been so scared his balls would've crawled inside him like two falafels in a pita pocket.

not at week five. At week five, she would've thrown her cigar at him and shimmied across the stage while we all cheered behind her. Dare I say it? Topless Tuesday was the *titz*.

Don't get me wrong—I don't think you need to be naked in front of your friends to gain more confidence. I'm just saying that pushing yourself outside your comfort zone a little only makes your comfort zone that much bigger. I am sure I just ripped off Oprah or some self-help guru with that last sentence, but fuck it. It's true.

And for all you folks still curious about Jacques, I never did find out how he knew about my club. But I did know how to get a solid grade on that two-hundred-word paper. Instead of the paper he wanted us to turn in on our favorite movie, I did him one better. Using the girls from my club, a black-construction-paper censor bar, and my club taking turns saying *"Oui!"* one hundred times, I created my own movie. It was titled *Filles Déchaînées à Paris.*

Girls Gone Wild in Paris.

I passed the class.

Quickshots: Terrible Comments

Y

Here is my first Quickshot! What's a Quickshot, you ask? Easy. For some of these stories, there is so much more I want to cram in, but I don't have the room (that's what she said).

So, rather than rob you readers of the exhilaration of my humiliation, I decided to include these countdowns throughout the book. No need to whip up simple syrup or buy some specialty endangered bald eagle egg liqueur; just pound a shot of your choice.

This particular Quickshot is about Internet comments! I don't think I'm breaking new ground here by saying that people can be HUGE DICKS on the Internet. And I'm not just talking about when you google-image the phrase "huge dicks."

I'm actually really lucky. For the most part the comments on my videos are super positive. And when someone does have the audacity to write something shitty, it is quickly thumbs-downed by so many people that it disappears. It's like a personal army of positivity. Despite my clique, a few shitty comments do manage to eke by on every upload.

Here are some examples of mean-spirited comments that have made me laugh. Let it be known that I've gotten some beyond-awful ones before, but I don't want those dicks who are secretly fans to read this book while wearing their *YDAD* shirts and have the satisfaction of seeing their comments in it. Instead, here are three different types of people who like to troll.

Please note that I left out their actual usernames so as to protect their identities. Please also note that more than one had a One Direction reference in their names. Them 1Ders are intense!

The Rookie

I bet ur a VIRGINA

First of all, in the words of every passive-aggressive southern woman, bless her heart. I would like to think that this is simply a case of bad AutoCorrect. Like when your mom texts you what she's cooking for dinner and it turns "meatballs" into "my balls." But if it is an AutoCorrect fail, riddle me this—why is "ur" still spelled like that? Hmmmm?

What we really have here is the case of the rude ten-year-old. She wants to say terrible things online. After all, that's what all the cool kids are doing. She just hasn't reached the point in her life where she knows how to be mean. She's heard girls call each other skanks at school and always looks shocked even though she doesn't know what it means.

Like when I was in fourth grade and the song "Baby Got Back" (a.k.a. "I Like Big Butts") was the jam of the summer. I have a very vivid memory of hanging out at the Yadkin County public pool and wearing my favorite peach-and-yellow French bikini because I knew my crush, Steel, was going to be there. Two things might've stood out to you in that sentence: The fact that I wore my cutest suit when I had the body of a cardboard cutout. And the fact that my crush's name was Steel. I have no idea what ended up happening to that guy, but I'm gonna guess he ended up a porn star or a comic book hero.

Anyway! A group of cool dudes were standing in a circle rapping about their love for big butts, and on the line "I get sprung," Steel said, "I get spermed." Everyone cracked up laughing. I had no idea why that was so funny. Not a clue. But you bet your ass I laughed. Probably too hard. Before anyone could catch on to my maniacal laugh of confusion, I excused myself to go get some more Airheads from the snack shop. Luckily, I got away with it. Unluckily, this was before the Internet, and I can never take back asking my mom what "spermed" meant.

This is that same scenario but in written form. She obviously wants to call me a "virgin" but doesn't know what it is or why it is offensive. Because if she did know what it was, I guarantee she would not be calling me that!

Really, chickadee? The girl who in this video says the words "Queefer Sutherland" has never been physically intimate before?

I guarantee ten minutes after typing this, our sweet commenter helped set the table for dinner, where her parents would ask her how her piano lesson went and her rascal of a younger brother would flick peas in her face.

And furthermore, since when has being a virgin been an insult? Even when Tai called Cher a "virgin who can't drive" in *Clueless*, the only part that seemed really mean was the "can't drive" part. When you are sixteen and someone calls you a bad driver, she may as well spit in your face.

Speaking of bad driving, when I was sixteen years old, I drove through a telephone pole. True story. I'd had my license for three weeks and had a cute little used green VW Jetta. One morning, I was waiting to pull out of my road when I noticed there was some gunk on my driver's side window. It looked like someone had hawked a loogie on it. I rolled down the window to see if it would scrape off, but no luck. I pulled out of my road, manually rolling the window back up. I looked again and saw the loogie had just smeared everywhere. Fucking gross! As I was staring at the Jackson Pollock of snot and holding back dry heaves, I ran off the road and smashed into a telephone pole. I wasn't even going that fast, but as soon as I hit and the airbags deployed, my knee-jerk reaction was to hit the gas. I broke that pole in half like "Macho Man" Randy Savage snaps a Slim Jim.* Pretty embarrassing. Pretty stupid. But, so help me God, you better not have told me I couldn't drive or I would've cut you out of my life.

I guess what I'm trying to say here is don't call someone a bad driver. But also, young girls, don't consider calling someone a virgin an insult. It's not. Having your virginity is nothing to be embarrassed by. In fact, it's more a bragging right than an embarrassment. It is way more embarrassing to put on a tough-guy act and call someone the misspelled name of a very respectable and beautiful American state.

The Weirdo

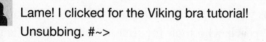

Lame! I clicked for the Viking bra tutorial! Unsubbing. #~>

Where do I even begin with this one? Seriously. This person is pissed because she was searching for Viking Bra Tutorial. I can't even be mad at her for unsubscribing. In fact, I want to slowly infiltrate this person's life via the videos she likes and gradually become her best friend.

I'll probably have to pretend to be into opera and wear a hat with horns on it for a while, but I really think it will be worth it in the end.

---

*Rest in peace.

The Hypocrite

Idiots with too much time.

Oh, man. I love this comment so much. You might be thinking, *But Mamrie! It's not that mean,* or *But Mamrie, there are no grammatical errors!* Look, when it comes to appreciating a ridiculous comment on YouTube, sometimes you gotta treat it like a chicken potpie. You gotta peel back a flaky layer or two to get to that real gooey goodness. I will admit that the potpie analogy is partially due to the fact that I'm watching Food Network as I type this. But it is true. Sometimes you've got to dig a little deeper to see where a person is coming from. And that is what I did with this gem of a user. I clicked on his avatar.

This is something that people forget is possible on YouTube. As easily as you can click on my username and see what videos I've posted, I can do the same exact thing to a commenter. I can also see what videos you've uploaded, or liked, or commented on.

This lil' peach who took the time to tell me that I am an idiot and that I have too much time on my hands didn't realize that (after drinking a few too many Rumple Minzes) I would click on that avatar of his.

What I found really knocked me off my orthopedic slippers. Homeboy, let's call him Reginald, had only one original video uploaded to his channel. Now, if I were to tell you that this one video was the most boring thing I have ever experienced, you probably wouldn't believe me. But I swear on my collection of tiny hats, it's the truth.

Reginald's only uploaded video was a montage of sunset pictures. Not a sweeping montage of time-lapse sunset footage. Not gorgeous sunsets over canyons, beaches, and other stunning landscapes with shots from a GoPro strapped to an eagle's head. No, no. Reg's video was a slideshow of scanned sunset photos he'd taken through a window with an old camera that still shows you the date in the corner.

Of course, he broke out every standard iMovie transition (star wipe, dissolve, even that weird spinning cube thing) to sandwich between each blurry sunset. It was set to a classic new age instrumental, to really get the viewer in the relaxation zone. But that's not all! Halfway through the vid it kicks into a more rocking number and switches to (get this) waterfall pics, but not before Reg cuts to a title card reading, and I quote: "Did anybody sad water?"

Guys. We all know good and well this was a painful and unfortunate typo. He clearly meant, "Did anybody *say* water?" but I think we can all admit the irony is heartbreaking. It *was* some supersad water. I felt so bad for Reginald. We used to live in a world where you could entice your friends and neighbors with a good cheese ball and a box of Franzia in exchange for them coming over and acting impressed with your boring-ass vacation slideshow. And you know, sunsets are the most boring vacay photos. Sunsets are the photography equivalent of people telling you what they dreamt.

But now, sans slideshow party, this man had to teach himself how to edit and scan old photos to throw them onto the World Wide Web, shouting into the void and hoping someone would watch it.

Well, guess what, mothafucka, I did watch. I am one of your sixteen views. And even though you called *me* an idiot who has too much time on her hands, I gave it a thumbs-up. Pay it forward, Reg.

The Backpedaler

NNNNNNNNOOOOOOOOOOOOTTTTTTTTTT
funny, you just copied graces editing completely
👍 👎

In case you who have been living under a rock (or picked up this book because it was on clearance and some smart-ass put Chelsea Handler's book cover on it), Grace Helbig is my cohort on *YDAD*. This is whom the man with the broken caps lock is referring to.

Let me take it back a little. Grace and I met on our first sketch team at the Peoples Improv Theater, in NYC. Grace was on an improv house team and I was in a sketch-writing class. For those of you who aren't total comedy nerds, improv is *Whose Line Is It Anyway?* and sketch is *Saturday Night Live*. The theater was putting together its first house sketch team and by some lucky streak, I was put on it.

Going to the first rehearsal, I was super nervous. Everyone else who was on the team had been in the theater awhile. They knew each other. They had been drunk together. I knew one person, my friend Steve, whom I'd met in my class. Fun fact! That first rehearsal, we read a sketch called "Everyone Loves Grace," in which we played ourselves pitching sketches, the whole premise being that every sketch Grace pitched, no matter how terrible, everyone loved. Every guy's pitch ended with Grace kissing him. Meanwhile, everything I said would be quickly shut down and ignored. This sounds a lot more mysogynistic than it was, trust me. Our sketch group was called Finger, and that is where the friendship deal was sealed.

Long story short, Grace and I remained friends after the group split up. We also became each other's daytime drinking buddy. She was making "Daily Grace" videos and I was bartending. Neither of

us had a normal nine-to-five job, and we lived four blocks away from each other. This meant we would get Bloody Marys at one p.m. on a Tuesday and not pass any judgment!

One day over drinks, I told Grace that I had a really dumb idea that would combine my bartending and bad puns. This was right when Charlie Sheen was going batshit fucking "winning" crazy. I thought it would be fun to create a cocktail based on his break-down and make a tutorial comedy video about it. And thus my first episode, "Charlie Sheen's Tiger Blood Gimlet," was filmed and my show *You Deserve a Drink* was born.

The reason why I give you this backstory is because when this comment was made, Grace actually edited my videos. That's like saying Chris Gaines copied Garth Brooks. It's the same damn person! And if you don't know what I'm talking about, do yourself a favor and google that shit. I took over editing shortly thereafter, but the first two years of *YDAD*, Grace was kind enough to edit for me. The only person copying Grace's editing style was . . . Grace. Actually, this is less of an insult to me and a compliment to Grace for having such consistent editing skills!

Now! Here is where I tell you my dirty little secret. Sometimes, and I do mean very rarely, I will have a few too many gin gimlets at home and end up looking at my comments. Of course, I check them the first hour I put a video up to make sure that I don't have two minutes of black screen at the end, or didn't realize my boob randomly pops out for a few frames. But once in a blue moon (or after too many Blue Moons) I get deep in them comments. Even less often, I actually respond to a comment. Most of these I type out, take another sip of martini, and delete. Type, delete, repeat. But there is the occasional ~~sip~~ slip of judgment. This was one of them:

 thanks darlin. Grace actually edits them, so good eye!

Notice the pet name, the impeccable level of passive-aggression with putting him in his place and then complimenting him. There's a saying in the South that you catch more flies with honey than with vinegar. I wasn't going to be mean about it. I wanted to make him feel bad! I wanted to slather him in honey. After all, there was already enough vinegar with that douche hanging out. Hey-yo.*

Ladies and gentleman, this is the response I got back:

ohmygod no no no no no that was one of my 'friends' who shares my account, I LOVE THESE VIDEOS!!!!! trust me!!!!! i know grace edits them, it says at the end:/ I LOVE YOU MAMRIE!!!!! THAT WASN'T ME I SWEAR!!!!

*For those slow on the upkeep, douches actually are made of vinegar. You're welcome. Take a sip for your ignorance.

Here's what I've noticed from these little responses of mine. Whenever I call someone out on crossing the line or just a sheer correction, nine out of ten times they have an excuse. It's never, "Sorry if that hurt your feelings, that's just my truth"; it's always . . .

- You totally read that the wrong way!!! I looooove you!
- My brother signed into my account and typed that!!
- I meant to type that on a different video!!!!!
- A SUPER bitchy ghost just possessed my body & typed that!!
- You misunderstood!! That wasn't English!! When translated into Klingdingdong it means "I'm OBSESSED WIT U!!!!"

It's always some lame excuse. Their thighs gotta hurt from all that backpedaling. But you have to remember (you being myself on YouTube, or if you are getting hate in e-mail, or anonymous messages in any form), these people would never say this stuff to your face. It's like when your friend drinks way too many margaritas and calls you an asshole. You take it with a grain of salt (or lots of grains of salt, when you promptly pound enough tequila shots to get on their level), because you know it's the booze talking. People who are constantly mean on the Internet are basically drunk assholes, word-vomiting out rude comments. You can't take them seriously.

The Genius

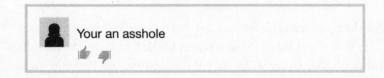

Your an asshole

YOU'RE a genius.

Leaves of Three Martini

3 oz cucumber juice
6 basil leaves
2 oz gin
½ oz simple syrup
Celery bitters

Time to break out that juicer you bought two years ago that's been collecting dust on your shelf ever since! Bust out that bad boy to make the cuke juice. And if you don't have a juicer (or a friend with lofty health goals), just sub lime juice.

Throw 3 basil leaves into a shaker with the cucumber juice. Muddle it together. If you don't have a muddler, you can always use a wooden spoon or a novelty-size baseball bat. Add the gin and simple syrup. Then swirl it all around—don't shake! Shaking the gin will make it bruise quicker than the knees of a hemophiliac after a blow job. Strain into a pretty glass, garnish with the remaining 3 basil leaves, and use an atomizer to spray 3 big mists of celery bitters over the top. If you don't have an atomizer or are allergic to class, add 1 or 2 drops of bitters.

In the film masterpiece *She's All That*, Freddie Prinze Jr.'s character is under a lot of pressure from his dad to go to Dartmouth. I think it's safe to say we've all felt that FPJ parental pressure when it comes to picking colleges, right? Umm . . . *wrong*! Where I'm from, the fact that I was graduating high school was already way impressive, so college was just icing on the Bo-Berry Biscuit.*

When it came time to apply to colleges, I really had no idea where to go. My initial plan was to get as far away from North Carolina as possible. True story—I had the option to have my pre-SAT scores automatically sent to a college of my choice, and I chose Brigham Young University–Hawaii. Yes, Brigham Young as in the Church of Jesus Christ of Latter-day Saints. I had no idea it was a Mormon school; I just saw the word *Hawaii* on the form and went for it.

My dreams of wearing a grass skirt and sipping mai tais during calculus went out the window when I got my scores back. There was no way I was getting a full ride on that number, never mind the fact that *I'm not a Mormon.* I was bummed. My GPA was higher than 4.0, but I guess SATs weren't my thing. It didn't help that they scheduled the SATs for the same day as prom. How was I supposed to be working out complicated analogies while I was daydreaming about my cornrows/French twist updo combo?

I turned my focus to schools that were in state. I *refused* to go to community college. Listen, there is nothing wrong at all with a good ol' CC. But I just couldn't stay in my county anymore. I come from a town with one stoplight, where guys attach metal nut sacks to the back of their trucks as a sign of manliness. Add to that the fact that I had dated most of those nut-sack sporters, and it was game over.

What about the University of North Carolina at Chapel Hill? I thought. *After all, I look super fuckin' good in light blue.*

In classic, responsible Mamrie fashion, it was the only school I

*If you don't get this reference, drop what you are doing and drive/fly as fast as you can to the southeast of America. Pull into a Bojangles', order a Bo-Berry Biscuit, and experience it. I recommend doing drive-through, because you might need to be alone for this one. . . .

applied to, and I put my application in the mail literally seconds
before the post office closed, on the last day it could be postmarked.
Part of this was laziness; the other part was that it was a forty-
dollar application fee at the time. These days, I will spend that
much on a bottle of blueberry vodka or a novelty pair of jumbo
granny panties, but those days? Forget it. That was a double shift
at the movie theater.

But the college gods smiled upon me.

Chapel Hill is a Norman Rockwell painting of a four-year university. Lounging under hundred-year-old trees in the quad between
classes, throwing keggers in our yard, winning the NCAA championship my senior year. Everything about UNC was perfect, including
the girls. Therein lay the problem—the problem of not getting laid.
These weren't just ordinary girls. These girls looked like they had all
just walked out of a J.Crew catalog. They were all in sororities, lived
in Lilly Pulitzer dresses, and had names like Catherine Louise Van-
derbilt Montgomery XI. Meanwhile, I was co-president of Topless
Tuesday, wore Poison concert tees, and openly burped in public like
I was being possessed by the ghost of a velociraptor.

Luckily for me, my roommates were all normal and not the
priss-pots in floral cardigans we'd see on campus. But being normal had its drawbacks. Let's just say guys weren't exactly forming
lines to date us. Being asked out was borderline impossible for a
"normal" girl like me.

While we spent the fall getting dolled up and squeezing into our
best velvet pants (it was 2001), by the time Thanksgiving rolled
around we all said fuck it. Winter of our freshman year was spent
in pajamas in my dorm, mixing up frozen margs and singing the
Dixie Chicks into hairbrushes.

We became such hermits that the only time we saw guys was in
class or the dining halls. We would have crushes on guys from afar
but never actually talk to them.

*Did you see Green Hat in the dining hall today? He asked me to
quit hogging the ranch dressing. I think we had a moment.*

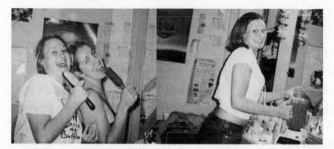

Sadly, I think the picture of Erika and me singing into hairbrushes is actually from Valentine's Day.

You guys. White Shirt is totally in my philosophy lecture. He sneezed last week, and I was this close to saying, "God bless you." Dammit, Mamrie! We could be engaged by now.

In our defense, we were screwed from the get-go. Unfortunately, not literally. While other college freshmen were basking in the scandal of living mere feet from the opposite sex, we were left out in the cold. The four of us had all requested a coed hall but were put together in an all-girls academic hall, or the "Virgin Vault," as it was so aptly called by the rest of the tower. I get that there wasn't enough coed housing, but putting us all in the same suite didn't make sense. They put the troublemakers in one place, like when Australia was a penal colony. Why stick us on the same floor as a seventeen-year-old getting her doctorate? Big mistake. We would be taking shots of room-temp raspberry vodka and making up a choreographed dance to Outkast, only to be yelled at by our hallmates:

Girls, seriously. I have heard "Ms. Jackson" on repeat for the last three hours. Can you please quiet down?

Aarushi, it's four p.m.! Get off our back. Here, take this. I handed her a shot. *It'll make you calm the fuck down.*

Later that semester, Aarushi would make her first B due to partying so much. I refused to take the blame. But I will take the credit for her record-breaking twenty-seven-second keg stand. When that girl put her mind to something, she'd do it really well.

Since meeting a guy on our floor was out of the question and putting on pants was required to leave the floor, dating was nonexistent. But in all truth I didn't want to go out with those frat chumps anyway. They wore pink polo shirts. Pink polo shirts tucked into *pleated* khakis. I am not hating on the Greek system in general. I spent many a wonderful night taking advantage of their parties with live bands and free beer. Hell, I even went with a friend to his frat formal in Charleston . . . dressed in full 1800s Southern regalia.* But frat dudes were mostly my friends, and not people I was interested in.

The only time I'd ever have luck meeting guys would be grad students or older guys. Lucky for me, I had the greatest wingman for all four years of college: a fake ID. That baby was my BFF. It wasn't fake so much as it was someone else's real ID, and I had to scrunch my face up and bug my eyes out every time a bouncer looked at me. But it always worked like a charm.

One night, my girls and I decided to peel the pajama pants off and go out. We got to the bar and right out of the gate I started having a super flirt session with a very attractive Italian guy. I'm not talking Italian like lives at home and lets his mom iron his underwear and cook him chicken parm every night. I'm talking the straight-up, plays *fútbol*, is named Piero, and barely understands what I'm saying kind of Italian. At this time, I was super into the show *Friends* (my roommates and I would make sure we were home at eight p.m. on Thursday, and if we weren't we would tape it on a *VCR*—yep, I'm that old, folks), so I often gleaned my life lessons from the wisdom of that Greenwich Village gang. I knew for a fact that Rachel didn't need to speak Italian to be able to date Paolo for almost an entire season. If she could do it, I

---

*Luckily, and honestly, I couldn't find a pic of that. But just imagine *Gone with the Wind*, except I'm gone with the whiskey. And my date was on acid, with a fake musket. FUN!

could do it. After all, I did look like Jennifer Aniston . . .'s overweight cousin, Tonya. I imagined going home with him to Sicily
and his mother having me try the marinara from a wooden spoon,
making sure the seasoning was right. I'd sip red wine as I helped
sprinkle the basil chiffonade on the caprese salad, looking out the
window at my new Italian boyfriend as he played checkers with a
table of old men from the village. (Like I said, it had been a while
since I'd gotten any male attention.) Naturally, I went home with
him.

Everyone relax! There was no stranger danger. I was going back
to a house with a group of people, including a girl from my sociology class whom the Italians were visiting. I *knew* her. I knew her
name and that she also needed sociology as a requirement. So, we
squeezed into their rented convertible, put the top down, and
cruised back to her house. About a half mile away, blue lights appeared in the rearview. Fuck, fuck, fuck. Our driver was sober, but
Little Miss Idiot in the backseat was eighteen and drunk as a skunk.
To be more specific, a skunk who'd just done five Jäger bombs.

The cop was actually cool (a sentence I never thought I'd say)
and told us if we left the car there and walked the rest of the way,
he wouldn't Breathalyze anyone. *Deal!* After all, we had a designated driver (the Italian Screech of the crew), but we'd been dumb-
asses to try and fit four people in the backseat. We all piled out and
started walking toward ~~what's-her-face's~~ my dear friend's house.
About halfway there, I had to take a major whiz. Being the classy
thing that I am, I politely excused myself and popped a squat in the
woods. Squatting down, listening to the breeze through the trees
and the pee hitting the ground beneath my feet, the night felt magical. I was finally gonna get some sweet, sweet ass. I couldn't risk
hooking up after a drip-dry!

I reached around me and grabbed a few leaves. Toilet paper is
technically made out of trees, I reasoned, so the leaves were like
the freshest one-ply TP available. #organic

RUTABAGA!

Once back at the house, the Italian and I had fun. I beat him at Ping-Pong, and then I beat on his ding-dong. I kid! That rhyme was *too* great not to go for. It takes a little more than that to put a notch on my lipstick case, but I was happy to "brush" up on him (makeup innuendo FTW).

The next day, the hangover was *painful*. But it wasn't as painful as being dropped off in front of your dorm by a convertible full of Italian men. Let me add that this was around nine fifteen a.m., right when *everyone* is headed to their nine-thirty class. Oh great, there's Green Hat watching me crawl out of this Miata full of dudes. Fantastic! There's White Shirt thinking I just played "Put Your Weenie in My Arancini" with five Italian dudes. But I played it cool (pretended to get a dramatic call on my flip phone) and hurried into the dorm. Once the elevator doors closed and I could finally relax, I noticed it. Something felt *off* in my pants. I fought the urge to panic and immediately drop my pants in the elevator, waiting until I got to my room.

There, on the toilet, is when I realized that nothing would ever be the same. Peering downtown, I saw that my hoo-ha was red and itchy and—holy fuck, I had Italian herpes! That was the only explanation. I straight-up had Italian herpes. Granted, it was probably much classier than normal herpes, with its affinity for high fashion and late-night dinners, but it was still *herpes*. And herpes is the one thing that lasts forever. Not true love, not diamonds—herpes. When the apocalypse comes, it won't just be cockroaches that survive. It will also be herpes and that random bottle of crème de menthe you bought years ago.

Upon learning about my new "forever friend," I took a shower hot enough to take off the top two layers of epidermis. I awkwardly crawled into bed. Just as I was about to finish filling out my online application to the nunnery, it hit me. That wasn't the herp; that was poison ivy! I must've, like an idiot, wiped with poison ivy leaves in the dark when I pissed in the woods!

I was so overcome with a sense of relief until I realized, *Hold up. I have poison ivy all over my vagina and butt crack*. It was like, *Phew, I thought I was eating poison but turns out it's only dog shit.* You still aren't exactly coming out on top.

And when I get poison ivy, *I get poison ivy*. When I was a little girl, I would spend a lot of time in the woods, and at least once a year my sister and I would come home covered in poison ivy. It would get so bad on our hands that my mom would have to feed us 'cause we couldn't pick up our forks. We looked like straight-up Garbage Pail Kids. We just never learned the adage "Leaves of three, let it be."*

Now, here's the superfun thing about having poison ivy all up in your butt crack. When you walk, the friction between your cheeks will cause it to spread. So I was pretty much detained from walking. And if I did, I was walking in a ballet second position with toilet paper separating my butt cheeks.

I missed a lot of class in those few weeks, and when my suitemates were questioned about where I was, they quickly made up excuses for me.

Mamrie? Oh, the poor thing got dumped. She's been eating Bagel Bites and watching The Notebook *for two weeks straight.*

Mamrie has been locked in our room, furiously masturbating to the first season of The Bachelor *all month. I've already called her parents.*

I'm Mamrie. We switched bodies. How's it going, y'all? Woot woot!

---

*When I was a camp counselor, I performed MC Hammer's "U Can't Touch This" but with all the words changed to be about poison ivy. I dressed like a poison ivy plant and made my campers be my back-up dancers.

I spent my days spread-eagle in front of a fan, with bright pink calamine lotion slathered all over my undercarriage. If you walked into my room, you'd think I was giving birth to a Pepto-Bismol baby. And it isn't until writing this *right now* that I realized the person who suffered the most during this whole ordeal was my roommate. What a sight to walk in to for two weeks!

If I wasn't laid out with my fanny to the fan, I was in the tub taking an oatmeal bath in hopes of drying out the rash. The dining hall workers must've thought I was a future subject for that show *Freaky Eaters*, judging by the amount of Quaker Oats packets I took from them. On the plus side, I smelled like maple and brown sugar for the next month.

Long story short, the whole ordeal was a nightmare. Watch where you squat, ladies. And for the love of God, drip-dry. Besides the pain and discomfort, it was just flat-out embarrassing—the most embarrassing thing I can think of. In fact, the only thing I can think of that could possibly be as embarrassing as having poison ivy on your crotch is taking a ten-hour flight back to Italy with it all over your *face*. That was going to be a tough one for him to explain to his mama. Sorry, Piero! But also, *thank you*, Piero!

Show Thyme

1 oz thyme simple syrup
Fresh blackberries
Juice of ½ lemon
2 oz gin
Champagne

For the simple syrup, combine a cup of water, a cup of sugar, and about 4 or 5 sprigs of fresh thyme in a saucepan. Leave on low heat until all the sugar has dissolved and the liquid is good and thymey (←not a word).

In a shaker, muddle 4 or 5 blackberries with the simple syrup. Add ice, lemon juice, and gin. Shake it all up and strain into a fancy lil' glass. Top with champagne. Then throw 2 or 3 blackberries on a toothpick to garnish. The drink will be a beautiful purple (the favorite color of all girls in the '90s), and the blackberries will resemble caviar, 'cause this shit is classy.

I have zero hesitation admitting that I am a complete and utter narcissist. A self-deprecating narcissist, but one nonetheless. I probably post at least one selfie a day. It's one picture—that I probably took fifteen times to get right. I talk into a camera at least twice a week, then stare at my face as I edit it, then continue staring at my face as I upload it.* But when I was growing up, it wasn't that simple. You took a photo of yourself and there was no checking it to see if your eyes were open. There was no, "Delete that. I'm making a derp face." You had to play the roulette of dropping off the film at a drugstore and waiting a week to get it back. Envelopes of pictures were more nerve-racking to peek at than pregnancy tests!

Disposable cameras have seen things. And touched things. There's something about disposable cameras that makes people stick them down their pants and take a crotch shot. All I know is if I worked at a film-development counter, I would put on a fuckin' hazmat suit if someone handed me a Kodak one-use. Back in my ~~whorey~~ glory days of college, I would straight-up get *anxiety* when I went to pick up pictures. I'd walk up to the CVS counter looking like the Unabomber—hat pulled down low, my hair in my face—and mumble, "Hi. I'm here to pick up some pictures. It's under the name Twila Falstaff."† Usually this was met with an "Mm-hmm" and a judgmental eyebrow raise as the clerk passed along the envelope, followed by me booking it out of there to check my pics in the safety of my car. Occasionally, the CVS employee would want to see me sweat, and I'd have to explain what was on the camera.

Ummm. They're pretty standard ones. Girls holding wine. Tailgating at the football game. Someone licking whipped cream off my neck as I'm dressed as Al from Home Improvement.

But of all the photos that have ever been taken of my face, there is one that holds a very special place in my heart. And that was . . . my Glamour Shot.

For those of you who didn't grow up going to malls (or were born

---

*And sometimes I look at it again when I get super drunk and watch my own videos (usually paired with me screaming, "I am a delight!" as I eat mashed potatoes with my hands).

†*Never* use your own name. As you can see, I use the fake name formula of A Southern Woman from the Civil War Era + Almost a Town in Arizona. Works every time.

after 1990), allow me to explain what Glamour Shots are. Glamour Shots are essentially the love child of head shots and the '80s prime-time soap *Dallas*. Real cosmetologists (more than likely beauty school dropouts) would style your hair and apply your makeup and deck you out in lavish costume jewelry and clothing. If that wasn't heaven enough, then you'd be placed in front of a crushed-velvet backdrop as the photographer snapped pics and said stuff like:

Beautiful! You are a natural. Just like Linda Evangelista! I haven't worked with anyone so talented since the JCPenney summer-sale shoot!

To ten-year-old Mamrie, the idea of Glamour Shots was a dream—my one-way ticket to Tinseltown. I had been begging to get an agent since the time I could talk; I'm almost positive that my first words were "lower commission." In my scheming brain, I could get my fancy Glamour Shots and mail them out to agents all across the US. Soon enough, a bidding war would erupt, and before you knew it, I would be replacing Topanga on *Boy Meets World* and changing the title to *Rider Strong Meets Mamrie*, because let's face it, Ben Savage might've had adorable curls and a charismatic old-Jewish-man vibe to him . . . but Rider was the babe.

I had been trying to punch my ticket out of Boonville since I was knee-high to a grasshopper, but there weren't a lot of agents scouting my area.* The only audition I went on as a kid was a cattle call for a lead in a made-for-TV movie. I wore my most adorable shorts overalls and my favorite Limited Too floral shirt. I even had my hair pulled back in a ponytail with a teeny-tiny stuffed animal bunny on the elastic. What could be cuter? We went to a hotel banquet hall filled with other ~~decent~~ adorable ten-year-olds and waited for two

---

*Although, just to be safe, I always dressed up when I went to the mall, and I definitely played my flattering angles when hanging at the food court. All those girls in *Seventeen* magazine would say how they got "discovered" when they least expected it. You'd better believe I wasn't going to be caught off guard in dirty overalls with a Cinnabon in my hand.

hours. Even though I felt like I charmed the casting directors and killed a Julia Sugarbaker sassy monologue from *Designing Women*,* I didn't get the part. In fact, they had thousands of little hopefuls like me come audition and then ended up giving the role to Anna Paquin. Anna Paquin—who had already *won an Oscar* when she was eleven. To this day, I can't watch *True Blood*. The fact that they chose her gap teeth over mine is too much to bear.

But I wasn't going to let one TV movie crush my dream. I figured I just had to change my approach. Forget overalls and bunny hair ties—I needed sultry backdrops and possibly a boa, the type of enhancements that only Glamour Shots could provide. But Glamour Shots weren't cheap, and before I could cruise on to bigger and better things, I had to convince my mom to shell out the dough. My first attempt was asked in what I thought was a very mature and reasonable manner, but she wasn't having it. I went back to the drawing board and came back with a rock-solid proposal.

"Moooooooom. PLEASE. For my birthday! I don't want a party, just Glamour Shots!"

"Mamrie, Glamour Shots make preteens look forty years old. If you want some pictures taken I can do it myself, here in the house."

But something told me it wouldn't be the same to just put on my mom's old eye shadow and stand in front of her flannel sheets. I had to go for a more severe tactic.

"First you and Dad get divorced. Then I lose the role I was born to play. And now I can't get Glamour Shots?!"

"Mamrie Lillian Hart . . ."

Uh-oh. The last time she used my full name was when she caught my friends and me prank calling our neighbor by asking if Mike Hunt was home. If I was going to get what I wanted, I had to go big.

---

*"And *that* . . . is the night the lights went out . . . in . . . Georgia!" Take a sip if you *don't* get that reference.

"I can't get Glamour Shots. I can't get an agent. I can't get an in-ground pool. Should I just write down all my dreams so you can set it on fire in front of me, or would you rather watch my pluck and optimism slowly disintegrate over the years?"

(Or something along those lines.)

Thanks to the massive guilt trip I laid, Mom agreed. In lieu of a birthday party that year, I would sacrifice my friends' good times and instead selfishly get pictures taken of myself. It was on!

Now, to help you fully understand the experience and what was going through my brain at the time, the next portion of this chapter will function as a diary entry. Why? Because I was always writing in a diary when I was that age—a Hello Kitty one, to be exact. I was on the Hello Kitty bandwagon *waaay* before everyone else, thanks to an exchange student my mom brought into our house. When I was growing up, my mom was always bringing exchange students to live with us. At any point, there would be an Irish kid or a German teenager in our spare bedroom. I'd like to say it was my mom's way of helping us to be open-minded and comfortable around other cultures, but I think she just wanted an in-house babysitter. To this day, I can say, "What do you mean I have to watch her?" in five languages.

Kyoto was my favorite, though—a supercool teenage girl from Japan who stayed with us for a whole year. I loved her, and when she went back to Japan, she would send me Hello Kitty stuff. Every time I got a little package from Kyoto, I was in heaven. I would obsess over my little erasers and notebooks and candies like they were gold. But that Hello Kitty diary was the ultimate import. I thought of it as my confidant, my best friend. Which means either that diary was magical, or I was very lonely. Possibly a little of both.

All right. Everyone take a moment, do some light stretching, and try to put yourself in the mind-set of a ten-year-old maniac. Can you feel the leggings and puffy-painted sweatshirt? Can you taste the Dunkaroos? Good. You are ready. Open your Hello Kitty diary and begin reading.

Dear Diary,

First off, I gotta say sorry for not writing in you for so long. I know I promised that I would write in you every day, but I've been so busy with school. And basketball. And building my Jonathan Taylor Thomas shrine. Anyway, allow me to catch you up on a few things since I last wrote. . . . Yes, I'm now in fifth grade. NO, I still haven't gotten my period. . . .

Anywho, last night I couldn't sleep at all. And it wasn't just because I stayed up late watching "Now and Then." I swear, every time I see that Devon Sawa I get this tingly feeling in my privates area. Almost like it fell asleep, but trust me, that thing is awake!

Anywhoozerz. I couldn't fall asleep because I was too excited. The reason I was so excited is because today I was going to get GLAMOUR SHOTS. That's right. My first-ever photo shoot! First step, Glamour Shots; second step, Oscar; third step, slapping that smile off Anna Paquin's face!

The drive to the mall felt like an eternity, and not just because my mom was listening to a Garth Brooks cassette. My mom let my sister, Annie, come with us. UGH. Annie is so annoying. She's two years older than me, and she thinks that makes her an adult. Also, she thinks she's hot shit since she got a water bed. Don't get me wrong, water beds are crazysexycool, but Annie doesn't need one. She gets seasick! Oh well, as much as I want to pinch her sometimes, she is my sister and I love her. And I didn't just write that because I know you are reading this, Annie. Annie, stop reading this!

We got to the mall an hour early, so I had a little time to hit up my favorite stores. First stop, Candy Express. I needed to pick up a new jumbo Everlasting Gobstopper. They are super popular right now. If you aren't sucking on an Everlasting Gobstopper the size of a softball, you might as well be invisible. It took me three weeks to get to the middle of my last one. And when I did, after three weeks of work, want to know what was in the middle? More candy. I thought there would at least be a ruby or some kind of precious gem inside, but nope. Oh well, it was worth it, even though my tongue bled for days and I couldn't really taste food for a week. Mom said I scraped off my taste buds, and I said, "I did it on purpose—have you tasted your meat loaf?" J/K. Mom's meat loaf is the shit. Annie, tell Mom I wrote good things about her meat loaf and then STOP READING!!

After Candy Express, I checked out the new styles at Abercrombie & Fitch. Have you seen the boys who work at that store? They smell like a woodsy daydream, and the models are barely wearing clothes! Once I get my period and my boobs come in, I think I'll model for them. If they're lucky! Speaking of modeling, I saw this episode of "Saved by the Bell" last Saturday where Kelly Kapowski starts modeling. She does a photo shoot and the photographer tries to convince her to take off her top, which she refuses. They wanted her to go to France and she turned it down! What an idiot! Your last name is clearly Polish, Kelly. The Poles have a hard enough time living down their idiot stereotype without you adding to it. UGH. Who turns down Paris? If it were me, and I had boobs, I'd be topless on the Eiffel Tower, flaunting my croissants faster than you can say "Slater, please cut your mullet."

Speaking of France, last weekend I went to Carowinds with Kristen.* We pretended to speak French with each other to look exotic around boys. Every time there was a cute boy behind us in line for a roller coaster, we would launch into French gibberish. A couple of boys tried to talk

---

*Carowinds is North Carolina's equivalent of Six Flags. There are crazy rides, and Dippin' Dots, and you can even stand in North and South Carolina at the *same time*. At the time, this was mind-blowing.

to us but we pretended we couldn't speak English. In retrospect, it was a terrible way to try to flirt with boys. They couldn't understand us at all, and we spent half the time talking nonsense to each other instead of actually hanging out. Back to the mall!

SO anyway, when we got to the pop-up Glamour Shots store, I was brought to a makeup chair. AN ENTIRE CHAIR JUST FOR MAKEUP! The mirror had all those little globe lights all around it like I was a real movie star.

"Hi, I'm Maureen," the makeup artist said, reaching out her French-manicured hand. She had beautifully teased hair and her fingers smelled like cigarettes. I knew I was in good hands. I said to her, "Look, I know it's very hard to improve on perfection, but do your best. Ideally I am going for a D. J. Tanner from 'Full House' look, but literally tanner. Let's say if D.J. were also a quarter Native American—that would be ideal." Just so you can get a full understanding of how well this mash-up was executed, here's the final pic!

As you can see, Maureen did an epic job in contouring my cheekbones, which was totally my idea. I asked her if she could shade in some striking angles to take away the chubbiness of my cheeks. I didn't want to get my proofs back and see myself looking like a chipmunk. Although, if I were a chipmunk, I would definitely be dating Alvin, the hottest of all chipmunks. Alvin is such a bad boy. He's always getting into trouble and can sing like crazy. However, if Alvin and I were to ever start dating, I would have to give him a total makeover. The dude wears long shirts and no pants. What's up with that?! Alvin, you look like you're going through a mental breakdown and have resorted to wearing only nightgowns. Not a good look. At least Simon has brains and Theodore found a chubby chaser. Get it together, Alvin!

I had a little bit of a tiff with Maureen while we were picking out wardrobe. I asked if it would be possible to stuff my bra and she "didn't think that was appropriate." You know what's not appropriate, Maureen? Chain-smoking a pack of Kools and not washing your hands before slapping bronzer on a 10-year-old.

At least I got to wear my favorite color. Metallic blue. They had this sweet jacket, which I can only imagine was 100% real leather, and they even gave me matching earrings! As you know, Diary, I don't have my ears pierced (I'm no slut), but luckily, these were clip-ons. They looked rad but I felt like I had two boat anchors attached to my ears. I imagined taking off the earrings and my lobes being totally stretched out. Just dangling on my shoulders like those women in Mom's "National Geographic" magazines. But sometimes you need to sacrifice for beauty, you know?

Once my cheeks were bronzed like a pair of baby shoes, it was showtime. Look, I always knew I was going to give great facial expressions, but I'll be honest, Diary. It was tougher than I thought. I was so happy to be in front of the camera, but I couldn't fully smile. I wasn't going to show the gap in my teeth! As soon as I turn 14, I'm going to get it fixed. . . .

All in all, the Glamour Shot experience was a success. Now I just gotta figure out how to find the addresses for agents. If only there were some way to look up information easily. Like typing it into a computer or something. But, no! Computers are just for Number Munchers and catching dysentery on the Oregon Trail.

Well, gotta go, Diary.

Peeeeeace!

Xo
Mamrie

As you can see, the picture turned out amazing. I could no doubt have been cast on *Kids Incorporated* from this head shot alone. But seeing how big a diva one hour in the hair-and-makeup chair turned me into, I am glad I wasn't allowed to be a kid actor. By the time I'd hit twelve I wouldn't have let anyone look me directly in the eye. I would've made my assistant spray my favorite perfume (Exclamation!) in every room or hallway before I entered, not to mention making sure the Dunkaroos in my dressing room were only icing, *no* cookies.

So thanks, Mom. You made the right move on that one, which helped me grow up to be a grounded and full individual. It wouldn't be until years later that my ego would be pumped up fuller than Annie's water bed.

Quickshots: Birthday Parties

This Quickshot is about birthday parties. Trading in a birthday party for that sick Glamour Shot was totally worth it. And this is coming from someone who *lives* for birthday parties. There are some people in this world who get embarrassed when their friends inform the waiters at a restaurant that it's their birthday. Screw that! I tell them it's my birthday when it's not. If there's an opportunity to wear a novelty sombrero while eating *free* flan, you'd better believe "today is *mi cumpleaños*."

Here is a list of my favorite b-day bashes through the ages.

Discovery Zone

Fuck Chuck E. Cheese's. Back in the '90s there was an amazing chain called Discovery Zone. Unlike the Chuckster, it had less of a focus on video games and more of a focus on a huge indoor jungle gym. I'm talking massive ball pits, slides, tunnels, all the top names. The kind of place that had shoe cubbies and the whole building reeked of children's feet. Even though I was too old to be hanging out in a place where most of the clientele picked their noses, I was *obsessed* with it. Other girls my age probably preferred hanging out at the mall, seeing what the latest fashions were at Gap Kids, but not me. If DZ were still around today and I could get a fake ID saying I'm under twelve years old, this book wouldn't exist, because there aren't electrical outlets for my laptop in the ball pits.

Every time my mom was going to Winston,* I would beg her to let me go to DZ while she ran her errands. Technically, I don't think you are supposed to drop off your kids, but like I said, I was of the older echelon of kids there (plus the staffers probably pitied me—let's be real).

Check it out, Dame DZ is back. She's gonna crack a hip one of these days.

I don't understand. Is this a brilliant ploy to get babysitting jobs?

Based on the way she just knocked that four-year-old over to get to the rope ladder, I don't think so.

When my eleventh birthday rolled around, I knew what I wanted: my ten closest girlfriends and five guy friends to all go to Discovery Zone with me. And, by God, my folks agreed. I don't blame them. After all, DZ was way less scandalous than the skating rink (my second choice). At the skating rink, there were way more dark corners. Plus they had designated songs for couples skates. Call me a prude,† but a bunch of fifth-graders holding hands while skating to Boyz II Men's "I'll Make Love to You" had to be a disturbing sight for parents.

The party was a *blast*. We climbed the ropes, crawled through the tunnels, and zip-lined into the ball pit. Which, I will say, is pretty brave of me, considering one time I jumped into a ball pit at McDonald's only to realize some kid had vomited right beside my landing spot. Have you ever tried gracefully getting out of a ball pit without the balls moving? It does not work. Those vomit balls avalanched on me, and my Happy Meal was not so happy anymore.

As thrilling as the obstacle course was, the real fun happened in

---

*The closest town with a movie theater and shopping—thirty miles away.

†BAHAHAHAHAHAH. That's a good one, me.

the bounce castle area. This was the part of the obstacle course most tucked away from all the *immature* eight-year-olds. It was also farthest from the chaperones' watchful eyes. It was there, among the primary-color tubes of air, that I suggested a game after a failed attempt at "Spin the Hat" (we were resourceful).

"I know a game we can play. I remember hearing that older kids would play it back when I lived in New Jersey." I had their attention. "It's called Sleeping Beauty. All the girls lay down in a circle with their eyes closed. The boys walk around and plant a kiss on each girl. If you are kissed and can feel like it's your Prince Charming, you open your eyes and scream out, 'Sleeping Beauty!'"

Here's why this game was brilliant:

A. Because even at eleven, I was figuring out ways to make finding love a competition, years before *The Bachelor*. There was no strategy. You could only "win" if you felt enough of a spark from that pop kiss to claim victory.

B. I made that shit up on the spot. This was no game I'd heard of in New Jersey. This was something I came up with in that bounce castle, 'cause let's face it, birthday girl wanted to get smooched!

I lay there on the bounce castle with my eyes closed. I was completely still with my arms folded across my chest, but on the inside I was freaking out.

Please don't be Jeff; let it be Eddie. Please don't be Jeff; let it be Eddie.

After the third or so kiss (three seconds long, closed mouth, basically an extended peck), I decided, *Screw it! I am going to open my eyes on the next boy.* I felt the face come closer to me. My eyes were closed so tight you would think I was watching *The Exorcist*. A perfect, sweet kiss was planted on my Dr Pepper Lip Smackered lips. Just as I was about to open my eyes and yell, "Sleeping Beauty!" I heard Leslie scream it first!

I instinctively shot Leslie my strongest evil eye. Trust me, if looks could kill, she would've turned to a pile of ash. The rage behind my superthick glasses cooled, however, once I noticed who her Prince Charming was.

It was Jeff! Boom! In ya face, Leslie. I had been secretly harboring a grudge against Leslie since she and Eddie had couples-skated to "Bump N' Grind" at her birthday party. But being the bigger person (literally; Leslie was seventy-five pounds soaking wet), I still invited her to my party.

Looking at Leslie with Jeff, I couldn't help but feel jealous. Sure, she had just risked injury by kissing those braces, but she won Sleeping Beauty! That envy lasted all of twenty seconds when I noticed that the prince I was going to open my eyes to was . . . Eddie. My big crush. Later that day Eddie would ask me to be his girlfriend while we played Skee-Ball. I played it cool and said, "Only if I hit the one hundred hole on this next ball." I hit it. I ruled at Skee-Ball then, and I do now. We lasted two blissful weeks, complete with holding hands that day and waving to each other in the lunchroom a total of seven times before calling it quits.

Once we were all DZed out, the boys went home and all the girls came back to my place for a slumber party. We sugar-rushed off so many M&M's that you would've thought they were cocaine flavored, and then we made up dance routines to En Vogue's "Free Your Mind." It wasn't until our sugar crash, when all of us girls piled onto a big pallet on the floor to give each other temporary tattoos, that I heard the news. Apparently it wasn't just any old pop kiss that had made Leslie wake from her sleeping spell. Jeff had slipped her the tongue. Looks like there were *lots* of things discovered that day at the Discovery Zone.

Studio 54

If you want your birthday to be a fun and memorable one, instill a liquor-only rule. If you want your birthday to be so fun and memorable that everyone blacks out and can barely remember it, instill a liquor-only rule.

This was the only regulation for my twenty-first birthday party. "No beer, no wine, only liquor, all the time."* I know what you are thinking. Twenty-first birthday? Lemme guess, you probably put on some dumb tiara and proceeded to take twenty-one shots along a bar crawl until you threw up in the streets. Ummmm, do you even know me at all? Of *course* I did that.

But I grand-marshaled that puke parade the night I was *turning* twenty-one. The birthday shindig was the next day.

It all started with a ridiculous green jumpsuit. For some reason, while I was walking through Nordstrom (I was feeling fancy that day), a lime green halter-top jumpsuit caught my eye. Probably because it was greener than a shaved kiwi. If I had accidentally rolled up on a green screen, I would've been a floating head and arms. I knew I had to have it. I looked at the price tag. Seventy-five bucks?! Well, that wasn't going to happen.

At the time, I was working at a bar called Woody's, which served cheap beer and cheap wings. In fact, I worked there the majority of my college days. I won't lie, it can be tough as a female to work at a place that is also a slang term for a boner. College guys aren't exactly the classiest folks after eight pints of Newcastle. Anyway! I worked hard at Woody's. My budgeting process for buying things would always end up being broken down into how many chicken-wing bones I would have to clean up to make that amount. At around a dollar tip per dozen wings, that jumper was looking like nine hundred bones. But I didn't care. When a mother goes

---

*Looking back, I was maybe a little too into *Coyote Ugly*. What can I say? That LeAnn Rimes soundtrack got me.

into an orphanage and sees the baby she knows is hers, she doesn't say, "What are the legal costs of this adoption?" She'll pay whatever it takes. And I felt the same way about this glorious getup.

Once I officially had the lime green halter-top jumpsuit in my life, the next issue to solve was where the hell I was gonna wear this thing. And so I used my old rule of thumb for ridiculous clothing purchases: If it doesn't work in everyday life, make it work by throwing a theme party! I knew immediately that the theme for my twenty-first was going to be Studio 54.*

Studio 54 is not only the inspiration for a terrible movie starring Ryan Phillippe and Neve Campbell; it was the name of a legendary club in New York during the '70s and '80s. It was disco! It was celebrities! It was eventually shut down because of tax evasion!

But for one fateful night in September 2004, I wanted to reopen the infamous hot spot in my shitty rental house. I told all my friends they had to dress in disco-era clothing. It can be tough to get good ol' boys whose idea of dressy clothes is their least stained basketball shorts to don polyester shirts and high-waisted pants. But after a little coercing (and me physically dragging them to Goodwill), everyone was game!

My roommates helped and we decorated our house with cheesy decorations from Party City. We stocked the bar with all the cheap liquor we could afford and filled the fridge with two hundred Jell-O shots. To really put the classy cherry on top, I filled a huge bowl with condoms, individual lube packets, and mints. Hey! I was single and it was my birthday. I wasn't taking any chances.

(Quick advice: If you are going to throw a party with lube packets as party favors, swiftly dispose of any that didn't get taken by

---

*In retrospect this is hilarious because Studio 54 was known for an insane amount of cocaine use, and I had never and will never touch cocaine in my life. Cocaine makes you cocky. I clearly do not need any help in that area. One bump and I'd be scared I'd become a dictator or cult leader.

I'm just assuming I didn't make any hors d'oeuvres for this party and that is why I'm biting a condom. Whore d'oeuvres, anyone?

guests. I would recommend doing this the following morning, or at least before you drunkenly eat french fries in the dark. Astroglide is no substitute for ketchup.)

Everyone got rip-roaring plastered within the first hour, and I couldn't have been happier. As things tend to do, the rest of the night got a little blurry. Thank God we had all those disposable cameras lying around so we could piece together the evening. Twila Falstaff made several trips to the CVS photo counter the following week.

A few things were obvious in the light of day: My roommates each had their crushes in bed with them, my friend Stacey ended up on my couch with a UNC basketball player, and I have *no* idea how he got word of the party. And this twenty-one-year-old birthday girl was the only party guest who didn't get laid.

Ping-Pong Tourney

I am a fiercely competitive person, which might seem surprising considering I don't give a shit about sports. I do, however, give a major shit about *tiny* sports. If it is a miniature version of a preexisting sport, I turn into a maniac. Seriously. I could be in a sports bar during the last game of the World Cup, and I'd ask the bartender to change it to *Ellen*. But if there's a foosball table in said sports bar? It's *on*.

But my true tiny calling is Ping-Pong. I think I love the idea that I can get super competitive while not really having to move my body all that much. The lack of movement, however, doesn't stop me from letting out backbreaking groans and wearing tennis skirts.

In New York, down in the West Village, there's an amazing bar called Fat Cat that has at least twenty Ping-Pong tables and always some random a cappella gospel and doo-wop group singing in the corner. The crowd there is great: guys trying to teach their dates how to put backspin on a serve, along with no-nonsense players who never talk and wear wrist sweatbands unironically. It was the perfect spot for my Table Tennis Tourney Birthday!

I set up the tourney March Madness–style, with sixteen people competing in a bracket that we taped up on the wall of our private room, away from the heated competition of the main room and the crooning of the a cappella gospel. Not that they didn't sound great—I love me a good bass voice—but it wasn't exactly pumping me up. I needed less "This Little Light of Mine" and more Prodigy's "Firestarter."

As in any good tournament, a trophy had to be awarded to the winner. Luckily, making trophies is one of my hidden talents. Pro tip: You can essentially make anything into a trophy as long as you have gold spray paint and a hot-glue gun.

This is the one I made for the party:

A jumbo can of black beans provided the necessary heft for the base, topped with a regular-size can of garbanzo beans for the second tier. The top is a dollar-store T. rex figurine. But a keen eye can see all the details that really set this homemade trophy apart from others. Upon close examination, you'll see that the T. rex is holding its own Ping-Pong paddle—and that, my friends, is the tiny magnifying glass from a glasses repair kit. In addition to the dino having the proper sports equipment, you will also notice that he is wearing a tiny bandanna around his neck. The very same bandanna that I was rocking that night. BOOM! It is those minute details that make a five-dollar trophy something that adults will fight over.

Competition got heated, and not just because a basement bar full of people in September is steamy as hell. We kicked off the first round of the bracket and immediately could tell that people were in it to win it. People were giving it their all—backhand serves, hard-core topspin, nonchalant nip slips for distraction. They were so hard core that I was knocked out in the first round. This is shocking for two reasons:

1. Me losing at Ping-Pong is like the 1993 Chicago Bulls not making the playoffs.*

AND FURTHERMORE:

2. Who the hell doesn't let the birthday girl win?!

I'll tell you who: my friend Alan. He came in wanting to win that night, and he wasn't going to let minor details like whose birthday it was stop his momentum. Alan is hilarious. He drives an orange Vespa, has a pipe collection, plays the ukulele. In fact, he got me into playing too—so much so that we had a group that would meet occasionally and play ukuleles, sing songs together, and have cocktails. We called it Uke Group, because obviously it needed a name (my obsession with clubs never wavered in adulthood). I have a very distinct memory of us meeting in Prospect Park in Brooklyn to picnic and play our ukes when the weather finally broke to spring. There we were, a bunch of semihipster adults surrounded by containers of hummus, playing "She'll Be Coming Round the Mountain" on our tiny instruments as a group of kids rode by on their bikes. We actually sang softer until the "tough kids" passed, like we were gonna get beat up by twelve-year-olds. As soon as we were in the clear, we broke into a rousing rendition of "Clambake." Alan was nice enough to even make a website for Uke Group so we could print sheet music before meetings. Depending on when you get this book, it might even still be up: www.ukegroup.net.

---

*I clearly had to google this, despite begging my parents for (and getting) Air Jordans every year growing up. What can I say? The boys loved them and I was a total poseur.

Alan's passion wasn't only for tiny stringed instruments. He wanted that trophy and spared no feelings for the birthday girl. I was bummed, sure, but the real job of the birthday girl is to keep the guests happy and get crunk. I watched the other rounds play out and noticed that someone else had the eye of the tiger:* my boyfriend. He was swinging that paddle like he was the long-lost Caucasian brother of the Williams sisters.

As luck would have it, Alan and Boyfriend were the final two in the series. At this point, I was D-R-U-N-K. As the fierce opponents took their respective sides of the table, I stood in the middle addressing the crowd.

"Listen up, ladies and germs! We have come to the championship round of my berfday Ping-Pong bonanza. The winner of this round will walk away not only with pride but also with this sweet-ass T. rex trophy that I hand-made. Gentlemen, take your positions . . . pe he he, positions . . . and play ball!"

I felt like Cha Cha in *Grease* when she lifts the handkerchief to start the race.

The match was neck and neck, the crowd watching the Ping-Pong ball like cats watching a laser pointer. There were oohs and aahs. It was like the live studio audience of *Family Matters*. When it came down to game point, I saw the fire in Boyfriend's eyes. In my tipsy brain, he threw that tiny white ball in the air and slammed his serve like Roger Federer. In reality, it was probably just a normal small Ping-Pong serve, but gosh darnit, he won! He took it home!

Unfortunately, I didn't want to take a certain thing home, and that was the trophy I'd made. What's the fun in creating such a dumb prize that people are vying for just to end up bringing it

---

*Tigers' vision isn't *that* impressive, TBH. They are basically color-blind. If any animal has good vision, it's actually a goat, who can see almost 360 degrees. But apparently, "Eye of the Goat" doesn't sound that badass in an '80s pump-up jam.

home yourself? I suggested we give it to Alan as a token of his hard work that night. It had been one of the greatest birthdays I'd ever had and I wanted to spread the cheer. But that wasn't going to fly. In fact, Boyfriend was straight-up offended.

Yeah, he and I fought for a good hour about how I didn't appreciate him defending my honor. I can only imagine the amount of eye rolling that must've gone on in the driver's seat of that cab as we argued about Ping-Pong in the back with a small golden T. rex between us, my boyfriend going on and on about honor like he was William Wallace defending Scotland! Like most drunk fights between couples, it ended with us both passing out, waking up the next day, and calling a truce mainly because neither of us could remember the fight enough to throw details in the other's face. The fight didn't last, but that trophy did. And on top of the fridge is where that T. rex lived for the next several years. It's currently defending my honor somewhere in a storage unit.

'80s Prom Kickball

Sometimes you just have to take the things you love most, smash them together, and see if it works. In the case of my twenty-third birthday, those things were kickball and '80s prom dresses. Don't think it makes sense? I'm sure the first person who combined peanut butter and bacon got some crazy looks from their friends. And on your birthday, of all times, why not combine two things you love while also making people bring you gifts and sing you "Happy Birthday"? It's an unbeatable idea. Other combination parties that I could have based on this theory would be:

1. White Wine and Watching Reruns of *How I Met Your Mother*
2. Making Crafts and Eating Kraft Macaroni and Cheese
3. Champagne and Shopping for Candles Online

4. Spanish Tapas and Swiffering
5. Margaritas and Masturbating

The greatest part about unlikely combo birthdays are all the looks you get from passersby. Take a moment to imagine walking through a park: the dogs, the joggers, the two dozen drunk adults playing an intense game of kickball in taffeta (which can be extremely chafing, FYI).

When all was said and done, our drunk *Footloose*-looking asses poured into a karaoke bar. Karaoke! One more thing that I love added to this birthday. Unlike my first night in New York, this karaoke session didn't end with a chipped tooth. It did, however, end up with us being kicked out of the bar as I wore a hot pink cummerbund like Rambo.

Ninja Night

At this point you've heard of my eccentric birthdays and thought, *Okay, I get it, those parties were in your twenties. You're allowed to be* *an idiot.* To that I say, hold on to your panties. Because my thirtieth birthday was the cream of the crop.*

When it came time to plan my three-oh, I knew I had to step it up. None of this child's play of dressing up in sequins or dancing to "Y.M.C.A." Hell naw. This was the first time people could legitimately give me "over the hill" cards, or a cane with a horn on it. I was over the hill and all about the thrills. So I decided I was going to have a Gun Party!

Okay, before you go all long-winded political Facebook post on me, I don't mean real guns. These were pellet guns; they couldn't do that much damage. I know, because I've been shot in the ass with one as punishment for losing a game, and it didn't break the skin.†

This shoot-out party was going to be one for the books. The only downside was that I was super busy at the time and needed some help. I knew the exact right person for the job: Topless Tuesday cofounder Melissa. You might recognize her from stories in this book that end with me being either half-naked or on drugs. She is the type of woman who goes fountain jumping naked in L.A. and regularly attends monster truck rallies, a girl you could call on a Sunday to see what she's up to and hear, "Not much. I ate a weed brownie and saw a show by myself at a marionette theater. What are you up to?" A word of advice, if you have a friend like this, your wild card: She is the *perfect* person to throw you a birthday party. Relinquish all control and just hand her a guest list.

We held the party at our friend Ryan's warehouse. Ryan owns a prop shop, which is basically a huge warehouse where he builds crazy shit for commercials. From the outside, there isn't much to look at: a random brick warehouse with a chain-link fence and a

---

*I am now realizing that you should never say "panties" and "cream" that close together.

†Despite my crying from anxiety, it was like getting a shot: a lot of buildup for not that much actual pain.

couple of cars parked outside. It looks like any typical canning factory or place for a murder, but on the inside it's *heaven*.

To paint you a dusty picture, one time when I was leaving Ryan's after a cookout he told me to watch out for the pack of wild Chihuahuas. I laughed and thought what a cute visual wild Chihuahuas would be. After all, I am the owner of a Mexican Hairless named Beanz.

Don't readjust your contacts. No, that is not the slow hyena from The Lion King. *That is my four-pound best friend.*

Can you imagine being chased by a pack of these? Worst-case scenario, you trip and get tickled to death by their tongues. But sure enough, I pulled out of his gate and a pack of tiny, grizzled Chihuahuas, hungry for blood and Pup-Peronis, stared me down from across the road. Individually they couldn't do much damage, but together they could destroy some ankles.

The party was set up with multiple shoot-out challenges. You had your pellet gun shooting out lightbulbs, a Chinese star being thrown at a foam bull's-eye, a blow dart you had to get through a hole in a piece of plywood to pop a balloon ten feet behind that. It was intense! We all took turns going down the roster, and lots of folks were decent shots.

Other highlights include getting an actual crossbow as a gift, swinging from a large hanging rope while singing "Wrecking Ball," and meeting my friend Tyler Oakley's mom, Jackie. Jackie was visiting Tyler from Michigan, and my party happened to fall on the last night of her visit. Tyler, not wanting a total case of FOMO, asked if he could bring her along. Of course, I immediately said yes! I had seen Jackie in a lot of Tyler's videos (he is also a YouTuber) and knew we would get along perfectly. I'm real good with moms, y'all. Here's proof:

They say the way to a mother's heart is teaching her how to shoot a gun while you're dressed in a Party City ninja costume. I aim to please.

Jackie ended up going home with a Best Effort belt. Yes, being the costume designer that she is, Melissa made (from scratch) leather-and-metal wrestling belts that I was able to dole out at the end of the night as the *Rocky* theme song blared through the warehouse.

Most people on their thirtieth try to class it up, but I'm never going to stop having ridiculous birthdays. I say make them over-the-top. Make them strange. If people ask you, "When are you going to grow up?" think about it for a second, then reply, "Probably in a couple . . . *eat shit*." We are always growing up. I'm growing up as I type this. An eighty-seven-year-old woman is still *technically* growing up. So be as immature as you want. Right now, you are the youngest you are ever going to be.

Hurry! Someone get me a motivational poster deal ASAP.

Frame the Cookie

Chocolate syrup
1 oz butterscotch schnapps
1 oz Irish cream
1 oz amaretto
2 oz cinnamon vodka

For the vodka: Fill a mason jar with 16 ounces of vodka (trust me, you will want 8 of these things). Toss in 5 cinnamon sticks (if you're feeling crazy, throw in a vanilla bean). Let this sit for at least a week, shaking it once a day.

First things first: Take your chocolate syrup and go all Spirograph on the inside of a martini glass. Stick that in the freezer to harden.

Then put all your remaining ingredients in a shaker full of ice, work those biceps that you pretend to have, and strain into the frozen martini glass. But beware, this ain't no Little Debbie bullshit. This thing will knock your pigtails into a Mohawk after four sips.

Marriage has never really been on my radar. It's not that I *dislike* it or anything. If you tell me that you're engaged, I won't look at you with dead eyes and say, "If you're going to tie the knot, better tie it on your noose because your life is over." That urge to say "I do" hasn't kicked in yet, and now that I'm thirty, I don't think it ever will. Then again, I started enjoying mustard at twenty-seven, so anything is possible.

These days, though, it seems like weddings are more "in" than ever! When it comes to their big day, bitches be cray cray. Some girls dream about their magical day their whole lives. They have Pinterest boards filled with DIY place cards or mason jar boutonnieres. These girls can't *wait* to slide into a strapless mermaid dress and walk down the aisle to Bob Carlisle's "Butterfly Kisses."* The thought of doing this gives me douche chills.

Part of me thinks I've never thought about my own wedding because I never got to be a flower girl when I was little. I have a theory that flower girls get such an insane adrenaline rush from tossing petals and the oohs from the crowd, that they're hooked for life. Forever chasing the dragon until their own big day. Not that I didn't want to be a flower girl; it just never happened for me, and understandably so. It's not like I was the cutest kid on the block. When you're picking a flower girl, you go for the most cherubic, not the most charismatic. I was always covered in dirt, and until I was four, I had the same haircut as Sandra Bullock in *Gravity*. Not cute. It was probably for the best that I was never in a wedding as a kid. At the end of the day, I would've taken over. I would've slipped the ushers a crisp fiver from my allowance to throw on "Motownphilly" as I did an original hip-hop routine down the aisle.

Once I aged out of flower girl, I still never joined the bridal party. I thought I would at least get to be in a wedding party once my siblings got hitched, but that ended up being a lost cause. My brother got married when he was twenty-two after he and my sister-in-law started randomly downloading each other's music on Napster, which blossomed into a long-distance love affair for ten months and eventually a marriage with two beautiful daughters.

---

*If you are thinking about using this song to walk down the aisle, do yourself a favor and really listen to the lyrics. They are fucking creepy. There's an actual line to her daddy that says, "If you don't mind, I'm only gonna kiss you on the cheek this time." Da fuck, Carlisle?

Come on, now. A marriage that sprang from Napster? That shit is more 2001 than Shaggy's career.

My sister has two kids with the same guy but never married him. Annie first became pregnant when she was nineteen. Normally in the South this would turn into a shotgun wedding situation, but we were fine with her not going the distance. If you aren't fluent in redneck,* a "shotgun" wedding happens when the bride is knocked up (i.e., the father of the bride will pull out his shotgun if that sonofabitch who put a baby in his daughter doesn't make her a bride).

Just because I don't want my own wedding doesn't mean I wouldn't love being in one. Some girls complain that they are "always the bridesmaid, never the bride." I, on the other hand, was "always a person who gets super wasted at the reception but is never close enough to the bride to warrant a spot in the professional photos." Here's the deal, guys: Even if I'm not in the wedding party, I'm always the *party* of the wedding. In fact, *I fucking love going to weddings.*

If I attend your wedding reception, there are some guarantees: I *will* convince your mom to take shots with me. I *will* flirt with your grandpa. I *will* get the Macarena started, and I won't leave until I am forced.

Given my enthusiasm, I've never really understood people who complain so much about attending weddings. We all know these people, the ones who bitch and moan about how their schedules are just jam-packed with nuptials.

No, fu' realz, Mamrie. Mark and I have a wedding, like, every freakin' weekend this July. It's, like, our part-time job.

*Speaking of redneck nuptials, one time I went to my high school friend's trailer. Apparently her mom had gotten engaged the night before. I immediately grabbed her hand to check out the rock, only to have her point to her ear. Yep, she and her fiancé had just bought a pair of diamond earrings and were each wearing one. I guess they were all out of engagement BB guns.

I had one too many at some nuptials and decided to try opening all my beers on various taxidermied animals. No one else thought this game was fun.

Oh, you mean a part-time job that has an open bar, mini–crab cakes, and a bumping dance floor? BRB. Gotta fill out an application.

But Mames, you have to buy so many gifts. I can't tell you how many toasters I've had to buy this year!

I'm sorry, but a sixty-dollar toaster sounds like a reasonable deal for a night of drinking. If I leave a bar with a tab lower than a cool hundo, I must've realized I forgot to set my DVR on a *Real Housewives* reunion. I wish bars had wedding registries as an acceptable form of currency. I'd be all like:

Rodney! I gotta close out, man!

(throws Cuisinart ice-cream maker on the bar)

Keep the change, ya filthy animal.

These people don't know how good they've got it. Going to weddings is the shit. I straight-up *train* for wedding season. I give zero fucks about ever buying a wedding dress, but you'd better believe I've seen every episode of *Say Yes to the Dress*. My favorite part of this show is when Monte, the silver lion of a man, "jacks up" the bride by slapping a veil and some costume jewelry on her and voilà—everyone explodes into ugly crying.

God, if only everything in life could be solved by jacking it up.

Parents don't approve of your homosexual lifestyle? Throw a veil on it! Recently found out you'll be spending seventeen years in prison for tax evasion? Quick! Grab one of those rhinestone ribbon belts to accentuate your waist!

I love watching these brides find their perfect dress as their bridesmaids cheer and hold up scorecards, even though I'd never had the thrill of holding up a 10 myself. But all that changed in 2011 when my high school best friend left me an excited voice mail.

"Mame-a-ho, it's Ash-hole!" She sounded like she'd swallowed a dog whistle, her voice was so high-pitched. "Call me as soon as you get this! I've got some superexciting news!"

I knew immediately that my bridesmaid curse was about to be lifted. What I didn't know was that despite having a Rolodex of sorority sisters who could throw a shower in their sleep, Ashleigh would choose me to be her maid of honor. I was instantly nervous. The spell had finally been broken, but I felt like Sleeping Beauty asking Prince Charming, "Can I get five more minutes? I'm still totally zonked."

I knew Ashleigh was going to plan a perfect wedding and I didn't want to screw up the MOH responsibilities. She didn't even ask me flat out. She sent me an adorable homemade card with a poem inside asking if I would.

"Ash, are you sure? You've seen me smoke weed out of a PBR can multiple times. Is this the person you want as maid of honor? I am totally cool just being a bridesmaid if that will be more comfortable for—"

"Mamrie, maid of honor is in charge of the bachelorette party."

There was no need to ask anything else. Ashleigh knew what she was doing. Unless you are standing in a bookstore right now and flipped this book open to this very page and this very sentence is the first one you've read in the book . . . you know that I like to party. And if you are said person in the bookstore, *buy this book!* Don't just get it all greasy with your dirty fingers and put it back on the shelf. Who raised you?!

Anyway, yes. Nothing makes me happier than planning a party, and this was going to be a big-ass one. In Charleston. With sixteen of Ashleigh's closest friends. I had met a few of them when I'd visited her in college, but that was almost ten years before and involved a lot of Goldschläger. I was basically party planning for Ashleigh and sixteen strangers.

Now, let me first preface this with the fact that these girls were wonderful and hilarious and are now my friends till the end. But walking into this crew as an outsider was intimidating. These girls were all southern ladies. Former debutantes who wore lace shorts and owned single-strand pearl necklaces. The type of girls who don't buy Anthropologie 'cause it's a little too "free spirit" for them. They knew how to sail, not shop at sales, and I felt like a dirty chimney sweep in their presence.

Now, I don't know if you've ever planned a weekend for sixteen women, but it can only be compared to herding cats. Everyone has an opinion on where to stay, what to do. *Let's stay in! Let's go out! I'm allergic to Mexican food! I hate beer! I will eat only while surrounded by beer-drinking Mexicans!* (That last one was my own request.)

There were a lot of opinions on everything from who should share rooms to what ply the toilet paper should be. And I did my best to accommodate all of them. But there was one thing I wasn't going to budge on, and that was the first day's activities. I wanted to be in charge of that, goddammit. I was in charge of that schedule and I knew exactly what we were going to do, the perfect activity to get everyone loosened up and comfortable around each other—a pole-dancing class! Granted, these girls had probably never even been to a strip club, let alone pole danced.

Let me take it back a month. Once I decided pole dancing would be the perfect icebreaker, I called the few places in Charleston that offered classes and settled on one that had good Yelp reviews. Now, since there were so many girls, the sweet-sounding but somewhat spacey teacher suggested we have the class in the back room per-

formance space of a bar. That way, we would have more room and
also, duh, a bar.

A month later with half a sorority in tow, I began to question my
plan. I had convinced all the gals to take a few shots before we would
head to the mystery activity. Once we got to the bar, however, that
loosening up got retightened. The place was empty. And no one
likes to enter a bar where you can still smell last night's vomit. Have
you ever been to a lush nightclub or other sleek place, accidentally
forgotten to close your tab, and then had to enter the premises the
next day before they opened? It's terrifying. What looks like plush,
classy velvet table service at night looks like someone jizzed all over
a black-light painting in daylight. Truly disturbing.

I asked the bartender for a round of tequila shots and had everyone lift their glasses as I announced the afternoon's activity.

"I just want to make a little cheers to Ashleigh." The girls *woo*ed
and lifted their well tequila. "I am so honored to be your maid of
honor and spend the weekend with all these girls. I still can't believe you are getting married. Jeff is a lucky man . . . and he's going
to be even luckier after today, because we're all about to take a
pole-dancing class! Woooo!"

I slugged back my shot, only to readjust my eyes and see a
bunch of not-so-excited faces. I hadn't seen that many confused
expressions since the time I auditioned for Claire Danes's role on
Homeland. I motioned to the bartender for another round.

"Pole dancing? Are you serious?" said the short one in the pink
gingham wrap dress.

"I'm totally serious! Pole dancing is, like, the hottest exercise
trend in New York right now. It's not just for high school dropouts
and Liv Tyler in Aerosmith videos anymore!* It'll be a blast!"

---

*The video for "Crazy" seriously changed me as an eleven-year-old. I
wanted to be as badass as Liv Tyler in that video. I wanted to ditch class,
go skinny-dipping, and strip in my father's band's music video—wait,
what? Gross in retrospect. Real gross.

Sarah S. chimed in, "Oh my god, do you remember that time Blake Foster sang the *Armageddon* theme to me at the Waikiki Karaoke Mixer senior year?"

With that they all started singing "I Don't Want to Miss a Thing" in each of their Blake impressions, which could've been great but how would I know? I wasn't part of any of these inside jokes! I took my second shot as they kept singing. And that right there is the main reason I chose pole dancing. Instant memories! Instant inside jokes that I would be a part of! Little did I know I would have instant regrets as soon as our instructor walked through the door.

The Aerosmith lyrics faded out as everyone turned to look as our pole-dancing goddess walked in with her boom box and midriff top.

"Everyone, this is Sienna."

I could tell Sienna was the best in the biz . . . mainly because she was old enough to have *invented* pole dancing. I had a flash of a young Sienna doing a jitterbug around a pole in the '20s.

She had long, flowy hair and tons of silver jewelry. I checked her wrist for a Life Alert bracelet but saw puka shells instead. But as the late Aaliyah said when she wanted to marry the world's grossest man, R. Kelly, "Age ain't nothing but a number," and I agreed. I couldn't judge Sienna because the first tip she'd ever gotten in her thong was probably a buffalo nickel. However, I could judge her because she was a total space cadet. You know how there are hippies who are really into the healing powers of rocks? Then there are the hippies who are really into smoking rocks? Sienna seemed like *that* kind of hippie. And homegirl had definitely indulged before this gig. She was high out of her mind and speaking in *sloooow* motion.

Let me remind you that this was my first impression with these girls attending the bachelorette weekend. These are the type of girls who have monogrammed tampons, so I can only imagine what they were thinking when Sienna walked in.

Oh, this is charming, what are we doing next? Breaking into someone's grandma's house to steal her medication?

Great planning, Mamrie. What's our dinner reservations? Canned pinto beans heated off a hobo's garbage can fire?

Before I could apologize to the girls for the live episode of *Intervention* happening before us, Ashleigh stepped in.

"I don't know about you guys, but I'm ready to learn how to dance! But first, let's have another drink!"

She winked at me and ordered another round for the group. With the bride's enthusiasm backing me up, everyone was on board and I felt a little relief. I treasured this feeling, as I knew it wouldn't last long.

The first thing Sienna wanted to teach us was a floor routine. It was your basic, run-of-the-mill lap dance, where every movement feels like it is dipped in molasses. By the time she started counting off "five, six, seven . . ." I could have taken another shot from the bar and been back without missing a pelvic thrust. Step by stumbling step, she slowly taught us choreography to the Ying Yang Twins' magnum opus, "Wait (The Whisper Song)." She incorporated chair work, but really I think she just wanted a rest.

I looked around the room. Every face looked like a what-the-fuck emoji. It felt sad. Like an injured animal that you just want to put out of its misery. Gingham Dress whispered in my ear, "Should we call a paramedic?" I stood there disappointed. I'd wanted it to be a fun bonding experience and now I was about to take the pulse of a meth-head hippie on a barstool.

I started to walk toward her, defeated, when she popped right back up onto her feet. "All right, girls," she let out like a death rattle, "time for the signature move. I'm telling ya, this move will have the boys eating out of the palm of your hand."*

---

*Two things: Sienna would have to scrub her hands like a surgeon right before an operation to have anyone consider eating out of them. Also, I've never really liked this phrase. I know it's supposed to sound sexy, but I just picture a guy eating out of my hand like a goat eats a quarter's worth of feed at a petting zoo.

I saw everyone's ears perk up. Maybe this wasn't a lost cause. She had us follow along (and I encourage those of you reading to do the move too).

"You take your hands and put them in front of you like a triangle, thumbs and pointer fingers touching." We did. "Then, you take that triangle and you put it right in front of your pussy." At this point I heard audible gasps. "This, girls, is called 'Framing the Cookie.' "

We all stood there with our hands framing our crotches, waiting for her to continue. . . . Nope. That was it. Framing the Cookie was her big move. You could've heard a pin drop if the Ying Yang Twins hadn't been screaming about sweat droppin' down their balls.

You know how when you look at a word for too long, it doesn't look like it's spelled right anymore? (I do this on every page of this book.) Or when you hear a dumb song multiple times in a row, and it just makes you laugh instantly (every Toby Keith song ever written)? This is what Frame the Cookie became to us. Sienna reminded us to frame the cookie upward of eighty times in twenty minutes.

Slowly run your hand down your thigh and frame the cookie. Take two steps left and frame the cookie.

The gesture looked more like "Put a Pizza Slice on Your Coochie" or like your vagina had just joined the Illuminati. Our cookies were framed harder than Roger Rabbit.

I stood there, cookie framed, wanting to crawl into a hole, when I heard Ashleigh behind me. "If this bitch keeps talking about cookies, I'm gonna have to leave and find me a Mrs. Fields." Everyone lost it and never came back.

This was the turning point! I had been so worried about everything not being perfect that I failed to see people were having fun. They were laughing and being good sports, framing their cookies as they were told. Maybe they weren't as uptight as I had feared. Actually, *I* was being the uptight one!

We were all dancing along, repeating after Sienna when she told us to frame the cookie, giggling so fucking hard. I think she thought we were giggling because we were so prudish that doing these dance moves made us uncomfortable. We were fine with all the moves. What got everyone was watching a senior citizen keep going on and on about her cookie while giving a lap dance that made her look like she was underwater.

Why a cookie? Sure, I can see how that might be a compliment in the "it's so moist and delicious" way. But there are several variations on the word *cookie*. She didn't say, "Frame the sugar cookie with pink icing," which would've made sense. She didn't say, "Frame that Double Stuff Oreo," which also makes sense (don't judge). For all I know, she was telling us to frame a dry, crumbly pecan sandie chock-full of nuts. Which actually did make sense in reference to her own goods. It would've made more sense if she'd told us to "frame the doughnut"—still a sweet treat, but at least a doughnut is glazed and has a hole in it.

If we're going to go ahead and assign a snack name to my vageen, there are a wide variety of other treats that work. And being someone who doesn't have a sweet tooth, how about:

1. Doritos: It's already a triangle shape and beloved by millions.
2. Pretzel: It's super bendable and of German descent.
3. Hummus: It's tahini-tiny (hey-yo!).
4. The popular '90s gummy treat Gushers (I had to).

The rest of the class was beyond ridiculous. We all self-medicated (drank) as one has to in these types of situations. After sufficiently twerking in slo-mo for a half hour, we moved on to the pole portion of the class, the part I was most excited about.

Just as I was about to hop on and show off to the girls what I had learned at that pole class in NYC, I heard a bloodcurdling "*Noooooo!*" from Sienna. At first I thought someone had opened a window and sunlight had hit her for the first time in years. Apparently, we weren't actually supposed to touch the poles in this pole-dancing class, which made zero sense to me. If I go apple picking, you'd best be assured I'm going to pick a damn apple (and then Instagram the fuck out of it so people know I do cool, active things).

Sienna had assured me during our previous phone call that she'd install her portable poles, which would work just as well as the dance-studio poles. Looking back, I'm not sure if there ever really was a "studio" like the website said. I wouldn't be surprised if I went back and found that those glowing Yelp reviews were by users Sienna69 and Sienna420. (I realize these aren't clever fake names. I wouldn't expect her to make up clever fake ones.)

These "stripper poles" we were supposed to be twirling on were looser than a rabbit in heat. Imagine trying to pole dance on a seven-foot-tall piece of spaghetti. They were so flimsy, in fact, that we weren't allowed to put *any* weight on them. We may as well have been wearing pigtails and lederhosen, framing our cookies around a goddamn maypole. It was a mess and only added to the giggle fest among the girls.

After a few songs of framing the cookie around the poles, I pulled Sienna aside. "Thank you so much for teaching us. I think us ladies are a little too inebriated to go any further, so we can totally call this one short." Sometimes I overcompensate for being shitfaced by using big words like "inebriated."

Then I tipped her generously and thanked her for teaching. She said it was no problem, that she was going straight from the bar to teach another class in someone's home. I, being just drunk enough to give unasked-for advice (my specialty), told her to bring mace and how dangerous I thought going to someone's home was. And then she left as quickly as she had come. Which wasn't that quickly, 'cause let's face it, she was a senior citizen and high on methamphetamines.

I went back inside to see all the girls laughing and framing their cookies. We left the bar and stopped by the grocery store to pick up snacks and booze. I rounded the chips aisle to see some of the girls taking a picture as they framed a Chips Ahoy! display stand.

"Mamrie, get in here!" one of them screamed.

I did it. I knew the inside joke. I had successfully wedged my way into this group of girls! The pole dancing wasn't just an icebreaker—it shaved that ice, threw it on a cone, and poured tutti frutti syrup all over it. We continued doing Sienna's signature move all weekend and even broke it out at Ashleigh's gorgeous wedding reception. Turns out, Ashleigh's Grandma Nuni frames a good cookie.

I think of Sienna often these days. I wonder if she found happiness, or if she went on to be an extra in the really fucked-up *Breaking Bad* scenes. Sometimes, I'll be walking down the cookie aisle at Vons and stop dead in my tracks. I'll pick up a box of Oreos, smile down at it, and think, *Oh, Sienna, you weird and wonderful woman. I really hope you weren't murdered at that other party.*

Ash and me on her perfect day. She was a vision. Later that night, she would get in a fight with her groom because of how badly she wanted pizza. That is why we are friends.

Angry Brazilian

4 lime wedges
1 oz simple syrup
Jalapeño-infused cachaça
Club soda

To infuse the cachaça, just throw a handful of whole fresh jala-
peños into it a week before you want to make this drink. Don't
slice them or it will be too spicy. Also, don't get freaked out if the
jalapeños turn white. That is the liquor sucking out all the fla-
vor like Bunnicula the bunny used to do to his vegetables.

Muddle the lime wedges in a tall tumbler. Add ice, simple
syrup, and however much cachaça you need to soothe your
wounds; top with club soda. Throw in a swizzle stick and give it
a swirl.

There are a lot of wonderful things about being a woman: The
miracle of birth. Supercute clothing options. Having three days
a month when you're allowed to be a total cunt.* But one of the
things that sucks about not rocking a Y chromosome is grooming.
Grooming is a motherfucker. Men can walk around looking partially homeless and it's considered hip—sexy, even. But ladies are

---

*Till a year ago, I didn't realize that "See you next Tuesday" was code for
cunt (C-U-Next-Tuesday). I thought it was an old-school compliment like
"She's really something else!" I shudder to think how many people I've
called cunts with a big smile on my face. My apologies, Vice Principal Brown.

expected to keep their bodies smoother than a swimmer with alopecia. It ain't fair.

When I think about the hours I've spent in my life shaving my legs, it makes me sad. I could've gotten a master's degree with that much time, specifically in women's studies, so I wouldn't give an F about having furry gams. But I do give an F, and it takes forever.

Now, I know, I know, guys have shaving responsibilities too. Pipe down, two dudes reading this! Whenever a guy hears a girl complaining about shaving her legs, he says, "Oh, but we have to shave our face every day!" Bitch, please. You are not Eric Stoltz in *Mask*. Your face does not have that much square footage and couldn't possibly take that long. Besides, if you decide not to shave, beards are hot. You lucky bastards can use laziness to your advantage.

Ever since I was little I've thought that beards were super attractive. This, of course, manifested itself in me having crushes on fictional characters, including:

1. The Brawny Man

This one is a stretch because it wasn't a full beard, but he did rock a major 'stache in the '80s. This was before Brawny modernized him and made him look like Dean Cain. A man who can pull off plaid *and* cleans up in the kitchen? Sign me up!

2. Johnny Appleseed

Admit it. If Johnny Appleseed were living today in hipster Williamsburg, Brooklyn, he would be dropping panties harder than he drops seeds. Urban farming is super in right now! That, paired with his eclectic choice of wearing a backward pot on his head? He's practically a two-episode love interest arc on *Girls*.

3. Paul Bunyan

This is a no-brainer. Paul was my first love. Right off the bat, you have his sheer size. The man was a giant, and there is nothing better than a large dude to make a broad like me feel petite. He also had a love for animals, which is the ultimate turn-on. And not just any animals—weird ones. I mean, his pet was a blue ox named Babe, so he clearly goes by my pet motto of Adopt, Don't Shop. And last but not least, the man liked to eat. I remember reading a story about Paul when I was little and it said that normal-size men would strap big pats of butter to their feet and then skate around Paul's massive cast-iron skillet, greasing it up for his breakfast. I want to skate with butter shoes! If Paul gave me the honor of letting me taste his massive pancakes, trust me, I would show him my flapjacks. Hey-yo!

But you know what isn't hot? Beards between women's legs. Wait, that didn't sound right, because thinking of a man's beard between my legs is *extremely* hot. I'm talking about if a woman let her lady business go wild for a few years, à la Bunyan & Co. No one wants to disrobe in the heat of passion and look like they are riding on the shoulders of Si from *Duck Dynasty*.

Rutabaga! Dad, this is the part of the chapter where you stop reading and tell me you're proud of me despite my life choices.

As far as my crotchal region goes, I would say I'm into light grooming. I'm not sporting dreadlocks or anything—it's more of a crew cut. But I'm definitely not hairless. My skin is *way* too sensitive to razor it on the regular. Fact is, I think a sexual partner would find my bush more attractive than the red, irritated, plucked-chicken look I would achieve from shaving.

Besides the sensitivity issue, the idea of going down there with an object that's used in street fights and just blindly swiping around is *terrifying* to me. You can't really see what you're doing down there! You might as well go to third base with Edward Scissorhands.

104 YOU DESERVE A DRINK

Things might be different if I could stroll up to an old-school barber-shop, be lathered up with a brush, and get the straight-razor routine, then end the whole shebang with a hot towel on my gal as a barber-shop quartet sings "Mr. Sandman." But that ain't gonna happen.*

Regardless, this story is about waxing. It was the summer of 2008 and the first time I'd had a boyfriend since college. I'd always heard about girls keeping their nether regions on point for their boyfriends, but the desire never really crossed my mind.

Oh, I couldn't care less, you hear guys say. *I prefer grass on the field. I don't want it to look like a twelve-year-old,* dudes-who-I-would-never-date-because-they-talk-like-that would say. But maybe there was something to making a little extra effort in the bikini area. I had never given it much thought until my friend Hely offered to do it for free when she started running an upscale sugar waxing place in Soho. You could get most of their treatments for free, because the girls in training needed to practice. Yes, you were a guinea pig of sorts, but it was a spa for God's sake. It wasn't like I was doing med-ical research testing and was going to grow a baby arm on my fore-head. Did I mention it was *free*?

At this point, I had been living in New York for almost three years, but someone had failed to tell that to my bank account. I was still living from one night's bartending tips to the next, and a day at the spa meant splurging for a three-dollar bottle of Mr. Bubble and putting some peppermint tea bags on my eyes. Sugar waxing was so fancy! If you don't know what sugar waxing is, it's simple. Instead of a traditional wax, it's actually a combination of heated sugar, lemon juice, and water. Lovely, right? Doesn't it sound like your cooter is popping by a lemonade stand? Think again.

I arrived at the spa, and it was gorgeous—all beautiful Indian silks and cozy places to sit. I was offered cucumber water from a bejeweled glass container. It was the coldest, most refreshing H_2O I'd ever put in my mouth, with just a whisper of cucumber flavor. What kind of

---

*Although I am working on a franchise called Shaved by the Bell.

sorcery was this?* I took my crisp cuke beverage and settled in to catch up on my reading: *Us Weekly*. Look, if you don't think that deciding whether Jennifer Garner or Kristin Chenoweth wore a bandage dress better is hard-hitting journalism, we cannot be friends.

So far, so good. I'd gone almost ten minutes already without making an "I'm so sari" joke. I was just about to find out the secret to Kingston Rossdale's effortless swagger when they called my name. Or at least they attempted it. Let's be real, no one ever gets a name like Mamrie right. I basically just wait for the person to make a weird face with a twisted-up mouth and then I save them the trouble. I know the look. From professors calling roll to Starbucks calling my order, it always looks like they are trying to hold a fart in their mouth.

Back to the spa! Two women escorted me into a small, dim room that smelled like lavender and had soft, soothing music playing. It was the type of atmosphere you always try to create when you need to unwind in a bath at the end of a stressful day. I, for one, love a hot bubble bath—filling up the tub, lowering myself in, and quickly realizing that the finale of *Master Chef* is starting in two minutes, and hopping out to track water all over my living room.

One of the ladies told me to take my time undressing from the waist down and then to lie on the table. "We will knock before coming in," she said, closing the door behind them. I won't lie to you. I was nervous. Every time you see waxing in a movie, it has more screams of agony than a war scene. But this place was so peaceful. Surely, I wouldn't be screaming with this harp CD playing in the background. I imagined the hairs coming off with ease, like a Persian cat being brushed.

Things started to feel not quite as harmonious once I was lying ass-naked on the table. Having your cooter on display in

*Later I would learn that cucumber water is just a sliced Kirby thrown into some tap water, but at the time I thought I was being served a royal Indian elixir.

front of two women speaking a foreign language makes you feel extremely vulnerable. We've all gotten pedicures and thought the women sloughing off our raggedy calluses were talking mad shit about our feet. This is how I felt, except this time, they weren't chatting about my feet. They were chatting about my lady meat. (Too far?) Needless to say, my butthole was clenched so tight that if you'd stuck a lump of coal up there, I would've shit out a diamond.

After a few rips of my epidermis, I settled into the fact that this was gonna hurt like hell and I just needed to take deep breaths and deal with it. But then began the slow parade of people. I guess there were quite a few ladies who needed to get their Brazilian tutorials in. So, before I knew it I was lying there with a wall of six women staring into my vagina like they were looking at an animal diorama at the Natural History Museum. I imagined this crew of students going room to room, looking at each vagina with audio-guide headphones on, nodding along to the voice-over.

As you can see here we have a Caucasian vageen. This one is particularly hairy, as it has been in the wild since 1983. Do not get too close. Unlike a skunk, it may not spray you, but it can project a foul odor. Next, we have the national vagina of our country, the great bald spread-eagle. . . .

As mortified as I felt with an audience looking down my hatch, the most painful thing of this experience was the actual *pain* of this experience. I guess I had expected that these women had had a little more training. You know the dummy heads that students practice cutting hair on in beauty school? I expected the same for waxing school—dummy vagina molds where these gals could get in their hours. But according to the amount of failed rips that I felt, I was gravely mistaken.

One woman just didn't have the strength to rip it off. She

poured on the hot wax and anxiously applied the paper. I swear I saw her mouthing a prayer, and then I watched her close her eyes as she pulled with all her might. It didn't budge. The only thing that hurts more than someone ripping deep-rooted hairs out of your crotch is someone trying and then *failing* to rip deep-rooted hairs out of your crotch. In fact, I think she pulled so hard that my hairs grew out an inch, like one of those dolls in the '80s that you could cut its hair then lift its arm to make it grow back out.

She tried again—still nothing. She and my vagina were having a high school courtyard catfight: two girls start pulling each other's hair and neither refusing to let go. I watched the instructor tap her out. A new one, clearly the teacher's pet, stepped in for clean-up duty.

This woman approached me with a smile on her face, totally at ease and super confident—a little *too* confident for my taste. There's something unsettling about a person who really enjoys administering pain as her job. You wouldn't want your dentist to say, "Oh boy! Looks like we've got a root canal today. This should be fun!" then crank up some AC/DC as he puts the laughing gas over your nose. I half-expected Teacher's Pet to crack her knuckles and have the instructor squirt water into her mouth as a bell rang. Round two!

She grabbed the paper with one hand, steadied my abdomen with the other, and ripped that motherfucker off like it was a burning car on top of her newborn babe. The entire peanut gallery gave an audible *ohhh*. Granted, I don't speak Hindi, but I'm pretty sure "Ohhh" translates to "I think you just ripped off that poor white girl's labia."

This is where I blacked out for a second. What I imagine happened is the Muscle held the wax strip above her head like a Mohican who had just scalped the enemy in a war.

Thankfully, all good things must come to an end, and the same goes for all horrific things. Everyone filed out and I was left to get dressed.

I lay there for a few minutes, gathering myself. I focused on my breathing like you do at the end of a yoga class, then peeked down to see the masterpiece. "That's weird. It looks like I had a manatee in a headlock." Holy fuck, it looked like I had a *manatee in a headlock*. Remember me telling you how sensitive my skin is? Well, after forty-five minutes of having essentially hot caramel poured on and ripped off of it, the poor thing had puffed out like Violet from *Willy Wonka*. I waddled out of that fancy salon looking like my crotch was shoplifting a neck pillow.

And for what? I sure as hell wasn't going to put on a swimsuit anytime soon, because (a) it would be painful, and (b) it would look like I stored a Bundt cake in my pants. There was no way I was letting my boyfriend anywhere near my vagina. I taped off my nether regions like a murder scene.

By the time the swelling actually went down, the hair was back. Here's what I don't understand. Your hair is supposed to be a good quarter inch before you wax it. So, women who wax religiously, are your bikini lines just a constant cycle of no hair, tiny hair? Are your vages like little front lawns of pubes you are constantly landscaping? I'd just rather spend my time doing productive things, like knowing the ins and outs of every single *Real Housewives* franchise.

In the end, that experience left me with some scars. Emotional scars. There might be physical ones too, but I've just never gone downtown with a compact mirror to check. Besides, they would be covered by hair. Like the good Lord intended. Granted, I am not a religious person, but if I were, I would argue that God wants us all to be bushed out. Why would we grow hair if we weren't supposed to rock it? He is clearly capable of making things hairless.

The same theory can be applied to weed. Why would God put weed on earth if we weren't supposed to smoke it? Why would he create a person with the brilliant idea for Salt and Vinegar Kettle chips if he didn't want me to eat them? Shortly after smoking that godly weed?

*Speaking of hairless, you can follow
Beanz on Instagram at @beanzhart.
I am more passionate about Beanz
becoming a star than all those Dance
Moms combined.*

At the end of the day, if someone doesn't want to be with you because you aren't perfectly groomed, then fuck that guy/girl! I mean, you can't literally fuck them, because they have rejected you, but fuck them emotionally. They aren't worth your time. Especially if the person wanting you to groom is a man with more hair on his balls than on his head. Let him know that you'll shave it all off down there as long as you can turn it into a tiny Afro toupee for his shiny dome piece. This might sound extreme, but the expectation of women to be hairless while men sit around with Rip Van Winkle nuts is unfair.

So, those are my thoughts on waxing. Now that we've all experienced this together, pour yourself an Angry Brazilian and allow me to *wax* poetic. . . .

*If you really want to go bare down there,
I suggest grabbing a bottle of Nair.
Smells like rotten eggs,
And goes on legs,
But at least it doesn't tear.*

Quickshots: Grooming Fails

As you know from the previous chapter, I have once, and only once, gotten my hoo-ha waxed. Perhaps that makes me unladylike. Perhaps that makes me the smartest woman alive. We may never know. But what I do know is that I am BAD at most lady things. Especially when it comes to grooming.

Side note: Why do we call it grooming? Is it because you need to get yourself looking fly if you ever want to land yourself a *groom*? That is probably a quick Google search, but who has the time? The tumbleweeds of pubes rolling around my bathroom aren't gonna clean themselves.

Putting on Makeup

I don't know if my problem is so much the actual application of makeup or the fact that my makeup bag always looks like Tatooine in *Star Wars*. I don't think I've ever owned a powder compact that did not explode in my purse. After its inevitable combustion, every time I go to pull something out of my bag, the item is covered in a fine layer of powder. I gotta take my blush brush and clean off my wallet like a paleontologist cleaning dinosaur bones.

This is why I never buy expensive makeup. I might be the only author in the entire bookstore who still buys Wet n Wild.*

Besides the general upkeep of my products, there is the whole having-to-put-it-on thing, which I am terrible at. As far as skin makeup goes—i.e., blending and contouring and not just slapping on foundation to look like an Irish geisha—I'm useless.

Also, blush is useless to me. I have mild rosacea that is exacerbated by drinking alcohol and eating spicy foods—which is pretty much all I consume. And most of the time my beverage of choice is spicy alcohol! At least once a week you can hear me say, "Fuck it. I know I look like a sunburned Santa right now, but give me another one of them habanero margaritas, kind sir!" A couple of those bad boys and I get an insane hot, red pattern on my body. See below.

This particular night was too many spicy pineapple margs. My skin broke out into a crazy maplike pattern. As you can see, I'm sporting the flaccid boner outline of Florida, but I'm hoping one day it will be a treasure map. Goonies *reboot, anyone?*

*Also, whoever came up with the name Wet n Wild for a company is my hero. Did the CEO want it to be edgy but thought Lubed n Crazy was a bit much?

And don't get me started on eyeliner! How the hell am I supposed to hold something steady and draw a tiny line on my eyelid? It is physically impossible for me to make it straight when half my vision is gone because my other eye is closed. I end up painting the eyeliner thicker and thicker to try and get both eyes to match, until I look like Amy Winehouse's trashier cousin. I really should save myself some time and just use a jumbo Sharpie.

Taking Off Makeup

This is a completely nonexistent concept to me. I wake up every morning looking like the walk of shame, all my makeup still intact but smeared.

Normally this isn't a huge deal because my daily look is tinted moisturizer, mascara, and lipstick; but there was a time in my life when I would rock half a MAC makeup counter on my face. And those mornings, my pillow would look like someone had tried to smother Tammy Faye. I'm talking, of course, about the glorious days when I was in a band.

"You were in a band? How is it possible that one average-size body could contain such a wealth of talent and charisma?" said No One.

It's true—for six years and two albums, I was a singer in a band called Cudzoo and the Faggettes. "Cudzoo" because it was the drunken misspelling of the vine kudzu, which grows rampant in the South. And "Faggettes" because our band asked us not to name them something "gay." It was the most fun. Our sound was the love child of a '60s girl group and the B-52s, with matching shiny dresses and choreographed dance moves. But our backing band were all punk musicians. So it was intense but also sweet. Kind of like a spicy margarita.

Some of our onstage antics included breaking pencils with our butts and making audience members bong beers out of a giant penis.

We were made up of me; my friend Jess, who I'd met in New York; Erin, who I'd known since third grade; and Sarah. Sarah was our drummer and also happens to be a neuropsychologist—NBD. While Jess, Erin, and I sang our harmonies about walks of shame ("Sequins Before Noon") and weird dance crazes ("The Toxic Shock"), we were backed up by Sarah and our rotating crew of male guitarists and bassists.*

We put on a damn good show, which of course meant wearing lots and lots of eyeliner. Six Jameson shots and eight Tecates during our set and you'd better believe I wasn't taking off my makeup before bed. I would be lucky to get off my sequined dress and pillbox hat. Spoiler alert: I woke up in my sequined dress 80 percent of the time.

*Shout-out to Lorenzo Potenzo, Beaux Berry Biscuit, and Tony Lofi—the greatest straight males who wore their Faggettes label proudly.

The mornings after our shows, I got to play my favorite game: Find the fake eyelashes. Usually they would be stuck to my pillow, making it look like some dollar-store version of Chairy from *Pee-wee's Playhouse*. But it wasn't always that easy. After a particularly raucous show, I could not for the life of me find my second fake eyelash. That is, until I went to pee. Apparently, in my sleep I had rubbed my eye super hard and then put my hand in my crotch. (Which, by the way, is my favorite sleeping position. Having your hand down your pants is comfortable. Al Bundy got it right. My fashion icon might be Peg Bundy, but my spirit animal is all Al.) There, perfectly placed in my vagina, were my fake lashes. If my pubes had been blond, it would've been the spitting image of Clitney Spears.

Haircuts

Some ladies absolutely love going to the salon. They have their particular stylist who is "the only person I would let near my bangs." I, however, don't think I've ever been to the same hairdresser twice.

Part of it is because I hate small talk. It's not the actual act of getting my hair cut that bothers me—I could sit still and have someone wash and play with my hair all damn day. But what I don't like is how part of a hairstylist's job description is essentially being Barbara Walters. "What do you do?" "Do you like California?" Even worse is having to feign interest if they are oversharers. Just cut my hair; I don't need to know your entire diet plan in the months leading up to your sister-in-law's wedding.

I'm sure I sound like a total bitch saying this, but dem's the facts. I am waiting for the day when a hair salon opens up called "Shut Up Cuts: You'll be cute, and we'll be mute," and I will have them put me down for a cut every eight weeks from now till eternity. But until then my normal look will be split ends and letting my mane grow so long that I look like I wandered off from a Phish concert.

Nails

I'm just gonna say it. My feet are disgusting. I am looking down at them as I write this and they resemble two turds attached to hairy tree trunks. These little piggies look like they've already been to the slaughterhouse. Both big toes have one little dab of red polish toward the tip, but the others are totally blank. This means that I have gone so long without a pedicure that my last pedicure is almost completely grown out. A quick google has told me that an average toenail takes about a year to a year and a half to completely grow out. That is how long it's been since my toenails were painted! I could've gotten a pedicure, gotten pregnant, and my baby would be crawling all before I'd gotten another pedicure.

Speaking of Google! If you type the name of basically any woman in the entertainment industry into the search bar, the third or fourth fill-in is that person's name and the word *feet*. Seriously. If you type in "Mamrie," Google will fill in the top searches of:

Mamrie Hart
Mamrie Hart Hannah Hart sisters
Mamrie Hart boyfriend
Mamrie Hart annoying
Mamrie Hart feet
Mamrie Hart owes me money

I hate to bust some people's bubbles, but there is no way you want to click on pictures of my feet. You could have the most intense foot fetish imaginable and that one search would make it disappear. It's like one of those camps that terrible Christian parents send their sons to "cure" them of homosexuality. Two pics of my feet, or one small whiff, and you'd be able to go to shoe stores without a boner. These dogs aren't just barking; they are starring in a Sarah McLachlan–scored ASPCA commercial.

On top of the general aesthetic, the general odor of my feet is that of a Dumpster that's been cooking in hell. If I have a long day of wearing flats sans socks, I have to leave my shoes outside my house. My neighbors probably think I am a traditional Japanese woman or OCD with white carpeting.

I need to get a proper pedicure, but it's almost been too long. It's like when you go seven years without seeing a dentist (What? Just me? Pardon me, princess.) and you are terrified of what the dentist is going to say. There's a moment when you think, *Fuck it, I'll just let my teeth fall out. I like soup!* I would rather never eat solid foods again than have the following conversation with my dentist:

Ma'am, I hate to tell you but your teeth have so many cavities, for a second I thought they were tiny cubes of Swiss cheese.

I don't understand. I brush two or three times a day and always use Listerine despite thinking it's a sin to spit out alcohol.

When's the last time you flossed?

Hmmm . . . What year is this?

Followed by me being replaced with a cloud of dust as I bolt to my car.

I feel at this point if I went in for a pedicure, the poor soul having to do it would pull out a file. Not for my calluses, but to just take off my feet because they have no hope.

But it's not just pedicures that a well-kept woman is supposed to have. No, no, there are also manicures. Women are *obsessed* with manicures. You cannot go on Instagram or Tumblr without seeing an elaborate manicure that someone shelled out who knows how much for. I have never been that girl. A lot of it has to do with the fact that my twenties were spent bartending. There is zero point in putting on polish, let alone paying money for it, when your hands are going to be in a sink washing martini glasses 70 percent of your shift.

And some girls are obsessed with always having their nails done up elaborately. (*cough*) Zooey Deschanel (*cough*). I'm all for rocking a themed look, but is it really necessary to have each nail painted with a different Duggar for the season premiere? Do you really gotta have someone slave over your cuticles with a toothpick to have a different disciple on each nail for Easter? Are you nervous you won't remember to attend the Oscars if you don't paint all the nominees for Best Picture on your hands?

I could understand if the painting served a purpose, like painting answers to questions on your nails before a big test or a list of emergency contacts. But there's no way I'd spend eighty bucks on an accessory that goes away in a week. I would never pick out a cute scarf for eighty bones if it had a warning label that read, THIS SCARF DISINTEGRATES IN 7 DAYS. Not for me, no thank you. If you see me and it looks like I have a manicure, look closer. You'll probably see it's just leftover buffalo-wing-flavored pretzel residue that I've yet to lick off.

Plucking Eyebrows

As you guys already know, hair removal on my body is not my strong suit. But the only thing worse than having to shave off your fur is having to pluck it off. It's exhausting and tedious, the grooming equivalent of the board game Operation.

I inevitably get my eyebrows waxed, they look banging for a month, and then I spend the next two months watching the Grouchos slowly come in like weeds in a backyard. But hey, at least it's not like my senior year of high school when I discovered waxing and then went *way* too far with it. If I'd taken eyeliner and drawn two dots over each pencil-thin brow, they would've looked like two frowny-face emojis.

As bad as my eyebrow game can be, it is nothing compared to my sweet, late Grandma Nette. Grandma Nette was the older of two sisters, her baby sister being Audrey. If you've ever seen the movie *Gypsy*, consider my grandma to be Louise and Audrey to be Baby June. They were living together in their seventies, and while my grandma had slowed down, Audrey was still a wild child, going out dancing, rotating boyfriends, rocking a cute bleached-blond bob, the works. And Audrey wasn't afraid of going the extra mile to improve her looks.

One year she decided she was sick and tired of having to put on makeup every day (I guess it's hereditary), so she done went and got it *tattooed* on. Yes. I do mean an actual tattoo needle went on her eyelid to give her eyeliner. By the time all the elements were finished, she had more tattooing on her face than most inmates. It actually looked nice (Still does! Hey, Aunt Audrey!), but the process sounds like some lost *Saw* torture.

And Audrey somehow convinced my grandma, in a moment of weakness, to get her eyebrows filled in. Grandma Nette kept her eyebrows shaped, but she'd always have to fill them in with a pencil. Not anymore. She went for it. It was good for a couple of years—that is, until Grandma Nette stopped caring about keeping her eyebrows plucked and let them grow free. Only problem was, they were growing slightly off from where the tattoo was. The only thing worse than one set of eyebrows to maintain on your face is having to keep up with two.

#godbless #family #justbrow'sing

Getting a Tan

Everyone looks better when they have a little sun kiss to them, right? Spoiler alert: I have never looked sun kissed. Ever. I've looked sun *sexually assaulted* before, but never kissed. I'm either white as a ghost or lobster red. Totally solar bipolar.

If I'm on vacay, I always try to "lay out" at the beach. I sit there with my Corona, moving my bathing suit bottom every five minutes to see if I'm starting to show color. On the beach, it looks great. But when I go inside and shower to get ready to go out for the night, I'm redder than an embarrassed lobster.

People say, "Well, the sun is super harsh but you can always get a little color in a tanning bed." Trust me, I tried. Granted, this was before it was a known fact that getting into a tanning bed is basically about as safe as crawling into a jumbo George Foreman grill. When I was in high school, tanning beds were all the rage. Everybody wanted that caramel-colored, slightly burned–smelling skin for their prom dress, and my skin always paled in comparison.

For whatever reason, the tanning bed places in my county were always tanning/video rental stores. Whoever first decided that people were missing the convenience of getting a base tan and renting *Troop Beverly Hills* in one place is a genius. If there were more convenient combo places like this, I would be better at grooming. Places such as:

Eyebrow Waxing and Computer Ink Replacement Store
Bangs Trimming and Belated Birthday Cards
Teeth Whitening and Tire Rotations

Luckily, I've grown to like being pale as a ghost. There's something regal about it, plus it'll prevent me from having wrinkles when I'm older. Sure, I might've been the pasty girl at prom, but when I roll up to my twentieth high school reunion, all those sun-kissed gals are going to look like California Raisins in cocktail dresses.

But Even with All These Gripes, the Fact Remains . . .

. . . I still look fine as hell.

Right in the Nuts

Glass bottle of Coke
½ oz homemade grenadine
2 oz white rum
Salted peanuts

For the grenadine, all you are going to need is unsweetened pomegranate juice, sugar, and half a lemon. We aren't making that radioactive shit that people put in Shirley Temples—this is the real stuff. Take 1 cup of your unsweetened juice and put it in a saucepan over medium heat. Add ¼ cup of sugar, stir till it dissolves, then crank that puppy to a boil for 5 minutes. Remove from heat and allow to cool before adding the juice from your half a lemon. Ta-da! Grenadine.

Now, get one of those adorable glass bottles of Coke. Take a big swig out of it, then add the homemade grenadine and the white rum. Then drop in the peanuts.

Throw in a straw and enjoy your delicious, boozy, old-school drink. Bonus: At the end you get boozy cherry-soda-infused peanuts.

Classic me, one cocktail deep and I already got a mouthful of nuts.

The phrase "We need to talk" in a movie usually means one of three things. If it's a boss to an employee, your ass is fired. If it's girlfriend to boyfriend, your ass is dumped. Parent to child, and your ass is about to get two Christmases. I got my "We need to talk" the summer of 1993.

I am a child of divorce. I wish I could say this is traumatic and makes me unique, but these days almost half of American marriages end up in divorce. Getting hitched is basically like playing the roulette table. Both are a fifty-fifty chance of losing a shit-ton of money, but at least with roulette you have a waitress bringing you free White Russians. I am actually taken aback when I meet someone my age whose parents are still together. It's like seeing a unicorn, or meeting a virgin on the Jersey Shore. I can't help but think there must be something super fucked-up in their family to keep up this charade. Are both parents so closeted that this loveless marriage will go with them to the grave? Did they accidentally murder a pizza delivery guy in the early '80s and marriage is the only guarantee that neither will rat the other out? People like to say it's actually things like children and eternal love, but I'm willing to bet they've got a body in those floorboards.

I learned that my parents were splitting up a couple of months before starting fifth grade. The summer started off normally. As far back as I could remember, my mom would take us to see my dad for a few weeks while he shot *In the Heat of the Night* in Atlanta. It's true. My father was an actor when I was growing up. On this show, which ran over eight years, he was the comedic relief. His character was a goofy, sweet cop named Parker Williams. Goofy? Actor? I guess the apple doesn't fall far from the tree. Except my apple can be quickly carved into a pipe in a pinch. Anyway, I spent those eight summers on the set of the television show, terrorizing craft services and begging the hair and makeup trailer to glam me up. This year was no different, except that first we were making the trek to Texas for my mom's family reunion, which my siblings and I all groaned about for various reasons. First pain in the ass was finding food along the way. It's tough enough getting any nourishment while on the road, but put a pack of three picky eaters in your backseat and you're screwed.

My brother, Dave, who had recently discovered black hair dye and *deep-rooted angst*, refused to stop at any large chain restaurants that contribute to the homogenization of our vapid society, or something along those lines.

"Well, I for one don't know what the heck Dave just said, but I am craving the hell out of some Cracker Barrel and I think there's one just past Charlotte off Interstate 77," my sister, Annie, added to the mix. She was a few weeks out from having to get braces and was ready to get her corn on the cob on while she still could. Meanwhile, I was already a vegetarian and knew my meals for the next five days would consist mainly of french fries and other words that restaurants use for their version of french fries.

There was no light at the end of the tunnel. We were driving twenty-four hours to meet a bunch of old fogies who wanted to pinch my cheeks. Even at nine years old I knew that my whole extended family was broke, so the possibility of charming prehistoric Aunt Millie and ending up in her will was nonexistent. Besides, I didn't want to be the heir to the *Mama's Family* cassettes she taped off the TV. But there was one bright spot to our trip: We were going to be staying in a hotel. And hotels had *pools*.

The promise of a pool could get childhood Mamrie to do anything. If a kidnapper had approached me in a sketchy van and said, *Do you like candy, little girl? I have tons of candy in this van*, I would've asked him what type of candy he had in there and then given a manifesto on how much I hate watermelon flavor. And I had a *lot* of opinions about it. Like how watermelon is delicious and refreshing but watermelon *flavor* tastes *nothing* like it, how sickeningly cloying it can be, how it gave me headaches . . . I would've been left in a cloud of exhaust before I could finish. But if a kidnapper pulled up in a sketchy van and told me there was an inground pool in the back of his house? Forget it. Sorry, parents—call Soul Asylum to stick me in a music video, 'cause my ass is halfway to a basement cage.

In addition to us Hart kids and Mom, my aunt Debbie and cousin Josh were going to drive in their car. This would save my mom from having to have all three of us kids in the car at the same time.

We would be meeting my aunt and cousin a few hours down the road, so the trip started with all of us piling into my mom's Maxima. This was no ordinary Maxima, though. When my mom had gotten it new a few years back, she'd made a classic Hart move and immediately fucked it up by rear-ending another car. A parked car.

Normally this would be frustrating, but my mom took it in stride when the guy at the garage said he could get her a deal on a new front bumper. Cut to two weeks later, my mom shows up to the garage and she's got a mustard yellow bumper on her burgundy Maxima. It looked hideous. But since my mom is a mom and wired to bring as much embarrassment to her kids as possible, she loved it. She thought it looked like her car was smiling! So, we were the family with the yellow-bumper car.

The trip down was surprisingly uneventful—lots of singing along to the B-52s, cheering every time we crossed a state line, and seeing who could get the most truck drivers to honk their horns. The only sliver of drama that occurred was when I found myself in my mom's car, having left my beloved stuffed animal, Chee-Chee, in my aunt's car. That cheetah and I were inseparable. I went on adventures with it, brought it on every trip, made watercolors of it. My brother knew that I loved this toy more than my own siblings, so he took this sweet bond and used it to torture me. One time, I walked into my bedroom and Chee-Chee was hanging from a noose from my ceiling fan. Not traumatizing *at all*. As soon as I realized that Chee-Chee was in Aunt Debbie's car, it was over. Dave and Josh proceeded to reenact *Rocky* in the back window with Chee-Chee as I screamed in horror until my mom got my aunt to finally pull over. Mind you, this was before cell phones, so any car-to-car communication was done solely with charades. Besides that incident, we were able to get to Texas safe and sound.

We arrived at the family reunion and proceeded to . . . ya know . . . reunion. To be totally honest, I don't remember very much about those three days. The only things that really stick out in my brain were that I hit it off with a distant cousin who brought her Treasure Troll doll collection, and I had to constantly explain why I didn't want to try deviled eggs.

I'm not sure if you guys know this, but the Deep South has a serious boner for deviled eggs. Like a "call your doctor if your erection does not go down after eight hours" boner. For a region so rooted in Christianity, I find it surprising that the most scarfed-down app has the word *devil* in it. People *cannot* believe it when I say I don't want one. And it's not because I'm a vegan (yes, yes, I know—pelt me with chicken fingers as I beg for forgiveness), but because I think it's a real risky move to put a bunch of people in a small church rec center and have them stuffing their faces with boiled eggs. If, God forbid, someone should light a match, the church would be left without a congregation.*

I also got practice in the art of learning how to avoid conversations with octogenarians who want to talk about your namesake.

Oh, the original Mamrie once saved a Confederate soldier? Well. I once conquered the six-pound burrito at Bandidos Taqueria. So suck it!

But those interactions with the old folks weren't all bad, considering the amount of candy I was given. A piece of taffy from Great Aunt Roberta here, some caramels from Uncle Leroy there. Seriously, why is it that all the candies aimed at senior citizens are tasty tooth extractors? It wouldn't surprise me if Mary Janes and Bit-O-Honeys were made by a top denture manufacturer.

Candy was all right and all, but there was a different treat that really stuck with me from that trip. The particular part of Texas we were in was known for its peanuts. Honestly, there was peanut everything. Peanut candy. Peanut barbecue sauce. Peanut-oil fried chicken. If you were a kid with a peanut allergy in this region, then you were going to be a straight-up Boy in the Plastic Bubble à la John Travolta.

---

*Did you know in France they call them *oeufs mimosa*? That's right, eggs mimosa. Doesn't that sound nicer? Kind of like how the French coined the term "french kissing" instead of the Carolinian term "tonguin'."

There was one southern tradition involving these legumes*
that I became obsessed with. And that, my friends, is peanuts and
Coke. Yep, you read that right. Peanuts and Coke.

I can't remember which old relative showed it to me at the reunion, but once he did, I was hooked. What you do is you take a
small glass bottle of Coke, like the ones you can find at a general
store,† and a single-serving pack of shelled and salted peanuts.
Take a couple of swigs of Coke, then use your hand as a funnel and
drop the peanuts in. It'll fizz up for a second, but what you're left
with is a salty-sweet palate party. Your Coke is the slightest bit
salty, and then when you are finished, you shake out your sweet
peanuts. Sounds weird, but it turns out it's a pretty old-school tradition from all around the Southeast. Trust me, I've dated boys
who play the banjo, and they have confirmed it.

Anyway! Once everyone was full and ready to part ways and
fart for days, we all piled back into the smiley Maxima and were on
our way. But instead of heading straight to Dad's place in Atlanta,
my mom decided to take my siblings and me to San Antonio for a
few days. Having been obsessed with Pee-wee Herman since the
tender age of three, all I wanted to do was go to the Alamo and ask
to see the basement. We did go to the Alamo (no basement, story
checks out), and we had the time of our lives eating our prepubescent weight in queso dip and swimming in the pool at the quaint
little Crockett Hotel. I was all about that diving board. Endless
hours were spent with my sister daring me to touch the drain in
the deep end, since we had both just seen Stephen King's *It*.

On our final night, after my mom made last call on the pool, my
sister and I went back to our room to start packing up our little

---

*Peanuts are legumes, not nuts. Doesn't the entire world feel like a lie
now?

†Yes, I did say "general store" nonchalantly. There is still a general
store in my hometown with big glass jars of candy, glass-bottle sodas, and
weird hillbilly tchotchkes. Oh, and flyers for upcoming Civil War reenact-
ments, but we'll just skip past that.

suitcases (Dave had his own adjoining room, no doubt scouring the channels for Skinemax), when my mom told us that she "needed to talk to us about something." Straight out of an after-school special, she sat us both down at the foot of the bed.

Like the wonderful woman my mother is, she used every sweet, generic way to break the news of the divorce to two young girls sitting in wet swimsuits. She made sure we knew how much she and my dad both loved us, and how it was in no way our fault, but they were no longer going to be together.

"Your dad and I are still very good friends; we just aren't going to be married anymore. Do you understand?"

After a few seconds that felt like months, Annie cleared her throat. My sister was known for being a drama queen (I'd seen her have a category 4 meltdown over gum in her hair), so I braced for impact. She started to speak, her voice breaking. My mom clutched her hands as she finally got the words out:

"D-d-does this mean we get two Christmases?"

I almost slow-clapped. My mom was so worried about us being heartbroken about the news, but Annie just got to the fucking meat of the matter. My mom seemed a little taken aback as I looked at her, waiting for an answer.

"I'm not sure how holidays will work yet, girls. But I just want to make sure you understand everything I'm telling you. Your dad and I will no longer be together as a couple, do you understand?"

We both looked at her with what can only be described as "naw duh" looks. That was the level of our shock—a.k.a. not very much. I think I cried for a second because you're supposed to, you always see it in TV and movies, and if I didn't cry, that would be weird, right? I mean, *fuck*. At *this* point in my life I can cry from a sentimental Subaru commercial, but for some reason, over-the-top emotions weren't happening for me at that time. It's like when you see a toddler bust his face and he just sits there dumbfounded. He's only gonna cry if you acknowledge his fall. If a toddler falls in the woods and no one's there to see it, trust me, that kid doesn't make a sound.

My parents hadn't really lived together since I was three. My dad would come home every few months or on holidays, but he'd sleep on the couch. I didn't know this wasn't normal. My mom was dropping us off at my dad's Georgia apartment, not staying and hanging out with her husband. Being a little kid, I never really caught on that my parents had been separated for over five years. They decided to tell my sister and me when we were old enough to understand. Kind of weird? Yes. But I've never been a parent before, so there is no judgment. (But I will say that my parenting methods will involve a lot less wool over my kids' eyes, and a lot more gin in my mouth.)

So now it was all out in the open. I was one of the statistics. I didn't need to ask if it was my fault. I didn't need to make sure they still loved me. I didn't need to milk this thing like an old, dehydrated cow. To prevent confusion down the road, my mom did encourage us to ask questions. I obliged, asking her things like, "When can I get back in the pool?" "What time does the pool close?" "If you remarry, do you think your new husband will have an inground pool?"

The next day, we left San Antonio bright and early. My aunt Debbie and cousin Josh were heading back to North Carolina, so it was just us Hart kids back in the car. My mother put on her peppiest front.*

"All right, kiddos, I really think we can make this fourteen-hour drive in one day. Who's with me?"

Shockingly, we didn't hit the road with the same gusto that we had on the way down. My "honk honk" arm motions to truck drivers were in slo-mo. It was more of a "honk if you get around to it, but don't stress yourself." "Love Shack" didn't have the same spirit behind it after I found out my home was no longer a shack of love. The tin roof of my parents' hearts? Rusted. My mom did what any

---

*Did I mention that my dad wasn't the only thespian in my pack of parentals? My mom was an amazing theater actress before she gave it up to birth us idiots. In fact, my mom and dad actually met in the theater department at college.

good parent does to cheer up her kids: took us into a convenience store and let us pick out whatever we wanted. Fuck chips. Fuck pretzels. I was getting peanuts and Coke.*

I sat in the back of our yellow-bumpered Maxima, sipping on my treat. And hey, at least we were making good time—that is, until we heard a loud *bam!* Either Emeril Lagasse was cooking gumbo in our car or we'd hit a major road bump. Sure enough, it was a flat. We all piled out of the car and stood ten feet back on the shoulder as my mom attempted to fish out the spare.

After my mom had said about the fifth cuss word I'd ever heard her say, an 18-wheeler slowly pulled onto the side of the road and parked twenty yards behind us. We all stood there frozen as the driver descended his massive truck and started walking toward us. My thoughts went once again to *Pee-wee's Big Adventure*. Remember how fucking terrifying the truck driver, Large Marge, was in that movie? Even if this driver wasn't going to be a ghost with a Claymation face, he was at least going to have a hook for a hand. Or a glass eye that he'd pop out and clean in his mouth. As he walked closer, I stood behind my mom, clutching the shit out of Chee-Chee, hoping the driver would be scared of my brother. Looking back, there was no way a crusty truck driver would be scared of a fourteen-year-old with a sarcastic attitude, but hope was all I had at that moment. The mystery man walked toward us, silhouetted by the setting sun. Once our eyes had focused and we could see his face, we saw before us something I couldn't have imagined: a really nice dude named Tom who had kids of his own back home and just wanted to help us get back on the road.

Phew! Crisis averted. By the time we finally had the spare on, Mom decided to call the rest of the day a wash and just get us to a hotel. That was enough excitement for one day, and the crankiness level had reached an all-time high. Plus, I was *way* too dry from not

---

*This part of Texas had glass-bottle Cokes in regular gas stations. I'm telling you, it was old-school. You could've found Crystal Pepsi if you would've reached deep enough into the cooler.

having been in a pool all day. So we got back on the road and started looking for a hotel.

Here's the thing about eastern Texas: The towns are super far away from one another. Like, multiple marathons distance. You might not have to pee when you pass one exit, but that's risking having to hold it for another hour. If you are hungry and see an exit, just stop. If you wait for the next exit for better options, you might be rolling through that Chick-fil-A drive-through as a skeleton. After about forty miles of desert, my mom declared that the next sign we saw for a hotel was where we were staying. Finally, a sign for a Motel 6 appeared on the horizon.

Even as a nine-year-old with low standards (my all-time favorite game was to play "Homeless Kid" in the woods), I knew that this motel was a shit hole. The woman at the front desk had more cigarette butts in her ashtray than teeth in her mouth. We stayed close to my mom as we walked to the room, constantly looking behind us like we were being smuggled out of Eastern Germany.

I looked down at the pool, half-expecting to see a dead body floating in it. Luckily, it was just a couple of deflated clear balloons, which I would later realize were used condoms. And listen, I don't mean to trash-talk Motel 6. I'm sure they've come a long way since 1993. Motel 6's motto has always been, "We'll leave the light on for you." Well, that they did. Good thing it wasn't a black light, because Lord knows if you'd let one of those suckers loose in there, it would've been a Jackson Pollock painting of bodily fluids.

In fact, probably acknowledging this fact, my mom had us sleep on top of the covers. That is, until we spotted several cockroaches in our room. Then I tucked myself into those covers so tightly that I created a personal panic room.

Despite all the cockroach eggs that were about to be laid in our nostrils, we all fell asleep, but not before setting an early alarm. (Remember when you had to set actual alarm clocks instead of using your cell phone? How archaic!) None of us wanted to be there an extra second beyond what was necessary. So at five a.m., we bolted out of bed. Not because the alarm clock went off . . . but because the *cops were banging on our door*.

Apparently, someone had been shot at the ol' Motel 6, a.k.a. Château Skid Row, and they wanted to see if we had any information. You could see the pity in the cops' eyes. All these kids crammed into a Motel 6 with a woman who looked like she just had the shittiest day of her life? They must've thought we were on the run from our superdangerous father, like Jennifer Lopez's kid in the movie *Enough*. Finally, all that practice of pretending to be homeless in the woods was paying off!

We used this as our cue to get the fuck out of there. First stop was a garage to get a real tire put on, and then we were back on the road. Once again, my mom was alleviating our pissed-off moods with whatever snacks we wanted! You know what I was drinking/eating in that backseat. Five hours in and we were making up for lost time. At this rate, we'd be in Georgia by dinnertime. And with the inherent guilt of putting his kids through a divorce on his shoulders, surely my dad would take us to Billy Bob's Pizza Circus for dinner.

Billy Bob's was essentially ShowBiz Pizza. Once ShowBiz started to go under, it would sell its animatronic animal bands to other arcade-type places. The one in Conyers, Georgia, was named after that band's lead singer, Billy Bob the Bear. He had the quintessential one tooth to show he was from the sticks. I loved that place. Nothing made me happier than awkward robot animals playing original songs, and spending forty bucks in tokens to win a fruit-shaped eraser set that probably would cost a dollar at Walmart.

I was finally starting to get in an okay mood, imagining my pockets filled with tickets from Skee-Ball, when *bam*! *Another fucking flat tire*. What were the chances? Apparently, the garage in ol' Murder Motel 6 town had sold us a janky wheel. So once again we were roadside, playing truck driver roulette for someone to stop and help us. Total déjà vu . . .

We got the spare with no time to . . . spare (pe he he), and we were going to ride that puppy for the next five hours into Georgia.

If that spare blew out, we were royally fucked, but we were gonna chance it. Why? Because my mother was going to straight-up put a brick on the gas pedal and send her offspring into a lake if she had to spend an extra hour with us.

As luck would have it, we actually did make it to Georgia on that spare. As we cruised our way through Atlanta, only thirty miles from my dad's place, I could taste the cheap, greasy pizza. I could almost feel the Skee-Ball in my hand. I could see the blue light going off everywhere when I was crowned the air hockey champion. . . .

And that's when I realized we were being pulled over.

"What the hell?! I wasn't even speeding!" my mom yelled as she pulled onto the shoulder. Another curse in the Mom records. I looked at Annie and held up six fingers. She was both unaware of my cursing tally and too enthralled with the cop situation to pay me a lick of attention. As an avid watcher of *Cops*, Annie stared at the front seat like she was back on her water bed, eating Starburst and watching a shakedown.

The cop approached our car and we all held our breath. He agreed that my mom wasn't going over the speed limit, but apparently spare tires can't go as fast as normal ones—he was pulling her over for her own safety. What a superobservant po-po! So observant, in fact, that he noticed my mom's tags were expired. As much as she promised she would fix it the next day, he wouldn't let up, even going as far as saying, "I pulled over a mama with three young 'uns earlier today that had expired tags, and you know what I had to do? I had to take her into the station."

Looking back, this was a crock of shit. There was no way he just happened to pull over two moms with kids for the same offense in one day. Unless this guy was living the lamest version of the film *Groundhog Day*, he was just trying to scare my mom.

Just like Puss in Boots in the *Shrek* movies, she broke out her big, sad eyes, telling the cop all the crazy shit that had gone down in the past twenty-four hours: the roach motel, the cops, the first flat tire, the *second* flat tire. We followed suit and looked up at him like three

Tiny Tims. By the time my mom got to the emotional crescendo of "And I just told them their parents are divorcing," the cop had melted. Mission accomplished. He sent us on our way, and Mom quickly snapped back to normal. I was only nine years old but I remember thinking to myself, *Umm, who took my mom and replaced her with Dianne Wiest? This woman can act!* I shot Chee-Chee a "check this bitch out" side-eye.

Thirty minutes later, my mom was dropping us off at Billy Bob's to meet my dad. In my head she told us she loved us unconditionally, then opened the doors to her Maxima and told us to "tuck and roll," without ever dropping below thirty miles per hour. When she retells it, she assures me that she took me inside, had a totally normal and nice convo with my dad, catching him up on the past forty-eight hours, then kissed our foreheads and drove the last six hours home.

With my overalls pockets filled with tokens, a fountain Coke in hand, and a pack of peanuts from the snack bar, I was happy again. This was going to be an okay summer. . . .

Oh! That is, until we found out my dad had a psychotic flight attendant girlfriend who was about to take over our summer like a Somalian pirate. Cynthia. She was downright batshit, but hey, at least now I had a hookup for peanuts. That's the thing—with that summer and hard times in general, you've gotta take the salty with the sweet. It's always a balance. My parents were divorcing, but at least I had never once seen them fight.

If you'll allow me to make one more analogy, which even if you don't, I'm going to anyway because I can't hear you: Like this tasty cocktail, don't keep everything bottled up. Sometimes you've got to let the nuts out. In this case, Cynthia was the nuts and luckily my dad let her out real quick. 'Cause dat bitch was cray cray!*

---

*Thank God, 'cause soon he would meet my future stepmom, who has been an absolute beacon of strength and encouragement in my life. Plus, she's really to blame for my sailor mouth. Love you, Anne!

Piña Colon-A

3 oz white or coconut rum
½ cup pineapple juice
1 tbs cream of coconut
½ cup ice
½ cup cubed frozen mango
1 chilled shot espresso

Combine everything except the espresso in a blender and blend. Pour your frozen best friend into a fun glass, shaping the top into a peak. Then pour your chilled espresso floater over the top. It'll swirl in and mix with your drink as you go along—and it'll look a lot prettier than mixing it in to begin with, which will leave you with a brown drink. Gross.

This is your classic poolside piña colada, but we give it an extra kick of caffeine by adding espresso to keep things moving.

I love to travel. I *lurve* it. Whenever I'm in a new place, my adventurous side kicks in—I want to see everything, do everything, drink everything. But there is one side of me that hates to travel. And that, ladies and dudes strong enough with your masculinity to read this book, is . . . my *back*side.

That's right, this chapter is about one of the biggest pains in my ass: *travel constipation.*

For some reason or another, when I go abroad, my very regular digestive system ceases to function. And when I say "regu-lar," I mean military boot camp regular. Sing it with me, everybody!

I don't know but I've been told
I'll poop every morning till I get old.
I don't know but it's been said
I poop as soon as I get out of bed!

When I wake up in the morning and have my coffee, it's a fuckin' go. It has become so Pavlovian that I can basically hear the name Dunkin' Donuts and have a solid BM. America runs on Dunkin' and Dunkin' gives me the runs. Fuck it, if I see a bra tag that says "DD" I'm probably gonna drop it like it's hot.

My regularity is so dependable, in fact, that my morning routine is scheduled around it. If I'm just chilling at home, writing in my underwear with my tiny dog in my lap (spoiler alert: like I am right now), then I drink coffee at my leisure. But if I'm headed to an audition and might be in traffic for an hour, I'd better down that cup of joe with a solid five minutes carved in to sit on the can playing Candy Crush before I leave my house.

When it comes to relieving myself, I am shameless. I will go anywhere, anytime. If I need to go at a party and there is a line of fifty people behind me, you'd better believe I'm taking a seat. Number two is my number one priority. It's the healthy thing to do! When I was younger, I remember hearing that if you hold your pee in for too long, the toxins from the urine release back into your body. This *terrified* me. The phrase "If you gotta go, you gotta go" became my mantra—nay, my *lifestyle*.

But for whatever reason, my dirty work goes on strike when I'm abroad. Can butts get jet lag? Is my butt just super ~~racist~~ patriotic? Is my ass just so damn proud to be an American that it literally doesn't give a shit about other countries? The jury is still out.* All I know is that my bowel movements cannot get through customs. And because I am a thirty-year-old woman with the imagination of a ten-year-old boy and the pores of a newborn, here is how I think a conversation between my ass and customs would go.

Int. Any Other Country's Customs

CUSTOMS GUY

You look different from your photo.
Did you do something to your hair?

MY ASSHOLE

Yes, I was recently bleached.
(Customs guy looks at photo; story checks out.)

CUSTOMS GUY

Have you left the country before? It appears your passport
has no stamps.

MY ASSHOLE

If you want to see a stamp, go about a foot above me and
check out that horrendous Chinese symbol tramp stamp on
the lower back. She thinks it means "courage." It really
means "pork."

CUSTOMS GUY

There is no time for jokes in customs, ma'am.

MY ASSHOLE

Sorry, I like to keep things *loose.*

*CUT TO: A jury room full of very confused people wondering why
tax dollars were spent on this case.

CUSTOMS GUY
Okay, look, I'm not trying to be an asshole but—

MY ASSHOLE
(offended)
You sonofabitch!
*(Asshole is then detained and given a full cavity search, much
to her enjoyment.)*
END SCENE

Okay. Now that my parents have *officially* thrown this book
into the fireplace, let me regale you with a timeless classic. I call it
"A Tale of Two Shitties."

It was December 2011. Maegan and I decided to escape the
harsh New York winter with a lil' vacay in Puerto Rico. It was the
land of rum, beautiful beaches, Ricky Martin—and where I didn't
shit for *six days*.

We stayed on the island of Vieques, where my friend Stefanie
from NC had recently moved to. She pulled one of those "I'm on
vacation and I love it here so I'm not leaving" moves that regular
people think happen only in movies. At the time, she was living
with her friend James, another US expat, who happened to have
an old-school Airstream trailer on his property, right by his pool.
Stef hooked it up and Maegan and I had a place to stay for free!
James was a total sweetheart and the poster child for old hippie
surfer dudes. He spent his days hanging by the pool and starting to
drink at two p.m. One night, we invited him out to dinner with us
and it took him two hours to find a pair of flip-flops because he
hadn't worn shoes in four years. His motto was "No shoes, no
shirt, no idea where I am right now!"

It wasn't until around day three that I realized I hadn't dropped
a deuce since arriving. I had hoped that since PR is owned by the
US, my ass would cut me a break. But no such luck. Apparently,

my butthole has stricter standards regarding PR than the Miss America pageant.

The first possible cure was, of course, coffee. I always say, once coffee hits my mouth, my drawers go down south. But even some Puerto Rican French press was no match for my stubborn bowels.

Next, I tried excessive amounts of beer, another old reliable. (Hey! It's not like I *wanted* to drink eighteen Medallas a day—it was for my health.) But sadly, that didn't make me go either, although it did make me almost accept a marriage proposal from a toothless local. James, knowing my struggle and being the gracious host that he was, found fresh aloe vera and peeled it for me to eat raw. Still nothing. He chopped down coconuts and watched me guzzle the fresh water in them, hoping that would lube up my tube. Nada.

James the Saint even offered to have butt sex with me to spark some movement. Although I politely declined, I was honored that he would've gone doggy style with me to make my stay more comfortable. That's hospitality! Take note, Martha Stewart.

I fucking loved those coconuts. Obviously rum was added to all of them.

Despite all the effort, I was still totally blocked. By day five, my full belly was stuck out so far that I looked like E.T. in a one-piece. I was rockin' a straight-up second-trimester pregnant belly while drinking a forty-ounce beer, floating on a pool noodle. The disgusted looks I got from strangers on the beach became a drinking game.

The constipation didn't let up the entire time we were there. We floated in the crystal waters on an empty beach, and I felt like I had an anchor holding me down. We canoed through the magical bio bay, and as I watched the water droplets that looked like stars, I wished on them that I could take a crap. No such luck. Despite all of my and James's efforts, I can honestly say that I've never gone number two in Puerto Rico. Obviously, as soon as the plane's wheels touched down on American soil, it was *on*.

Ahem. I would like to take this opportunity to formally apologize to the bathroom attendant at LaGuardia Airport. What I did in there was not okay. You didn't deserve that.

Although PR was painful, in retrospect, it was child's play compared to the first time this travel hex happened. This one is a doozy and lasted for over a week. Dare I say you'll need to exercise some constipa-tience for this story?

It happened when I went to Bali for Hely's thirtieth birthday. You remember Hely from facilitating my torture Brazilian? She had family there, and they were kind enough to let her and a rotating cast of friends take over their house for a month. She had invited us a year earlier, and I couldn't believe I'd actually saved the money and booked the flight. At twenty-four, I felt like this was the most adult thing I'd ever done.

I was *So. Damn. Excited.* Bali was supposed to be majestic. The beautiful beaches, the smiling people, but most of all . . . the peanut sauce. I FUCKING love peanut sauce. I'm gonna go ahead and say that peanut sauce is my number one condiment, but don't you dare say anything to hot sauce. If I lost hot sauce's trust, I don't know what I would do.

There's a joke in the South that goes:

How do you get a southern girl to suck your dick?
How?
Dip it in ranch.

Followed by a high five and those two dudes going back to playing *Halo.*

But me? I've always hated ranch. However, if the only peanut sauce left in Bali was on someone's ding-a-ling? Well . . . then I'd have me a new boyfriend.

While I've been an on-and-off vegetarian and vegan since the ripe age of nine, this trip was during the few years I fell off the conscientious wagon. In Bali most of my meals consisted of chicken satay and peanut sauce with a side of white rice with peanut sauce followed by some more fucking peanut sauce. I couldn't get enough.

It wasn't till about day three that I noticed all that peanut sauce that was coming in was not going out. Nothing was coming out, in fact. My butt should've been pumping out peanut sauce like one of those machines at Whole Foods that let you grind your own peanut butter, but alas, it was not.

I tried old faithful: coffee. Lucky for me, Balinese coffee is super potent. They brew it as dense as tar over there, so a couple of cups of that, and I was sure to be sittin' pretty. I jumped in headfirst. I probably had four cups of coffee in this serene, small back garden of a coffee shop. I caffeinated so hard that, I swear to God, I could feel my eyebrows growing. But I still didn't have to go. I take that back. I did have to go, in the sense that I needed to *leave* that fucking garden immediately. I had reached full-on panic attack caffeine levels and found myself in my own *Requiem for a Dream* but with fewer butt-to-butt dildos.

(Although, come to think of it, a couple of dildos probably would have helped the situation. Dammit, be-hindsight is always twenty-twenty.)

After a few days of not going, wearing a bikini was just straight-up embarrassing. Or, I guess, *more* embarrassing than usual.

I was more clogged than Bigfoot's shower drain, so I decided that I needed to take a more radical approach. Since I was in Bali and needed some medical attention, I decided to do what the Balinese do when they are constipated. And I knew just where to go.

The year I went to Bali was the same year the book *Eat, Pray, Love*, by Elizabeth Gilbert, came out. In case you haven't read it, the book follows the author's journey as she finds happiness through the food in Italy, meditation in India, and then love in Bali. If you haven't read this quintessential lady book, do it now.

In the book, Gilbert becomes friends with a woman named Wayan, who owns a Balinese healing center in the mountain town of Ubud. While Wayan helps her with her messed-up knee, the two become lifelong friends. I had to meet Wayan for myself. Why?

A. Because I had just finished reading the book and thought it would be cool to meet this character in real life.
B. Because I was backed up further than a subway line when someone falls on the tracks, and I thought maybe she could help!

I had a plan but I needed travel buddies. Going to Wayan wasn't like walking a couple of blocks to go to a drugstore. This place was three hours away, and in a country where I'm pretty sure I saw a macaque driving a Vespa.

"Jillian. Erika. Pack your bags because first thing tomorrow morning we are taking a car to Ubud!"

They looked at me, dumbfounded.

"Come on, guys! Ubud is the cultural center of Bali. We need to get up there and experience the art and music that makes this majestic country."

"Is it gonna help your butt?" Erika asked.

"Hopefully."

"Let's do this!"

We all attempted a three-way high five, which never works. Just like in a normal three-way, you are always left unsatisfied and someone gets accidentally slapped in the face.

The next morning we hired a driver to take us up into the mountains. I was ready to nip this thing in th'Ubud! We had no idea where to find Wayan's shop, but as soon as we started to ask a local, he rolled his eyes and pointed. Apparently, I wasn't the first person to seek her out because of the book.

I decided that I would not fangirl out. I was going to play it cool like, "Hi, table for three . . . Wait a second. Are you Wayan from *Eat, Pray, Love*? Well, I'll be! It's Wayan from *Eat, Pray Love*, girls! And to think, we almost just went to the Olive Garden. What are the chances?!"

We got to her little shop, and sure enough, Wayan seated us herself. One of the things Gilbert would always do in the book is go to Wayan's healing center for a Vitamin Lunch, which consists of small portions of superhealthy foods and juices. Each dish is labeled with a small laminated postcard, and then Wayan explains the health benefits of each. She presented us with a lovely platter and the cards:

Grilled coconut: rheumatism
Tomato chutney: healthy gums
Tempeh satay: strong bones
Bean sprouts: strengthens muscles, fights infertility
Water spinach: healthy blood, fights insomnia
Fresh papaya: healthy digestion

Digestion? What is this mythical digestion you speak of? I'll pa-PAY-ya for a second helping! I thought to myself. We finished lunch, which was clean and tasty (but severely lacking in peanut sauce), and then came time for the body reading. It's basically like a palm reading, but instead of a Romanian woman straight out of *My Big Fat Gypsy Wedding* telling you your future, Wayan gives you an overview of your health.

She started by picking up my friend Jillian's hand. After examining it for a while, Wayan concluded that Jillian has heartburn and should get more calcium. Erika was up next and her palm apparently said she should cool it with her intake of red meat and eggs, and also that she would have two children. Then came the moment of truth. She lifted my hand and studied it intensely. She was looking at it so closely, I got paranoid that I hadn't washed my hands last time I went to the bathroom and she was going to call me out for it. Three straight minutes went by in complete silence. My thoughts got increasingly frantic. *Do I need more calcium? Is she going to diagnose me with giving too many hand jobs? Oh shit, do I have a week to live? Speak to me, Wayan! For the love of God, I only have a week to live! SAY SOMETHING, DAMMIT!*

She finally released my hand, looked up at me with her sweet face, and said, "Your mind is in the middle. You're not that smart, and not that stupid."

And with that, she sashayed away.

B'scuse me?! I hadn't been that pissed and confused at a Wayan since I saw *White Chicks*. What kind of shit was that? I tried rationalizing what she had said. *Oh . . . mind is in the middle. She's trying to say I'm a very balanced and rationally thinking person. That's not that bad, I guess.* Who am I kidding? Wayan basically called me an idiot to my face while taking my money! I blamed it on the constipation. Perhaps she couldn't tell how many kids I was going to have or what dietary changes I should make because my body was so messed up. She couldn't read my palm because the creases were practically filled with shit, like the spine of an uncleaned shrimp!

Things were getting to the point of serious discomfort, and it was time to take my medicine back west. I'm talking laxatives. Being in a different country, and not being familiar with their medicine brands, I eased in. A couple on day six. A handful on day seven. By day eight, I was downing laxatives like it was 1987 and I couldn't fit into my prom dress. Finally, on day nine, I took the maximum amount your body can handle in a day. I washed those suckers down with the strongest Balinese coffee I could find.

Still nothing. That is, until six o'clock the next morning. The urgency woke me from my sleep, and my legally blind ass stumbled to the bathroom. The timing was perfect. All my friends were asleep so it meant that no one would be waiting for the bathroom or, worse, hear me testing the strength of Bali's plumbing system. After about fifteen minutes of me losing my shit (literally), a light knock came at the door.

"Hey, Mame. The car is going to be here in ten minutes."

Did I imagine that? Was I hallucinating from the sheer ecstasy of finally taking a shit? I've never taken Ecstasy before but I imagine the sensation I felt was similar. I was halfway to pulling out glow sticks and dancing to "Sandstorm" when I realized it was the very real voice of Jillian.

"I'll be right out." Followed by my ass sounding like a semiautomatic being fired down a garbage disposal.

Apparently, while I was manically gobbling Balinese Ex-Laxes the night before (which I like to think were called Bowel-and-Ease*), I had forgotten that we had an early start the next morning. Because we were going WHITE-WATER RAFTING.

I thought to myself, *Which of these idiots planned a white-water rafting trip knowing good and well I haven't pooped in over a—ohhhhh.* It was me. I had planned it assuming my issue would have cleared up. My mind was definitely in the middle. Touché, Wayan. Touché.

Now I had to live with the consequences. You know how people talk about "breaking the seal" when they start drinking? How you can hold your pee as long as you want, but once you finally take a leak, you are going to have to pee every fifteen minutes? Well, I didn't just break the seal on my ass. The seal had all but joined the witness protection program at this point.

Despite feeling like I could sit on the toilet for the better part of 2007, I sucked it up and joined my friends in the car. It was a miserable trip. I felt like I needed to give birth and the doctor was telling me to hold it in. After 120 grueling minutes, we arrived at

---

*Get it? Bowel-and-Ease? Like Balinese? If you didn't get it, take a sip.

the white-water rafting place. As soon as we pulled up, I peeled out of the car in search of a bathroom.

When I finally found it with my heat-seeking missile of a butt-hole, there was a twenty-person line. Not even just a normal line. Apparently, the lacrosse team of some American college had decided to come to Bali and all use that bathroom that day. There it was. One toilet and two dozen beautiful college athletes before me. It was like I had accidently stumbled into the premise of a *very* specific fetish movie. I couldn't do it. The thought of a gaggle of Abercrombie & Fitch models listening to me as I uncorked eight days of evil was too much, so I joined my group and suited up.

Here we are earlier in our trip about to attend a small village's Full Moon Festival. We had made friends with a local named Mangde (pictured), and his sisters dressed us up in their traditional garb. I put on a smile but, Lord knows, I was super uncomfortable with my own full moon . . . my butt.

We hit the river with a bang. Literally. It was the last month of the dry season in Bali and the water level was super low. This posed two problems. One, this whole excursion was going to take a lot longer than we had expected, and two, the river was gonna be *bumpy*. As soon as the raft hit the water, I felt like I was being punched in the colon.

I asked our instructor about how long the trip would be. He confidently and politely replied, "*Boom boom.*"

Yes, boom boom. No, he wasn't speaking in Black Eyed Peas lyrics. This was how he guided us. "Boom boom" roughly translated to "Hold on to your tits, girls, we're about to hit a boulder." I didn't want to be a negative Nancy and ruin the experience for my friends, so after about a half hour of almost boom-booming in my shorts, I decided to take action.

I dug deep into my river experience of tubing and began instructing everyone on our raft. I yelled at them to paddle right! I yelled at them to paddle left! I yelled at them because I was about to defecate in a rubber boat! The urgency of my bowels transformed me into an Olympic coxswain.*

The guide couldn't tell me how far away from the end we were, but he didn't need to. My ass could tell. Have you ever watched someone on the beach with a metal detector? The closer it gets to metal, the more intense the beeping becomes. That was my ass getting closer to a bathroom.

We finally reached the end of the river and I straight-up Usain Bolted to the bathroom. I won't go into detail about the wonders of what occurred in those following five minutes. (A girl's got to keep a little mystery, right? Said me, never.) But I *can* say that shit was orgasmic. If I'd had a cigarette I would have immediately lit it, then high-fived myself. When I had fully deflated and regained composure, I strutted out of that bathroom like a boy after his first blow

---

*Coxswains are those people on boats yelling out orders, the ones who get gold medals for being bossy. Literally *coxswain* translates to "boat servant," but if you only translate the second half of the word, it's the best porn name ever. Mamrie Hart stars in . . . *The Cox Servant.*

job. Part of me expected people to be applauding and lifting me up on their shoulders. Although that still would have been a risky move, considering the situation.

Once I got over the hump of the dump, my body went back to regularly scheduled digestion. I felt like a human! I could eat without being in pain again! I could actually get drunk again! (Apparently, when you have a Sizzler buffet's worth of food just waiting to exit your body, it's hard to catch a buzz.) Finally, I could enjoy Bali without feeling terrible. All I wanted to do that last week was be beachside in a bikini, piña colada in hand. But just to be safe, I threw in a *shit-ton* of coffee to keep things on track.

So, what have we learned from this chapter? For starters, there are no refunds upon purchase of this book. Second, I seriously missed my calling as a competitive white-water rafter. But there is more than that. I like to think of my constipation as a sort of metaphor for traveling. When you are in a new place and your normal routine changes, you've got to adapt to your surroundings.

You've got to go with the flow, and if that flow is blocked, *try anything.*

Except butt sex with James.

Quickshots:
Terrible Flying Experiences

Y

While blockage when I travel somewhere is always a pain, sometimes trying to actually get there is the worst. For whatever reason, homegirl right here has got some bad luck when it comes to traveling. I'm not talking that child's play of having a flight delayed by three hours or the Chili's Too being out of skillet queso. I'm talking travel hiccups that are EXTREME(ly annoying).

Here are my top three most awful stories.

1. Baltimore

People have issues. And 99 percent of them can be traced to something that happened in their childhood. My issues with flying are no different. I flew all the time as a kid and loved it. I was even a member of the Delta Air Lines Fantastic Flyer program. This basically meant that I got to meet the pilots and get a wings pin as I boarded every flight. They also sent me their knockoff version of *Highlights* magazine every few months and a birthday card. Delta even had a mascot. It was a lion named Dusty, and the way they styled his mane and stuck him in a bomber jacket, well . . . I'm not gonna lie. I thought Dusty was *hawt*.*

*Don't pretend you didn't have animated crushes as a child.

But my love affair with flying came crashing down. Not literally! Oh dear God. Not literally. Thank God. Everyone reading needs to put down this book and knock on wood. Then pick it back up and order another copy. My flight was fine, but my mindset was forever changed.

Check this out. I was nine years old and had been living in North Carolina for only a year. But my mom, being the amazing parent she is, let my sister and me fly to see our friend Kara back in New Jersey. It was awesome. I know a lot of people might think, *Wait a sec, you and your sister flew by yourselves at such a young age?* We did! In fact, we were old pros at it. By the time I was eight years old, I knew that if I had a layover in Atlanta that was more than forty minutes, I could easily get to Terminal A and get a Sbarro without being late to board my flight in Terminal C. Sometimes they would require a stewardess to take us from point A to point B, which, looking back, must've sucked for the stewardess. They've been listening to assholes complain about how cold the plane is for six hours and just when they think they're free, they've gotta take two preteens to their next gate. I always felt embarrassed when they had to attempt to make conversation with us. You know that the majority of conversation they had were:

Where you headed off to?

Then some pathetic kid with a runny nose says, *I'm going to visit my dad.*

That will be fun! Do you have anything cool planned while you're there?

The kid wipes his nose with his hand. *Not really. We'll probably just talk about my feelings since the divorce and hang out in his tiny studio apartment. My mom says he's a deadbeat who couldn't find a job if it hit him in the—*

Well, here's your terminal!

My sister LOVED talking to stewardesses. Annie couldn't wait to be a grown-up (the fact that she started smoking at thirteen proved this), and so she basked in the presence of these glorious, put-together ladies.

Here Annie and I are playing the classic children's game "Aerobics Instructors." As you can see, Annie looks stylish and ready to flirt while I love working out in turtlenecks.

But it was this flight back from NJ that the stewardess–unattended minor situation got weird. The flight was only an hour and a half long, but to a child, an hour and a half feels like eighteen days. Annie and I were sitting there with our little packets of peanuts and plastic cups of Coca-Cola (my peanuts dumped into the Coke, obvs) when the turbulence kicked in. This is before my extreme awareness and fear of mortality made every bit of turbulence feel like a speed bump on the road to death. The plane was being tossed around like a beanbag in a game of Cornhole, while Annie and I were smiling from ear to ear, making tiny "woo" noises. We were acting like we were on a Tilt-a-Whirl. Meanwhile there was probably some poor woman three rows back bargaining with God and doing her rosary beads.

The captain came on the PA system. "Folks, as you can see I've had to leave on the Fasten Seat Belt sign because we are experiencing some very rough air. There seems to be a pretty significant electrical storm happening below us and, sorry to let you know, we have been advised to make an emergency landing in Baltimore."

Do what, now? Emergency landing? Furthermore ... *Baltimore*? I looked at my older sister for comfort. She was busy doing that weird cross-over-your-chest thing like I'd seen Winona Ryder do in *Mermaids* when she wanted to be a nun. We managed to land without me shitting my pants, but then there was a whole new scary element. We, nine- and eleven-year-old girls, were stuck in Baltimore for God knew how long.

Once we deplaned, we were told that the storm was so bad there was no way we were getting out till tomorrow morning. And this is where the airline came up with a brilliant plan.* Annie and I were going to stay in a Red Roof Inn, along with all the other stranded passengers that night, and we would be chaperoned by two stewardesses. Annie could hardly contain her fist pumps, while I was fighting back tears. The only person freaking out more than me was my mother.

The airline reassured her that we were in good hands. The stewardesses, let's call them Tammy and Trish, were our chaperones. Tammy even got on the phone with my mom to let her know that we would be totally safe and on the flight first thing in the morning.

"We know you must be worried sick about your girls, but they will be fine. I practically raised my little sisters," Tammy told her as Trish comforted me by braiding my hair.

Talking to Tammy calmed my mom's nerves enough to not make the seven-hour drive in the bad storm. It was official. Our babysitters were stewardesses.

Before we made our way to the Red Roof Inn, we had to get

---

*I must let you know at this point that it wasn't Delta we were flying. Delta, and my dear cartoon lover Dusty the Lion, would never have come up with this plan.

some sustenance for us two growing girls. Luckily, the airline also provided both Annie and me a fifteen-dollar voucher for the airport. If someone gave me that now, I'd be all, "Mothafucka, that's barely a glass of pinot grigio." But as a nine-year-old, I thought I was rich. We stopped by the airport store to load up on Cheez-Its and sour cream and onion Ruffles. Things were looking up!

Once we checked in to the hotel, Annie and I sat on one of the full beds eating our snacks as Tammy sat on the other bed. Trish had gone out with some fellow stewardesses to "get some food," which was weird considering the amount of blue eye shadow she was wearing. And I'm pretty sure I had seen her spritz some Jovan Musk on her cleavage. Tammy flipped through the channels and finally settled on a rerun of MTV's *The Grind*. I wanted to speak up and ask her to change it. I wasn't opposed to the amount of booty popping happening on the screen; I was just bored. Why would you want to watch average, pedestrian dancers dance with each other? This wasn't like today's *So You Think You Can Dance*. This was "So You Think You Can Kind of Keep a Beat and Will Work for $30 a Day and Free Lunch." I looked to my left to see Annie in heaven.

After *The Grind*, I finally got sleepy. I was tuckered out after such a big night and was ready for a lil' shut-eye before our early flight out in the morning. Just as I was closing my peepers to say good night to my lord and savior, Jonathan Taylor Thomas, the door swung open. Trish was back.

And she wasn't alone. She was there with some rando dude (we'll call him Randy the Rando) who looked like an extra from *Silk Stalkings*. I can't for the life of me remember the conversation that was had (I was busy trying to teleport out of there as Annie literally drooled), but I imagine it went a little something like this:

Taaaammmmy. I'm back from the bar and look who I ran into!

Great, Trish. It's the random barfly you slept with last time we had a layover in Baltimore. Let me guess, he was at the same bar.

What are the chances, huh?

Annie was watching like it was an episode of *Melrose Place*.

Randy noticed there were kids present and did the pull-a-quarter-out-of-the-ear trick on me, but he pulled out a Budweiser bottle cap instead. That was the final straw for Tammy, who then suggested they leave.

After Randy and Trish left, we all conked out. It had been quite the adventurous evening, and we eventually made it back to NC the next morning—me with a newfound fear of flying, and Annie with a newfound dream of being a stewardess.

2. London

I was headed to London to do a round of #NoFilter shows (a.k.a. Saggy Tits Gate) and chose a red-eye for the eleven-hour flight. As I boarded the Virgin plane, which always feels more like an airplane-themed club than an actual plane, I realized my seat was in the middle. I'm an aisle girl. Yes, windows are great for sleeping, but there is something so comforting about being able to get up whenever I want without having to ask someone. By the eye rolls some people give in those situations, you would think you were asking them to carry a child for you. You know the type. The people who unbuckle the seat belt like it weighs eighty pounds, who have to demonstrate how difficult it is to get up with the person in front of them reclined, finally making it to their feet like they've been on a fuckin' space shuttle for six months and their leg muscles have atrophied. It sucks.

I made it to my row and did the "that's me" point to the Larry Bird look-alike in the aisle seat. His eyes lit up. And then his wife stood up across the aisle.

"Would you rather have my aisle seat? That's my husband. I'd rather sit with him."

Oh, thank God.

"That would be amazing. Thank you so much."

"Dammit," Larry Bird chimed in. "You sure you want to switch, dear?"

Lovely, he was flirting with me in front of his wife, who quickly elbowed the Bird harder than Magic Johnson during the 1986 NBA Finals.* I really dodged a bullet on that one.

I settled into my new aisle seat beside a man who was already passed the fuck out. Things were looking up. The flight itself was painless—no turbulence; Captain Zzz beside me literally did not open his eyes once. We started descending into London, and I was *shocked* that I'd made it the whole flight without one thing annoying me. The screen on the back of my seat was broken and not even that had brought me down. I drank wine. I worked on my laptop. I napped. The only tiny moment of panic I had was when I thought the guy beside me might actually be dead. I'm not gonna lie, I got real close to that random man's face to make sure he was still breathing.

This glee was fleeting, though. 'Cause the second our plane's wheels hit the runway, something hit *me*. I was a little disoriented but could only assume from the texture that someone had thrown their bag of overpriced Munchies Snack Mix from the force of the landing.

"What was that?" I said as I noticed that some got in my hair.

"Some guy just threw up on us," Larry Bird said in a super-pissed-off tone.

I smiled at him, still not processing what he'd said, and then it hit me. I was picking vomit out of my hair. I sat there frozen. What could I do? I didn't have anything to wipe it off with. I couldn't get out of my seat. I just sat there covered in this man's regurgitated dinner as the plane slowly taxied toward the gate.

The only good thing to come out of it was the possible corpse

---

*Shocker: I had to google that reference. Now "Who hates Larry Bird?" will forever live in my search history. Please, God, don't let him go missing!

lifting his head to say, "Oh, that sucks," then go back to sleep. It made me laugh out loud. Very hard. I was the girl covered in vomit, laughing hysterically to herself.

3. Kuala Lumpur

I am notoriously cheap when it comes to flights. If a layover in Kazakhstan on a plane full of goats means saving two hundred dollars on a trip, sign me up! This has gotten me into some layovers from hell. Let me regale you with the tale of the worst one, which happened in Malaysia.

I was flying home from visiting my brother and his family in Australia, and I was totally exhausted. Like all good flights, we were going the long way around the entire earth back to NYC. My first layover was a ten-hour stop in Kuala Lumpur. This probably sounds like hell to most sane people, but I was still a scrappy twenty-five-year old. I'd done Greyhound bus rides longer than that, and everyone knows that Greyhound buses are more dangerous than inmate buses. I could do anything for ten hours.

I figured I'd hit up a restaurant, drink my face off till it closed at midnight, and then sleep on the floor the rest of the night. Because I, for one, have zero shame in sleeping on an airport floor, especially if it's a morning flight. I distinctly remember sleeping on the floor of LaGuardia once and hearing a woman say, "Poor thing. She's probably been stranded here for days because of the blizzard." My flight had been delayed ten minutes. That is how quickly I will hit the deck. In fact, I make sure to pack my carry-on backpack specifically so that it will serve as a makeshift pillow. Ten hours was going to be a breeze.

When I landed in Kuala Lumpur at ten p.m., I knew my plan was kaput. The airport looked like a tomb. There wasn't a soul in sight who hadn't just exited my flight. Once the deplaning passengers had scattered, I realized that the airport was not only pretty much empty, but I was the *only person left in the terminal*. Sure, this sounds like the premise for an amazing '80s movie, but it caught me a little off guard. The place looked postapocalyptic except for the one old man vacuuming.

This was going to be creepy, but I was sticking to the plan. First order of business: Get drunk!

Visions of rum with pineapple and mango juice danced in my head as I strutted toward the dining area of the terminal. I couldn't wait to get a drink with a tiny umbrella in it. I would hold that tiny umbrella over my head like it was raining and say, "What recession?" as the patrons of the bar would laugh and laugh. I was already working on my encore joke when I rounded the corner to see all the bars were closed. Undeterred, I went in search of food. I found a vending machine. Lemongrass Bugles-type chips for dinner it was!

I swiped my card. Nothing. Again. Nada. I looked around to make sure there was still no one near me, then licked the stripe on the back of the card and swiped again. Still nothing. *No worries*, I thought to myself, *I'll just have to go to an ATM and take out some currency that I will never exchange back to dollars.**

But when I typed in my PIN at the ATM machine, my card was declined. It took me a minute to realize what was going on. I had warned my bank that I was going to be in Australia for a month, but I didn't say shit about Malaysia. This was bad. Not only was I stranded in a deserted airport for the next ten hours, but now I didn't have a dollar to my name. The next meal I was getting was the flaccid egg sandwich on the flight.

I sprawled out on the floor, stomach growling. The sooner I could sleep, the sooner that egg sandwich would be in my face. But as much as I tried, I couldn't fall asleep. Normally after five min-

---

*Seriously. I never exchange my money back, out of sheer laziness. If I took the time to round up all the random euros, loonies, and pesos in my house, I could buy a hot tub—the good kind with cup holders and massage jets.

utes of lying horizontal, I'd already be dry-humping the floor and drooling, but it just wasn't happening for me. Every time I closed my eyes, I imagined waking up to the old vacuuming man spooning me with his hands up my shirt. And no one would be there to tell him otherwise! I'm sure he was a great guy who would never do that, but the thought kept me tossing and turning. I sat up and noticed a cluster of computers a few gates down. I made a beeline to the lit-up screens like a moth to a lightbulb.

Oh my Gilbert Gottfried, there was Internet! I threw my arms up in victory. I felt like Tom Hanks in *Cast Away* when he learns how to crack open coconuts. Sure, he's still stuck on a desert island, but there's hope. These crappy old desktops were my coconuts.

I logged on and immediately checked my e-mail. I saw that Maegan was on G-chat and figured with the time difference, she was at work. We started chatting. She bitched about work and I bitched about feeling stranded with no money or food in Kuala Lumpur. Just take a second to visualize an empty airport and a girl lying on the floor, popping up every few minutes to type something into the free computers, occasionally laughing to herself. I was slowly going mad.

MAEGAN

I'm gonna go take my lunch. . . .

ME

Oh my god, what are you going to eat? I want to imagine it.
I am so hungry that this is like dirty talk to my taste buds.

MAEGAN

I'm thinking about going to get a big veggie dumpling soup from Republic but I might just grab a falafel sandwich from the cart. . . .

ME

BOIOIOIOIOIOIOIOING!

MAEGAN
Will you still be on in thirty?

ME
This is my life now. This is all I have.

MAEGAN
Hang in there. I'll be back.

I looked up the menu to Republic and read it to myself like it was *Fifty Shades of Grey*. By the time I got to "A tamarind-infused broth," I couldn't take it anymore. I felt like Sting must feel after a tantric sex session—my whole body was buzzing just imagining the broth in my mouth. Why oh why couldn't reality be like the movie *Hook* and all you had to do was imagine food and it would appear?*

Stomach roaring, I peeled myself off that hard tile floor and strolled through the terminal in my pink cowboy boots. (Could I be more American?) The clicking of my boots was the only sound. I found a row of fast-food places and thought about trying to convince the poor bastard on the third shift to give me a snack for free, but then I got a weird, foreign feeling in my stomach. It was pride. I couldn't be this American who was clearly flying around the world, wearing bubble-gum-colored cowboy boots, begging for yesterday's fried rice.

As I made my final turn, I spotted a Western Union in the distance. Random. I didn't even know they had Western Union in Asia. Shouldn't it be called Eastern Union? And that's when it struck me!

I took off like airport security was chasing me for stealing Corn Nuts. I got to the computers and slid to a halt à la *Risky Business*.

---

*Although, unlike in *Hook*, I don't think I want to eat neon cakes and pies. Like, seriously, though, why did all the Lost Boys' food look like it was made out of neon zinc oxide?

*Please let her be back online. Please let her be online. Please let— oh
thank Bejeezus, she's still online.* I started typing. . . .

ME

MAEGAN!!!!! ARE YOU THERE? HOLY
FUCKBALLS!*^&%#$! Can you do me a huge favor??

MAEGAN

As long as you never say "fuckballs" again. What's wrong?
Did you accidentally "The Secret" the vacuum guy to touch
your boobs?

ME

LOLZ! No, seriously. I am desperate. Is there any chance
you can sneak out of the office and Western Union me
some $$$$? It would be to the Kuala Lumpur airport
branch under my name. . . .

MAEGAN

That's a sentence I never thought I'd read. Of course I will!
Leaving now.

Sure enough, after an hour and a lot of broken English and sad
rounds of charades trying to explain myself to the night-shift
worker at Western Union, I had a crisp hundred dollars' worth of
Malaysian ringgits in my hand. There were only three hours left
before my flight started boarding, but I was going to treat myself.
This meant buying way more snacks than I could possibly consume and then going straight to the rent-by-the-hour hotel in the
terminal. I was essentially paying sixty bucks to take a three-hour
nap, but desperate times call for desperate measures. I was in a
strange room in an airport terminal, covered in a confetti of snack
crumbs, but I didn't care. I felt like Eloise at the Plaza.

And that is the last time I ever booked a layover longer than two cocktails' worth.

In the End

I still have some bad luck when it comes to flying. That's out of my control. But I did decide to take matters into my own hands when it came to my fear of flying. I needed to face it head-on. *So*, I bought myself a flying lesson for my thirtieth birthday.

Turns out, flying is a lot less scary once you know how to land a plane. Although I'd still much rather be back in coach taking down tiny vodkas and watching Netflix on my laptop, so please don't count on me.

Tannin Bed

**A shit-ton of fresh blueberries, raspberries, and
    pitted cherries**
Bottle red wine
1 cup simple syrup
Juice of 2 lemons and 1 orange

*Throw everything into a punch bowl or novelty-size wineglass.
Stir together, add ice, and sippity-sip. These fruits are known
to help reduce anxiety. Grapes are good for it too, but I'd rather
drink my grapes than eat them. If you don't have or don't like
red wine, sub white or rosé or sparkling or whatever the fuck!
Just don't let it stress you out. That defeats the entire purpose,
ya dumbs.*

This chapter is about one of the banes of my existence: panic attacks. If you've never had a panic attack, it's very hard to understand and almost impossible to explain. Kind of like when someone is visiting you and you want to watch *The Real Housewives of Atlanta*, but they don't watch it, and you try to catch them up on the details. It doesn't work. You end up getting so frustrated that you just change it to *Friends*. Everyone gets *Friends*. An imprisoned Taliban member could watch one episode and agree that Chandler is underrated.

All that said, in this chapter I'll try to explain panic attacks to you from my personal experience. Allow me to set the scene. It was winter in New York City. I had been living there for a handful of months and was pretty comfortable in my routine of working ten a.m. to six p.m. as a receptionist at a recording studio, living on a supertight budget, and going out for cheap drinks on the weekend. When I say cheap drinks, I mean the bar I frequented was actually named Cheap Shots. Our other haunt was a spot on St. Mark's called the Continental. Their deal was ten shots (of total shit liquor) for ten dollars. I *lived* there my first year in NYC.*

It was a Friday night and Maegan and I were strolling toward the East Village doing what any two fabulous twentysomething gals do on a night off from work: bitching about coworkers.

"I swear to God, if I hear Fred from accounting do his Borat impression one more time, I am going to eat staples," Maegan complained. Normally I would do my impression of Fred doing his impression, but I was preoccupied. Something weird was happening.

Suddenly, I became very conscious of my legs. And not in that "Damn, my legs look gooooood" way I am usually conscious of them. Specifically, I was aware of how I couldn't feel them. I couldn't feel them, but somehow they were still working. Left. Right. Left. Right. How did they know how to keep working? Maegan kept talking but it just sounded like the adults in Charlie Brown—totally nonsensical noise.

Maybe my legs were just cold. Winter in Manhattan is colder than a popular girl at a "Magic: The Gathering" party. We continued walking and I bent over and hit my legs with my hands a few times. Yep, still there. And somehow still working.

Not only are my legs being weird, I thought to myself, *but why is my mouth so dry?* It felt like I had just slept all night with my mouth open in front of a fan in the Mojave Desert. *I hope I don't have to*

---

*But don't go looking for those places or those deals when you are visiting the Big Apple. That was the stretch of time in the mid '00s before St. Mark's was turned into fro-yo shops and automated cupcake machines. Now it straight-up looks like Little Tokyo sprinkled with leftover gutter punks. Kind of like that Avril Lavigne "Hello Kitty" video.

talk, and oh shit. My hands have stopped working. I need to shake my hands and slap them to make sure they still work. And Mame? Mame?

"Mame!" Maegan shouted, finally getting my attention as I stood there slapping my legs like I was being attacked by mosquitoes. "Are you okay?"

I could've played it off like my tights itched—it was no secret that I never did laundry. But I decided to be honest. "This is going to sound totally crazy"—I could speak! Sweet Jesus, I could speak—"but I feel really weird. Like, I'm very aware of my legs right now, and everything feels . . . just strange. Like I'm a little underwater."

"You're having a panic attack," Maegan said matter-of-factly, as if she had just ordered lunch. *Yes, I'll have the Caesar salad, extra croutons, and you are having a panic attack. Also, I'll take a Diet Coke.* I stared at her, not knowing how to respond. "You're totally having a panic attack. We need to get you inside ASAP."

I continued to look at her in wonder. I'd always heard about panic attacks but didn't know what they would feel like. She linked her arm through mine and talked me down as we walked to the closest bar. Somehow my legs were still moving and keeping up.

I was very aware of my speech pattern but was nervous that no sound would come out. Like, have you ever spent an entire day by yourself? You're chilling at home, watching a *Catfish* marathon, judging these idiots who could fall in love without ever video-chatting. (Meanwhile, you haven't put on pants all day and just ate a block of Gouda like an apple.) Then it happens. Just as you are about to watch Jimbo Jenkins find out his fiancée is actually a French bulldog who's learned to type, you remember that you have to go to a coworker's birthday party in an hour. Fuckity fuckity fuck! You have a brief moment when you think, *Do I still remember how to talk to people? When I open my mouth, will full-fledged thoughts and sentences form?* This is exactly how I felt during the panic attack.

We got to a bar and Maegan ordered me two white wines. I focused on my breathing, which felt like it wasn't coming naturally, as Maegan spoke to me calmly and stroked my back. After I ~~chugged~~ drank my pinot grigios, the weirdness started to lift. I felt normal enough to speak.

"So, that's what a panic attack feels like, huh?"

"Yep. You feel like everything is crazy and you might die. Just a really fun time overall," Maegan said sarcastically.

The next few weeks were stressful. I walked around nervous that at any time I was going to have a panic attack, but without Maegan there to lead me through it. After all, I didn't know what had caused the first one. There hadn't been any obvious trigger that set it off. I wasn't feeling particularly anxious at the time. Would my panicking about having a panic attack send me into a panic attack?!

Later I would try to trace it back and would realize that the first time I had really experienced anxiety was, no lie, because of *Saved by the Bell*.

Be honest with yourself—you fucking loved *Saved by the Bell* as a kid. I, for one, watched it probably every single day from 1992 to 1995, and I wasn't alone. I guarantee most American females ages twenty-eight to thirty-two could sing the *SBTB* theme song from start to finish.

Obviously I had a major lady boner for Zack Morris. He was handsome, suave, a delightful troublemaker, and a good boyfriend. Plus, as cool as he was, he wasn't afraid to be in the glee club or star as the prince in Bayside's production of *Snow White and the Seven Dorks.**

Sure, *SBTB* had its flaws. I was painfully aware of the inconsistent use of Zack's ability to freeze time. I would watch it and just

---

*Even as a nine-year-old, I thought it was embarrassing that the entire production was in rap form. Like, I was a preteen, in the middle of nowhere North Carolina, wearing a shirt of Minnie Mouse and Daisy Duck that read OFFICIAL MEMBER OF THE BOY WATCHERS CLUB and it was STILL too white for me.

be face-palming at why he wasn't using that power constantly. But it was wholesome fun. I didn't want to deal with eating disorders and coke problems like those skanks on *90210*; I wanted to have pep rallies in an oddly small burger joint and throw secret surprise parties in my principal's office because for some reason there wasn't anywhere else to throw them.

What I think I've adequately proven is that my love for *SBTB* was endless. Until one fateful day.

Riding on the success of the sitcom, *Saved by the Bell* decided to come out with a two-hour made-for-TV movie where the gang goes on a Hawaiian vacation. It was called *Saved by the Bell: Hawaiian Style*. (The execs at NBC really took a risk with that edgy name.) In it, Kelly brought her cutest bikinis. Screech, of course, accidentally became some Hawaiian deity, because that's what always happens on trips. But the gang did forget one thing back at Bayside . . . the laugh track.

I remember being nine years old and watching my favorite fake high schoolers, the ones I would rush home from school to watch every day, and feeling extremely uncomfortable. Why wasn't there laughter? And *woo*s when someone kissed? And groans when Screech did anything? My heart started to race. Without the cues from the live studio audience, I didn't know when to laugh. To make matters worse, without the built-in guffaws, Screech seemed mentally handicapped. And judging by the self-made porn tape he released years later, that assessment is apt.

Everything seemed like a lie in my nine-year-old brain. Was *Saved by the Bell* not actually funny? This was worse than learning Santa Claus wasn't real. I had to turn it off, and that's saying a lot. This was a girl who thought *Ernest Scared Stupid* was a goddamn masterpiece.

And that, folks, is the first time I experienced anxiety. Luckily, it didn't turn into a full-on panic attack. I was young and innocent enough to think, *I feel weird. Better do a floor routine on my trampoline and pretend I am Dominique Moceanu during the Atlanta Olym-*

pic Games. My trampoline was basically my home base to get my mind off anything.

Two things you'll notice from this picture. That building behind us is my elementary school. That's how close we lived. On days I didn't have to go to school because of a dentist appointment, etc., I would jump on my trampoline and wave at my classmates. Also, I'm wearing a hat with my name embroidered on it. Clearly I've always been very modest.

Unfortunately for me, there weren't a lot of jumbo trampolines lying around New York City to create a panic attack diversion. And once I had my first one with Maegan, they crept up about once a month. And without warning. It was worse than getting my period. In fact, I called it getting my exclamation point.

Occasionally they would happen on the subway. I'd be sitting there, reading *Us Weekly* and minding my own business, and *boom*! Suddenly, those familiar feelings would start to creep in and I'd start sweating. It was going to happen and it was inevitable and I had to get the fuck off the train. Trust me, when you are freaking out about your breathing, the inside of a New York City subway train isn't the ideal place to be. You already feel like you can't get enough air into your lungs, and then you look down the car to see an old lady coughing, a discarded dozen chicken-wing bones on the floor, and a homeless man taking off his ten pairs of socks across from you. It's game over.

I'd also have them at parties where I was meeting new people. This really threw me off because I am an extremely *un*-shy person. But for whatever reason, during those few years they would creep in.

Oh shit, here they come, I would think. *Ain't no stopping this emotion train. Just hope that it's quick.*

Those anxious feelings would start to cover me like molasses. There would still be full sentences coming out of my mouth, but I had a completely different inner monologue happening in my head, kinda like when you are reading a book and realize that you haven't been processing the words for the past five minutes. There was this disconnect between my brain and mouth.

I learned the proper etiquette in that situation is to excuse yourself to the bathroom (while grabbing a cup of vodka on the way), splash some water on your face, and sip said vodka until you feel confident enough to Irish-good-bye the shit out of that party. And for the love of God, take a cab home. Never go back underground with those residual feelings of panic. As soon as you get through the turnstile, the underground music from *Super Mario Bros.* will start playing in your head and you'll imagine all the rats at the station banding together to form one large Transformers-style super rat.

But more so than in social situations or on the subway, the worst panic attacks would happen before I had to perform live. Good thing I decided to become a comedian! Until the past year, every show—and I do mean every show—I would be beyond nervous to go onstage. As soon as I was actually onstage and heard the first laugh, all the nerves would settle. But until that moment, the anxiety was through the roof. And nothing made me more anxious than when I hosted my show *Celebrity Funeral* at the Upright Citizens Brigade Theatre.

I started performing shows at UCB back in 2009. If you haven't heard of this theater, I'm sure you've heard of the many, many successful folks who've come out of it. Amy Poehler was one of the founders, for God's sake. This fact had me occasionally licking random spots in the dirty theater, hoping to ingest some of her leftover DNA. The space itself was a basement theater underneath a grocery store and a McDonald's. Was it glamorous? Nope. Was getting to perform on that stage for four years magical? Abso-fuckin'-lutely.

After doing a few duo and group sketch show runs, I decided that I wanted to host and produce my own show. And from that came *Celebrity Funeral*. Every few months I would host a mock funeral for a celeb who was still alive. Other comedians would perform eulogies as surviving family members, costars, and totally made-up acquaintances as I served as master of ceremonies. For example, some eulogies at the Mariah Carey funeral were:

1. My girl Alison Bennett being wheeled out as a postal worker who'd had her arms and legs chewed off by dogs because she was playing the song "Emotions" and the high note made them go insane.
2. The ridiculous Hannibal Buress playing P. Diddy. Diddy used his eulogy to set the record about his and Mariah's hit single "Honey." Mariah was supposedly super into entomology, and the song was actually written to warn folks about the impending bee crisis.
3. My friend Eliot Glazer closed out each show by reciting a poem as Maya Angelou. This would always derail into sexy territory. If you've ever had doubts about a Jewish gay man pulling off a spot-on impression of a late African American poet laureate, you have not met Eliot.

It was essentially an old-school roast, and I loved it. But no matter how exhilarated I felt onstage, no matter how proud and satisfied I was after a sold-out show full of laughs, I would be nervous as fuck the next time we performed. I'd go through the same song and dance: I'd talk to folks backstage while having a totally different, freaked-out conversation in my head. I wasn't able to feel my legs. I'd have to focus on my breathing because it felt like my body wasn't going to do it itself. But a new, fun addition came along with the stage fear. And that, ladies and gentlemen, was taking nervous shits.

Don't judge me. What I was experiencing is known as fight-or-flight. In fight-or-flight, your body thinks it's in such extreme danger that you are about to die. It rushes a bunch of adrenaline into your bloodstream in case you need to fight or get the hell out of the situation. Your palms are sweaty. Knees weak, arms are heavy. There's vomit on your sweater already, mom's spaghetti. Wait a sec! My mom doesn't make spaghetti. Sorry, guys, sometimes I lose myself in Eminem lyrics. But that is how I'd feel, minus the pasta puke.

It's this fight-or-flight adrenaline dump that makes mothers lift cars off their babies and helps people outrun bear attacks. For me, it was a lot more literal. It was an adrenaline *dump*.

Every time before I went onstage for those few years—every single time—I would give myself a little pep talk in the mirror (more specifically, my powder compact as I sat on the toilet). It would go something like this:

"Mamrie. First of all, you look great. Honestly, that lack of exercise and late-night Kettle chips eating is really paying off. Also, you are gonna be amazing in this show! Quit freaking yourself out. As soon as you hear your first laugh, all these crazy feelings will melt away. And hey, worst-case scenario, you shit onstage. Right there in front of everyone, you shit your pants and it splatters on the floor underneath your dress like an unexpected prom birth. If that happens, you'll move back to North Carolina. No problem. Change your name. Everyone probably thinks Mamrie is a stage name anyway. You can take a couple of years of courses at the community college to become a dental hygienist. Marry a man who is intellectually beneath you but loves you to death and makes decent Crock-

Pot meals. Not your ideal life, but you'll still be mildly unhappy. Now, get out there and make 'em laugh."

Okay, so I'm no Tony Robbins, but there *was* something comforting about giving myself the worst-case scenario options. Every show, I would have to take over the bathroom, and every time I'd get the pep talk. It got to the point where no matter what time I was on, even up to my live shows today, the people around me knew that I was gonna need a solid ten minutes in the bathroom by myself.

Here's my advice to anyone who experiences panic attacks. Be vocal about it. I'm not saying stand up in the middle of class and pull a Kanye. ("Mr. Ginsberg? Imma let you finish but I just want you all to know I'm having a panic attack. I can't feel my legs, and learning about WWI is not a good look for me right now.") But I am saying be open about it with your friends, your family, even your coworkers. My friends no longer bat an eye when I have a panic attack. Some have even turned it into a drinking game. If I start to feel the wave of anxiety coming toward me, whether we are grabbing a martini or doing an interview, I will just casually say, "Heads-up. I'm experiencing a panic attack so I might get quiet for a while, so just take the lead on talking."

It isn't something to be embarrassed about. In fact, more than likely you already have a friend who experiences the same thing. They might just not have a name for it yet. They could've been calling it "kooky floating maniac time."

For example, there was one night when I was still bartending at a seafood place on Park Avenue, before I booked my first commercial and hightailed it the fuck out of there. This was when I still reeked of steamed crab legs and would fill a coffee cup full of Baileys and vodka as soon as I got to work and pretend it was a latte. For five years, I bartended at this restaurant.

Word to the wise: Never work at a restaurant where you can't eat the food. The other waitstaff would drool over tasting the daily specials, picking each other off like they were basketball centers to get an extra bit of the shrimp cocktail or lobster mac and cheese. I stood behind that bar selling people on how sweet the Kumamoto oysters were and how well they paired with champagne. Meanwhile, I would dry-heave at the thought of eating those barnacle-looking loogies.

I remember one shift when a new waitress on the floor looked like she was having a major struggle. I watched her almost drop plates of empty lobster carcasses all over a table she was clearing and then walk into the bathroom on the verge of tears. When she came back out, I decided to get the scoop, expecting to hear she had lied in her interview and this was the first time she'd waited tables, or that a table just screamed at her for a two-dollar surcharge for mixed greens as a side.

"Mary, is everything okay? You look upset."

"I'll be fine, don't worry about it."

"Is it because they've started making us wear these ties with crabs on them and ninety percent of the male customers make an STD joke about it?"

She went silent for a second. Maybe I had cracked the case, and not just the case of Modelo I was pounding behind the bar to deal with the incessant onslaught of crab jokes.

"I don't know. Everything feels weird and off. Seriously, there's no way I can balance three martinis. I'm gonna drop the tray," she said, clenching and unclenching her hands like they were cold.

Bingo! Panic attack. I could finally pay it forward for that first panic attack that Maegan so calmly walked me through years before.

"Okay, have you ever had a panic attack before?" I asked as she shook her head no, tears welling up in her eyes. "Well, I think you're having one now. Here's what you need to do. I'm gonna pour you a glass of tequila. You're gonna go into the private room, sit, sip, breathe, and it will all feel okay in twenty minutes. I'll drop off these martinis and finish up your last table, okay?"

She nodded, clearly taken aback by how quickly I'd whipped up a plan. Poor thing had probably been hiding her first panic attack for the past half hour. I couldn't even wait tables hungover, let alone with mounds of adrenaline coursing through my body. And there she had been shakily tying lobster bibs on customers and balancing trays of twenty coffees all at once.

When I finished up her table and the restaurant was officially closed for the night, I went and checked on her. She was relaxed and a little tipsy. But she wasn't alone. Three other servers were around her, telling her how they got panic attacks and sharing their stories.

Here's the deal, dudes: No matter how bad you are panicking, it's going to eventually subside. It's scary as hell! But it will pass. Take this analogy, for example:

In the summer of 2014, I got to shoot a travel series called *Hey USA!* with my partner in crime, Grace Helbig. It was seriously a dream job. How many people get to travel around the US all summer, having their days filled with adventures that they don't have to plan? I'm not going to lie and say that waking up at five a.m. to whale-watch, meet Iditarod dogs, and learn to trout-fish all before four p.m. and all while having to be "on" in front of the camera isn't exhausting! But it's a very rewarding type of exhaustion.

This is from the first episode. NBD—just having a snowball fight on an Alaskan glacier. Sometimes I pinch myself at how cool my job is. Also, because I'm super pinchable.

Now that I have made sure I don't look like an inconsiderate asshole, here we go. Grace and I were on day three of our stop in Portland, Oregon. Unlike other shooting days, when we packed four or five activities into one day, this entire day was going to be spent white-water rafting. I was pumped.* I love doing stuff on the river, especially floating on a tube with an inflatable cooler of cheap beer beside me. However, I learned real quick that this wasn't going to be rafting with a coozie. These were straight-up *rapids*. Thirty seconds on the river and we were going down a class IV (out of six) rapids. I almost fell out, and our cameraman cracked his helmet against a boulder. But that wasn't the craziest part.

We were shown a small waterfall before we got on the river, to assess whether or not we were comfortable going down it. The guide told us about half the people decide to go down it, and the other half chicken out. As soon as I saw the falls, I thought to myself, *Somebody grab the Shake 'n Bake, 'cause it looks like we're having chicken today.* But I couldn't do that! There was a film crew with us! There are two things I never want to do on camera.

1.   Show da pussy.
2.   Be a pussy.

Plus, Grace was gung-ho to go down them. "We'll regret it if we don't do it," she said as we were stationed on the bank about a hundred yards from the falls.

"You're right. I'm in."

As soon as I agreed, I immediately regretted it. I think it goes without saying that I started panicking. How was I going to paddle hard enough for us to go over the falls if my arms felt like two Sour Punch Straws? Everyone else on our crew had already gotten out;

---

*Mainly because we were in the continental US and my digestive system wasn't demonstrating a sit-in.

they weren't going over them.* It was just going to be Grace, me, and the guide. He started feverishly repumping the raft. I started feverishly asking questions. "What's the ratio of rafts that flip? Has anyone died going over the falls? How long are you in the air? I've bungee jumped, is it scarier than that?" After the thirtieth or so question, he cut me off.

"Look, the only thing you really need to worry about if we flip is getting sucked back into the falls. That's why we have to paddle super hard and get some air going over them."

"What happens if you get sucked in?"

"If you get sucked into the falls, you are stuck. The pressure of the water will hold you down, but it's going to release you after fifteen seconds if you don't fight it." Fifteen seconds of being stuck underwater sounded like an eternity. "Just remember, it *will* release you. You just have to stay calm. What I like to do is sing the Indiana Jones theme song when I'm stuck. It keeps me more calm than counting." And he kept pumping up the raft. I looked at Grace in complete shock.

"One last question," I added. "How many times have you been sucked under?"

"About three," he replied nonchalantly.

"Okay, three times. You said you've worked here for three years. Those odds aren't that bad—"

"No, no. Three times this month."

I turned to Grace, who now looked like a ghost in pigtails.

"Grace? You really want to?" I asked her, hoping the desperation in my voice would assure her she could drop the act and we'd get the fuck off the river and go drink in our hotel bar.

"Yeah, let's do it," she replied like it was no big deal, but I knew it was, because when Grace is uncomfortable her eyes bug out and

---

*I later learned that the guide in the other raft let them know that going over the falls feels like being in a car crash and lots of people knock out their teeth. FUN!

her mouth turns into Grumpy Cat's. But thank goodness she was putting on her tough-girl act, or else I would've been a mess.

"Okay," I said, slowly turning back to the front of the raft while white-knuckling my paddle. We had said we'd do it (on-camera, no less!) and we were going to see it out. There was no pep talk. No emotional halftime speech. We nodded at each other like two kamikaze pilots agreeing to their fate. When all was said and done, no one got sucked into the falls. Grace and I paddled like we were trying to qualify for the Olympic rowing team, and our raft sailed over those falls with ease. But I took our guide's advice to heart.

The waterfall, while scary, would've released us. The panic attack will also release you. Just relax, and don't feel weird about being vocal about your feelings. Also, no one has ever died from a panic attack. Just breathe. And if possible, drink the nearest thing to you.

And one more word of advice: If you ever hear me singing the Indiana Jones theme song onstage, pull a tarp over yourself Gallagher-style, or slowly back away. Things could get real.

Spears-Mint Mojito

1 lime
10 mint leaves
½ oz elderflower liqueur
2 oz white rum
Club soda
1 oz Bacardi 151

This is like a classic mojito but with a couple of added bonuses to Vegas-ize it. Before you do anything, cut your lime in half horizontally. If the lime is the Earth, cut through the equator. If you do not understand that reference, then you shouldn't be drinking anyway. Put down the bottle and pick up the books!

Start out by muddling your mint leaves with your elderflower liqueur in a shaker and squeezing in the lime juice. Add the white rum and lots of ice. Give the shaker the action from which it gets its name and pour into a tall glass. Top with club soda.

Then, take a spoon or your fingernails (depending on your personal level of hygiene) to one of those lime halves that have been squeezed, and scrape out all the pulp and white rind. You'll be left with a tiny green bowl. Put that 1 ounce of 151 inside and lovingly place it on top of your mojito. Carefully set that shit on fire, and voilà! Drinks and a show! You can use a straw to dunk the fiery rum whenever you feel like it. Eventually it will all burn off, but the sooner you submerge it, the stronger your drink will be. By the time you finish two of these bad boys, you'll be wearing those lime cups as nipple hats.

When I heard that Britney Spears was going to be doing a residency at Planet Hollywood in Vegas, the first thing I thought was, *Who the hell is watching Jayden and Sean?* My second thought was, *I have got to see this.* I had just moved to L.A. six months earlier and hadn't yet made the pilgrimage to the City of Sin. I didn't care that Britney would dance like a marionette version of her former self. I didn't care that I would be paying major dollars to watch someone lip-sync their greatest hits or that her abs would require more paint than a *House Hunters* fixer-upper. Goddammit, I was going to get to that show dead or alive. Fortunately, I did end up getting to the show, and I was alive . . . but just barely.

First, let me take you back a few years.

Britney came into my life back in 1998, when I was a freshman in high school. ". . . Baby One More Time" hit MTV, and everyone was enamored by this cute girl with her little Catholic schoolgirl uniform and Muppet voice. She was the girl all the girls wanted to be and all the boys wanted to jerk off to. I couldn't believe that she was only two years older than me. If you had done a split screen of the two of us, I would've looked like a prepubescent troll next to that bare-midriff vixen.

Britney was pretty much the soundtrack to my teens and early twenties. Obviously I listened to cooler music than Britney (no offense, Britney Jean, if you're reading my book. And if you are, hey, girl! Did you get the picture I sent of me dressed as you for Halloween in '01 and '08?), but I still had a soft spot for her. I might've just left a Modest Mouse show, but the second I got back in my car, I'd be cranking up that former Mouseketeer, blaring "Toxic" the whole way home. Complete with dance moves from the video, which is always fun for whoever pulls up beside me at a stoplight.

If you have any doubts about the level I commit to Brit, you can use my freshman year spring break in Panama City as a prime example. While everyone else was bonging beers on the beach, I went to see *Crossroads*. Not that bad, you say? I went by myself. And I was the only person in that theater. If you don't know the cinematic masterpiece that I am referring to, allow me to brief you.

Crossroads is your run-of-the-mill post–high school road trip movie in which a pop star tries in vain to be an actress for two hours. Just kidding. It's about three former best friends, along with the possibly dangerous guy driving them, going on a cross-country trek together for their own personal reasons. It stars Zoe Saldana, a.k.a. the chick from *Avatar*; Taryn Manning, a.k.a. the crazy Christian redneck from *Orange Is the New Black*; and in her feature-film debut, Britney Spears. The movie itself is god-awful. Like, for a road trip movie, this is a car crash. . . . Shit—that was pretty good. Maybe I should ditch this whole book-writing thing and become a snarky movie reviewer.

I knew it would be bad before I went, but in an innocent, cheesy way. I needed a break from the type of bad that was happening outside that Regal Cinema's doors. On the way to the theater, I walked by a girl giving a blow job to a fire hydrant. Obviously I was going to dive headfirst back into the spring break grossness as soon as I left the theater (I had tickets to see Master P that night), but for that ninety minutes, I could feel pure again. By the end credits I was belting out "I'm Not a Girl, Not Yet a Woman" right along with Brit Brit.

Clearly, I've loved the Spears for years. Luckily, I had two friends who were just as amped at the idea of seeing her Vegas show as I was. Enter Grace and Joselyn. I was going to hit the road with my two dear friends for an adventure. Which sounds oddly similar to a little film I mentioned before. Yep, this was our *Crossroads*. If you are familiar with the movie, Grace was obviously the Britney character in this trio. Sweet and kind, but tough when she needs to be. Joselyn was Zoe Saldana (yes, I *am* going to refer to them by their real names and not their roles; get over it): tough, has her shit together. And by process of elimination, I will assume the role of Taryn Manning. Would I rather be Britney? Of course. Taryn's character is brash, speaks her mind, and . . . It's official, I'm the Taryn.*

For those who are terrible with geography or have never seen *Swingers*, Vegas is only a four-hour drive from L.A. That's it—four measly hours! I have sat on a broken-down stinky subway car from Brooklyn to Manhattan longer than that! The plan was for Joselyn and Grace to meet me at my place at noon on a Saturday, we'd take a few Bloody Marys to the face, then the three of us would hit the road. But we weren't going to drive ourselves. No, no. We were taking a car service.

I know what you're thinking. *Oh la la, Mamrie! A car service? Did it come complete with a top hat and fox trained as a butler?*

Settle down. There was a car service at the time that was giving "social influencers" (*God*, I hate that phrase) credits toward rides if you mentioned them on Twitter or Instagram, so we weren't paying completely out of pocket. Also, they had a deal going for a Vegas trip. In it, a driver would pick up you and your friends and drive you to Vegas, where you'd get a complimentary one-night stay at the Cosmopolitan and then get driven back the next day. This was an ideal setup because there are few things I hate more than driving when I am super hungover. I always have terrifying out-of-body experiences where I can't believe I am operating a several-ton vehicle, and it distracts me from, you know, being a good driver. And Lord knows we were going to be violently hungover, because we were seeing Britney, bitch!

As planned, Grace and Joselyn met me at my place for some Bloody Marys first. Because, let's face it, we were about to drink our faces off in Vegas, and you can't drink on an empty stomach.

---

*Remember when choosing which *Sex and the City* character you were was a thing? The girl in every group would be bummed when she had to be the Miranda. Miranda was the shit! A lawyer, hilarious, hot husband, tiny red-headed babe. Fuck being Carrie and her emotionally unstable, cheating ways. Still love ya, SJP!

You can, however, drink a Bloody Mary and stick a bunch of pickled veggies in there and kill two birds with one stone. So, we were drinking our Bloodys, chatting about the night ahead in my living room. Grace called the car, and it was officially on its way.

"I can't believe we are taking a car to Las Vegas. Who are we?" Grace chimed in.

"Assholes," Joselyn answered without skipping a beat.

I didn't care if we were assholes for splurging on such a luxury. I had come a long way since my first ride in New York City, when I sat on a stranger's pizza crust. I could already picture rolling into Vegas in a sleek black car, everything going in slow motion as all eyes panned from my foot stepping out of the car on up to my face to see who I was. Obviously there would be lots of fans held by bellhops to give my hair just the right amount of breeze. Right before I could get to the paparazzi portion of my fantasy, I was snapped out of it by a car horn.

"It's here! Let's move it, ladies!"

We gathered our bags and feasted our eyes on our car and driver. The moment can only be described as the physical form of that losing noise from *The Price Is Right*.

Enter . . . Gabriel.

Gabriel was sent by Company-That-Rhymes-with-Boober to pick us up. When he pulled up, we noticed that this town car was a little more beat-up than normal. The inside wasn't much better: There were rips in the leather, and it smelled like there was a moldy towel in the front seat. It wasn't the ideal road trip car, with the ceiling material sinking down like a weird belly above our heads, but we would make do.

Gabriel, bless his heart, matched his car in terms of dishevelment. He looked like he'd been sleeping in his clothes, and his pants had dust on them like when you eat a powdered doughnut and then accidentally wipe your hands on your pants. His hair was doing an early *Friends* Joey Tribbiani thing, but unlike that womanizer, Gabriel wasn't really pulling it off. It was gelled back so intensely that he could have legally driven a motorcycle in California with his 'do serving as a helmet.

He awkwardly tried to open the door for us but got out of the car a little too late, so we did it ourselves as he stood and watched us get in. Once we were all inside and Gabriel was in the driver's seat, he turned and asked, "So! Where are you girls going?" We were a little surprised that his boss hadn't given him a heads-up that he was about to embark on a four-hour drive, but we cheerfully replied that we were going to the Cosmopolitan.

He started to type "Cosmopolitan" into his GPS. "Is that downtown?"

Joselyn gave Grace and me a look. Just like Saldana, she was a little apprehensive of the situation. "Umm, it's in Vegas?"

Gabriel's eyes lit up in the rearview mirror. "Vegas? Holy shit! I told my friend that I didn't think I was ever going to get one of the Vegas deals. This is *awesome*!" We soon found out from good ol' Gabe that drivers really wanted to be called to drive on Vegas deals. They got paid a superhigh rate and also got put up for the night. It was like a last-minute bender surprise.

"I can't believe it! Vegas, baby! Vegas!" Gabriel continued. That was the first time I'd ever hear "Vegas, baby" said unironically. But not the last, as Gabriel repeatedly said it for the next four hours.

We were excited that he was excited. Sometimes you can get a car-service driver, or cab driver, who is *pissed* when you tell him how far you are going. It would've been terrible if Gabriel had been dreading the Vegas call and we were stuck in the backseat while he sulked for four hours, but he couldn't have been happier. Gabriel had almost a childlike excitement about him. He didn't seem like the sharpest tool in the shed, but he definitely wasn't dull. This guy was a *character*.

"Do you care if I call my girlfriend and let her know? This was supposed to be my last ride of the night."

"Of course not! Do your thing. *Vegas!*" Although I *was* a little surprised that he had a girlfriend. I pictured her as an older woman, someone his mother wouldn't approve of her "baby boy" being with. Yep, I was definitely getting a *Moonstruck* vibe, and I couldn't snap out of it.

Gabriel pulled out his iPhone and began making calls. I couldn't help but notice that his screen was completely shattered glass. When I say it was shattered, I mean it was one drop away from being glitter.

I'm not trying to say this in a judgy way, but more from a place of understanding. One time I was in such a rush to an audition that I left my phone on top of my car as I threw on a semiclean shirt I had in my trunk. After several miles, I realized what I had done, so I drove back to my parking spot and searched frantically for it. No luck. It was a goner. I headed to my audition, but unfortunately for me, the role wasn't for a supergrumpy bitch, so I didn't nail it. As I sat in the turn lane on Melrose about a mile from where I had lost my phone, I looked down at the five-lane road and saw a glimpse of leopard print. My phone case! I jumped out of my car like my baby was in the middle of the road and on fire, and grabbed my now-demolished iPhone. Hell, if it was a damaged phone it could be replaced for two hundred dollars, but a lost phone would cost me five hundred to replace. You'd better believe I mailed that Ziploc bag of glass to AT&T and got my discount! I felt like the luckiest unlucky girl in the world!

I didn't dwell on Gabriel's phone long, though, because soon I was too overcome with terror. He couldn't drive worth a shit, and it was terrifying. Maybe it was the adrenaline of *"Vegas, baby!"* Maybe it was the difficulty of looking through his contacts on shards of glass while also swerving between tractor trailers. But Gabriel was cruisin' at ninety-five miles per hour, driving about as well as I play *Mario Kart*, and I'm fucking *terrrrible* at *Mario Kart*. The Crossroads 2.0 cast was complete with a driver we thought might kill us.

We weren't five miles from home and my anxiety was through the roof. I wanted to scream but decided to approach the situation with the calmest and kindest version of my voice. The one you put on when you meant to order your enchiladas without sour cream but then they come out with sour cream and you know it's your fault but still want them to fix it. That voice.

"Gabriel, honey. I'm going to need you to drive safer. I seriously have car anxiety and you're *kiiiinda* driving like a maniac. I want to arrive alive." And he did drive safer. For about three minutes. I tried to block out almost crashing into the back of a Smart car (which would've *certainly* killed the people in it) with happy thoughts of blackjack and backup dancers. Every ten minutes or so I would try to sweetly crack a joke to get him to pump the brakes.

"Hey, Gabe! Could you speed up a little? We haven't gone into the future yet!"

"Gabriel, did you have to join the union to stunt-drive for *The Fast and the Furious: Tokyo Drift* or just sign a waiver?"

"Gabriel, knock knock? Who's there? *Slow the fuck down!*"

He'd apologize and slow down, then, sure enough, he'd accelerate right back up.

Luckily, I had filled a twenty-four-ounce travel mug with champagne and was sucking that thing down like a malnourished newborn. The three of us were glued to our phones. When we weren't texting our loved ones good-bye before our imminent fiery crash, we were texting each other.

```
I can't believe I'm going to die
without having seen Britney live.

I can't believe I'm about to die with
a 24 oz can of Corona between my legs.

I can't believe I'm going to die
before winning a Webby!

I think Grace just farted.
```

We spoke only through these secret communications, like Dayanara and Officer Bennett leaving notes for each other in the first season of *Orange Is the New Black*. This texting wouldn't have been so awkward if the car wasn't completely silent. While we'd had visions of jamming to the entire Britney anthology all the way to Sin City, we had no such luck. Gabriel's auxiliary input was broken, and radio was the best he had. But there's not a lot of radio in the middle of nowhere. So we rode in total silence, except for the clacking on our phones, big swigs of beer, and the occasional *"Aw fuck!"* of Gabriel's almost running off the road.

About two hours into our drive, we asked Gabriel to pull off at the next exit so we could pee. We were in the straight-up desert at this point, but we eventually pulled into a mega gas station surrounded by nothing.

I love big gas stations like this. The South is filled with them, and whenever I was on a road trip as a kid, I asked to stop and check out the selection of tchotchkes. In North Carolina this meant How to Speak Redneck books, Native American figurines, and confederate flag bottle openers. For the weird stretch of desert between L.A. and Nevada, this meant slim pickins. I tried on a few trucker hats but decided I didn't need to put WHAT HAPPENS IN VEGAS STAYS IN MY BLOODSTREAM on my forehead.

"Mame! Check it out," Grace said while holding a teeny gun above her head. It looked like the world's cutest stickup. "It's a tiny Taser gun." God bless Grace. She knows a miniature can always brighten even my worst moods.

"Be careful," the clerk said from behind the register, "that thing hurts like a motherfucker."

Must've been his desert accent, but I heard that as, "Try it with reckless abandon!" Needless to say it shocked the living hell out of me. No, really—the actual living hell that I was in. Because for a brief second, I wasn't focused on imminent death in Gabriel's car. It's all about distraction. Like when you pinch your leg while getting a flu shot. I had to buy that baby Taser.

We finished buying our bags of chips, adorable Taser, and tall boys of Corona (NECESSARY), then headed back to the car. Once we got there, Gabriel was nowhere to be found—but the car was completely unlocked. Completely unlocked as all of our laptops lay in full view. For three girls whose careers are the Internet, this could've been real bad if someone had stolen them. Gabriel got lucky, but I still felt like I had to say something to him, make him understand that this shit was not okay.

He looked dumbfounded. "It's a safe area," he assured us as a gang of motorcycles pulled in and a buzzard circled over our heads.

"It doesn't matter, dude. Our stuff is in here. You have to lock the door when—" Before I could finish, Gabriel was sprinting back toward the gas station.

"I think I left the keys in the bathroom!" he yelled over his shoulder.

I looked at Grace and Joselyn in disbelief. It was official: This man was an idiot. I felt like we were on *Punk'd*. And not even the classic *Punk'd* with Ashton Kutcher, but the bad remake version hosted by Kellan Lutz. All we could do was pray to get to Vegas safely and take a bunch of beers to the face to numb the anxiety. Defeated, we got back in the jalopy, and after screaming at Gabriel to not enter the highway on the off-ramp, we were back on the road.

Sixty miles outside Vegas, we were miraculously still alive, but we encountered another situation. A text on my phone came through from Joselyn: "Has anyone else noticed that we have zero gas?" Sure enough, I looked and saw the gas meter hovering just above the "we're fucked" line. At that point I had more gas in my system from all the Bugles I'd housed.

"Hey, Gabriel, you might want to stop for gas."

"We're only sixty miles away, though."

You could practically hear our eyes collectively roll into the backs of our heads. Did this motherfucker think that you could drive for sixty miles with the gas light on? Driving was literally his job. I took a deep breath and tried to speak calmly without being condescending.

"Gabriel. You need to get gas. I want to see Britney Spears tonight, not be stuck on the side of the road with coyotes."

He pulled off at the next station and we watched from the backseat as he struggled to pump the gas. He looked like a virgin on prom night. I kid you not, he went into and out of the gas station three times trying to figure out how to prepay, and he stared blankly, as if he had never pumped gas before in his life. I could've offered to help him, but I needed to stay put and focus on my breathing because I was *this close* to spraying gas all over him and lighting a match. I would've straight-up *Zoolander*ed that Chevron.

After his third trip to the cashier, he finally got it pumping. *At least we aren't going to be stranded roadside!* I thought, the small things in life seeming so meaningful. He got in the car, then looked dumbfounded.

"Shit! I think I left the keys in the bathroom."

"Dare I say, oops, you did it again?" Joselyn said as Gabriel slammed the door, completely ignorant of her fabulous joke.

Gabriel eventually realized he'd just left the keys on the roof of the car (I slipped Grace a five-dollar bill because she'd called that one) and got back in the front seat. There are few things as satisfying as watching the gauge on the gas meter rise all the way back to the top, particularly in situations of distress. Gabriel cranked the engine, and we collectively gave a sigh of relief watching the meter climb, but after two seconds, it stopped. It wasn't even at a quarter tank. I looked at the gas pump to see that Gabriel had put a whopping *ten dollars* in the tank. *Ten!* Mind you, this was the same car that was supposed to be taking us back to Los Angeles the next day. Why wouldn't he just fill up the tank?

I couldn't bite my tongue. I had to speak up about this last hour we were going to be on the road. Joselyn wasn't even going to Britney with us. She had a stand-up show in a few hours and we needed to get there. Gabriel was about to get a piece of me.

"Okay, Gabriel. Before we pull out, there are some rules for this last hour." Gabriel nodded, listening intently. "First, you are *not* to go over eighty miles per hour. Next, you are *not* allowed to text and e-mail from your phone. We need to get to Vegas alive and you need to drive safely. This shit is not okay."

He began to rationalize his driving, but we weren't having it. Joselyn cut him off, but not before he got out one excuse: "I've been driving since eight o'clock last night, so I'm a little tired."

What. The. Actual. Fuck.

He had been driving since eight p.m. the previous day? By my approximation, when we got in his car and told him Vegas, he had already been driving for sixteen hours.

We all squeezed each other's hands in the backseat. It was like there was an unspoken agreement among us to just make it to our hotel and not bother voicing our unhappiness.

As we finally pulled into the Cosmopolitan, he had to get in his last words. "I know we had some bumps in the road"—to which I burst out laughing and Grace, being the nice one, kicked my ankle to shut me up—"but I really need you to rate me five stars. If not, it could be bad for my job." I was about to point out how killing three women after driving warp 7 would also have been bad for his job, but before I could, Grace kindly told him not to worry about it, and we got out. I was tempted to drop to my knees and kiss the ground like an astronaut returning from a tough mission.

We checked in to our rooms and immediately ordered room service cocktails. Normally, on a night when I knew I would be drinking for hours and hours, I would just drink beer. But not after that ride. I needed something stronger. Lemon Drop martini it was.

That night in Vegas was a blur, but allow me to recount the evening's events for you. I don't want you to feel like you missed out, but I also don't want this chapter to be as long as *War and Peace*, so here's the recap of debauchery:

1. We saw Britney and it was so much fun. She kind of danced like she was being *Weekend at Bernie*'d and didn't sing a single note the entire show, and we loved it. We knew we weren't going to see Celine. This was Britney. And bless her heart.

2. We found out our British YouTube friends from the Sorted Food channel were also in Vegas that night from London. We met up with them after the show, and I drank eight hundred Lemon Drops. Even though it was a girls' night, what can I say? Boys. Sometimes a girl just needs one.

3. One of their handsome British dads was there. I flirted with said dad and warned Barry that I was his new mama. I may or may not have made him call me Mama all night, but that's a pretty standard Drunk Mamrie move regardless.

4. All of us decided it was a good idea to go get our dance on at the club Marquee. I was wearing a Snoop Dogg sweatshirt and leggings, which was shockingly not up to the dress code, so Jamie, being the chivalrous British chap he is, gave me his blazer to wear over them. I was the most clothed woman in Vegas, looking like the office manager at Death Row Records. That's My Prerogative.

5. We danced. A lot. The kind of drunk dancing where you're not even doing real moves. I think I just marched for a good two hours, and I may or may not have told a girl wearing a Tupac dress that she didn't know shit about hip-hop.

6. Grace and I left Marquee at four a.m. and *neeeeded* to play blackjack.

7. I stopped in at a gift shop to grab an electronic hookah and told the security guard that he was a "tall drink of water." At least that's what Grace says I said.

8. We sat at electronic blackjack for an hour, talking about

how we couldn't wait to get back to the room and eat our room service leftovers, like we were chained to the machine or something. We were in the zone. Grace won a hundred bucks and I ordered a White Russian because I forgot I was a vegan for a minute.

9. Back in the room we stuffed our faces, then moved the room service table outside someone else's room so we didn't look like pigs.

10. The next day, Joselyn told us that she'd gotten so black-out drunk after her show that she'd accidentally shattered an entire bottle of Ketel One and gotten kicked out of the club. As she was telling us about her misadventures, she reached behind the microwave and found a cup of sweet potato fries. Apparently, I had hidden them in my wastoid state because I wanted them all to myself. I'm guessing my game plan had been to wait for Grace to fall asleep so I could eat them, but I didn't follow through.

Early mornin' comes way too soon when you go to sleep at five a.m. It felt like there was a pissed-off gorilla in my brain rattling my skull like a cage. Which means we had done our eighteen hours in Vegas perfectly. Lucky for us, our Sorted Food friends were headed back to L.A. that afternoon as well and could give us a ride. I can't tell you how much of a relief this was for me. The only thing left to do was tell Gabriel. So, like the mature and rational adults we were, we broke up with him via text message. Nothing mean. Nothing shitty. Grace simply texted him, "We found another ride back to L.A. Thank you!"

The trip back to L.A. was downright lovely. Handsome boys with British accents cracking jokes as I shoveled potato chips into my mouth? Heaven. Poor Joselyn didn't speak the whole time, she was so busy fighting off hangover nausea. The only thing she could do was take deep breaths and stare at the horizon.

It's no shocker that we made it back to Los Angeles safely and faster than we had gotten there. We pulled off my exit and just as we came to a stop at the first light, Joselyn bolted out of the car and ran to the entrance of Griffith Park. That poor thing had held off for the entire ride and now she was puking her guts out less than a mile from home.

Eventually we got a text back from Gabriel. It was borderline awful, and he said that Grace was a bad person. But we had zero regrets. We had successfully had our own *Crossroads* adventure!*

---

*At least that's what I thought until I Wikipedia'd the *Crossroads* plot to write this chapter. *You guys!* For being a sappy, cheesy movie that I cried to when I was eighteen, it sure has a lot of rape, abuse, and tragic pregnancies in it. In fact, *Crossroads* made our trip look like a kids' movie. . . . And I am totally okay with that.

Nightcap

1 oz lavender-and-honey simple syrup
2 oz chamomile-infused vodka
Juice of ½ lemon

For the simple syrup, all you have to do is combine 1 cup of water, 1 cup of honey, and ½ cup of lavender buds into a saucepan on medium heat. Let it simmer for about 5 minutes, then remove from heat and strain out the lavender.

For the vodka, throw in 2 chamomile tea bags for every 12 ounces of vodka you want to infuse. So if it's a regular-size mason jar, throw in 2 regular-size tea bags. Let it sit for an hour.

Combine all the ingredients and take that shit to the face, be it over ice, shaken and strained, or warmed up in a mug. You do you, girl/guy/dog that likes booze.

Since I was a little girl, I have always had problems sleeping. On television, you always see kids get tucked in and immediately fall asleep. Does that happen in real life or is this strictly a Stephanie Tanner scenario? 'Cause when my mom tucked me in and turned the light off on her way out, I was awake all night, *convinced* that Bigfoot was about to crawl through my window. (Side note: My mom let me watch *Unsolved Mysteries*, so I spent the majority of my childhood terrified of every noise in the night and also wanting to be a re-creation actor when I grew up.) I distinctly remember being a fifth-grader and lying in bed at three a.m. thinking, *I am the only kid awake in the world.* The insomnia feeds the anxiety, the anxiety feeds the insomnia, and my night would become a human centipede of sleeplessness.

One side effect is sometimes I would be extremely hungover at school after a long night of staring at the glow-in-the-dark Troll stickers on my ceiling, wishing I could sleep.

No amount of shoelace barrette or sweetheart neckline gonna cover up the fact that this fifth-grader was running on four hours of sleep.

But it wasn't all bad—like when it came to slumber parties! There are a few precious years growing up wherein birthdays are either at the roller skating rink* or are slumber parties (or Discovery Zone if you're a badass bitch). When it came to slumber par-

---

*I *lived* at the skating rink most Fridays of my childhood. It was owned and DJed by Ernest (who was at least eighty), and I would always request tons of 2 Live Crew, not knowing it was dirty. Picture nine-year-old Mamrie on skates: "Ernest! Can you please play 'Me So Horny'?" "No." "What about 'Pop That Pussy'?" "Again, Mamrie?"

ties, I was in my element. I already had the prank calling in the bag. "Ummmm, can I speak to Seymore Butts?" Incredible. One time I called a random number and didn't ask for anyone. I just pretended I knew the woman who answered and hoped I sounded like one of her friends or that she would be too polite to ask who I was. We talked for fifteen minutes.

And forget about the sleeping shenanigans! I was *always* the last kid up. At the beginning of every slumber party, everyone is warned that the first person to fall asleep is gonna have a prank pulled on her. First one to go to sleep gets shaving cream in her hand and then we'll tickle her nose. First one to go to sleep is getting her hand put in warm water so she pisses the bed. First one to go to sleep gets her bra put in the freezer. Needless to say, that never happened to me. And that wasn't just because I didn't need a bra till I was fourteen.

I was the kid playing all the pranks. I was like a small female George Clooney, and the party was my *Ocean's Eleven* set. I would have my coconspirators, the naive bastards who thought they could be on my level, helping me at first. But one by one, they would drop like flies. There'd be a whole finished basement of girls with toothpaste on their foreheads, while I was outside jumping on the trampoline as the sun came up. By the time everyone would wake up pissed, I was in the kitchen making cinnamon rolls with the mom, looking innocent as fuck.

When I didn't have people to torture at night, I had other ways to entertain myself. Besides gluing my own photo into *Tiger Beat* magazines, I watched infomercials. Fact: In fourth grade while all the other little girls were writing to Santa for an Easy-Bake Oven or Suzy Q's First Yeast Infection doll, I asked for a food dehydrator. That's right, a food dehydrator. And I got it too! Dried banana chips? Check my lunchbox, bitch. Homemade potpourri? Fuck you—you want lavender or rose petals? I have received so much joy from Tony Little's ponytail bouncing around on a new workout machine, or an unnamed British dude hawking the latest circum-ventilation roaster (#restinpeaceRonPopeil). To this day, if I am awake after two a.m., I am totally content to watch an infomercial that I've already seen ten times.

Now that I'm an adult, I no longer worry about not sleeping. Instead, I relish it. I am night owl, hear me hoot! Granted, I might not feel this way when it's four a.m. and I have a six a.m. call time. But that is what coffee and adrenaline are for. In fact, my insomnia comes in handy on those mornings. When I was filming my first movie, *Camp Takota*, Grace had a decent amount of crying scenes. Her trick to get herself to Teartown? Not sleeping! The lack of sleep and subsequent overcaffeination could get her to cry on cue. It's been said that this is also Meryl Streep's technique.*

And who really needs sleep when you can just have coffee? I believe that I can do anything with a big-ass cup of coffee. And I ain't no coffee snob. Fuck that. My ideal cup is straight-up blueberry flavored from 7-Eleven with three of their tiny amaretto-flavored creamers. I don't get it when people talk about how amazing a certain brand of coffee is. Or when I go to a trendy coffee shop and have to wait ten minutes for a cup, watching it go through a version of the board game Mouse Trap. The barista will assure me, "Because of the elevation of these beans, we have to fully evaporate the impurities for the truest taste. It'll just be, like, forty more minutes." Excuse me? Fuck to the off. Maybe my taste just isn't sophisticated enough. It's the same way people discuss the bouquet on a certain pinot noir as I sit nodding and drinking Two-Buck Chuck from Trader Joe's through a squiggly straw.

Now, a lot of people ask me, "Mamrie, why don't you just take something to make you fall asleep?" Good question. Yes, I know all about natural sleep aids like melatonin. But they too have side effects. Apparently melatonin can cause extremely vivid dreams,

---

*This is a complete lie. Go ahead and take an extra sip if you fell for it.

and the last thing I need is my dreams of Ryan Gosling to be more vivid. Lord knows, I'd wake up on the floor in a pile of feathers and sawdust because I would dry-hump my bed down to nothing. Okay, what about a powerful FDA-approved sleep med? There's everything from pills I can't pronounce to the adorably named ZzzQuil. But here's the deal. I don't want to build up a tolerance to them. I understand this may sound strange coming from a girl who can finish a round of Edward 40 Hands and then go out for cocktails, but I have my limits.

While it may take me a long-ass time to fall asleep at night, once I finally drift off, I am out. I apologize to any future partners or roommates who live with me, because if there is a fire, our asses will be burnt to a crisp. An intruder? It was nice knowing you. This bitch can sle-e-e-ep. Unlike my mom.

Don't worry, this isn't the part of the book where I divulge my mommy issues. My mother happens to be an adorable southern woman who is a loving grandma and makes a mean Crock-Pot of pinto beans. She also happens to be a severe insomniac. Ever since I can remember, she has taken hard-ass drugs to be able to fall asleep. If for some reason she runs out while the pharmacy is closed for a three-day holiday weekend, she does not sleep for three days. It's an actual *waking nightmare*. So the last thing I want is to love me some sleeping aids and then not be able to sleep without them. Although, it does provide for some great stories.

There's a witching hour when my mom's sleep meds kick in, but not enough to knock her out. This is the closest I've ever come to seeing my mom high. She usually just saunters around in her little robe, watching TV and doing the whole "I'm not sleeping; I'm resting my eyes" routine. You know the one. You and a friend are watching a movie, and to make it appear like you aren't falling asleep, you throw in an occasional laugh or "mmhmm." One time, my mom did this, but she laughed and said, "Oh, those Polacks!" I don't remember what we were watching, but I do know it had nothing to do with Polish people. And *that* is the moment I learned of my mother's burning racism for Polish people.*

The best witching-hour story is "The Night of the Choco Taco." Picture this. It was 2003. I was a sophomore in college who only lived two hours from home; so, every couple of months I would make the drive to get a home-cooked meal and watch cable. At around "pull out my hidden bottle of wine, my mom is asleep" o'clock, I heard the mom-shuffle. Sure enough, she rounded the corner in her robe and slippers with a cup of hot tea.

Caroline joined me on the couch to watch *Iron Chef*. As she sat down, she immediately spilled her hot tea all over herself. While I was worried she had burns from the scalding hot water, she was cracking up.

"I'm gonna fix me another cup," she said, and walked out of the living room, laughing like we were watching a Dave Chappelle special.

"Grab some paper towels!" I yelled after her as I went back to my beloved Food Network. A few minutes later, just as the chairman was about to announce the winner, she was back. She handed me the paper towels to help her wipe up the spill, but before I could get it off the floor, I looked back at her. She was eating something.

"Mom, what are you eating?" I asked.

"What does it look like? It's a choco taco." The woman was eating a taco shell filled with chocolate ice cream and topped with sour cream. Yep, an actual taco shell. Tell me that ain't some straight-up stoner shit right there.

The best part is the next morning, she was dead set that my stepdad ate all the chocolate ice cream and didn't leave her any. 'Cause that's right, folks, some sleep meds make you *sleep-eat*. That's the last thing I need. And this is coming from a girl who once got high and ate Funyuns dipped in butter.

*I'm kidding! My mom has no issue with the Poles. It's the Chinese she hates. . . . Still kidding! I love you, Mom.

Sometimes my mom being on sleep meds was a major advantage for me, especially in high school. During my senior year, we had one of these incidents. I had a humongous exam on *Hamlet* for my AP English class the next morning, and while I should have stayed in and studied (like any of you reading this who are still in school should do), I had other plans. Our neighboring county didn't have school the next day, so my friend Ashleigh and I headed over the bridge to a house party. Not the wisest choice, but we figured we'd socialize for an hour or so and be back in time to study for the final.

Once we got there, it was a full-on house party. Ashleigh wasn't drinking, since she was driving, so when the party ran out of mixers, she volunteered to do a grocery store run. By the time she got back, the scene was a lot different than before. . . .

ASHLEIGH
Mamrie, what the hell are you doing?

I'm sitting at a table across from George, a six-foot-four-inch lumberjack of a man. Empty shot glasses covered the table and people cheered around us.

ME
Whadduz it look like I'm doin'? George challenged me to a
shot-off and I'm kickin' his assssss.

Yep. In the course of twenty minutes, I decided it would be a good idea to go shot for shot with a giant. Luckily, Ashleigh carried me to the car, but not before I told the guy I was seeing at the time, and I quote, "I don't want no one-minute man." What can I say? Missy Elliott was super popular at the time, and that dude had the bedroom skills of Urkel. Not Urkel's suave alter ego, Urquelle; I'm talking pure "Did I do that?" Urkel. Yes, yes you did do that. And you did that way too fast. Moving on . . .

We drove back over the county line, and Ash served as a crutch, leading me up the stairs to the bedroom. Once we got to the top we heard, "Mame, is that you?"

My blind-as-a-bat mother was holding on to the wall to lead herself up the stairs. Now, in any normal scenario, I'd have been caught. I just hoped that my mom's sense of smell wasn't heightened since her sight was gone, as I smelled like I'd taken a long soak in a batch of bathtub gin. Add to that the fact that it was a weeknight and I was coming home at one a.m.? No *bueno*. But luckily for me, my mom had taken her sleep meds.

Once she managed to reach the top of the steps, we went for a T. rex attack route and tried to hold as still as my drunk ass would allow. Which wasn't even close to still. Ashleigh took charge.

ASHLEIGH
No, Caroline. This is all a dream. Mamrie and I have been in bed for hours. Now, go back to bed.

MAMRIE
Yeah, Mom. You're dreaming.

And then I straight-up *Wayne's World*ed her, jazz-handing up and down in front of her face, with the "doo doo da loo" dream sequence sound effect.

MOM
Oh, okay. Night-night, girls.

And without a moment of hesitation, she turned and carefully headed down the stairs. *Success!*

What wasn't so successful was my performance the next day at school. I was so hungover that I hit Snooze a million times, until Ashleigh physically forced me out of bed, with no time to shower. I sat there in class, answering a hundred questions about *Hamlet*, all while wearing sunglasses with little rhinestones in the shape of a heart in the corner. I would like to say I was just rocking a vintage look, but the truth is they had just become popular again because of *Charlie's Angels: Full Throttle*. I was a mess.

Since my brain was on a slower speed, I was last to finish my test. Everyone had already left for afternoon break when I sauntered up to Mr. Parrish's desk. Mr. Parrish was the toughest, greatest teacher at our school. People feared him but also respected him. Kind of like Mr. Feeny from *Boy Meets World*. Or Michelle Pfeiffer in *Dangerous Minds* but with fewer Coolio jams playing. I turned in the exam, and as I was walking out the door to go destroy some Baked Lay's in the cafeteria, Mr. Parrish called out to me.

"Excited to see how you do, Miss Hart. I've never graded a test taken by someone reeking of vodka."

With that I slowly pulled down my shades and said, "Mr. P., in the words of Shakespeare, 'The teacher doth protest too much . . . methinks. And . . . me drinks,'" then walked out the door.*

These days I still have a hard time falling asleep, and I'd still rather depend on my big cup of gas station coffee in the morning to keep me going than resort to choco taco–level drugs. The only difference with my insomnia now is that I don't let it bother me. "Jesus, take the wheel," as they say.†

Instead of tossing and turning at three a.m., I crawl out of bed and snuggle into the couch just in time to hear the magical phrase "The following program is a paid advertisement" as I take a sip from a cold martini. With the mayhem of everyday life, sometimes it's nice to be the only kid awake in the world.

---

*Whether this actually happened or not is questionable. I was still pretty loaded at the time and didn't sober up till we skipped second period to go to Bojangles'. Also, *study*, kids. Do not follow my lead!

†I really just want to get rich enough so I can hire a driver named Jesús and be able to say this phrase to my heart's content. Look, everyone's inspiration for success is different.

Sorry Camp-Ari

1½ oz Campari
1½ oz mescal
Juice of ½ tangerine
1 oz orange liqueur
1 sprig rosemary
**Some sort of fire-making device (matches, a
      lighter, a caveman)**
***Bonus ingredient: a broom to sweep up all the
      panties that will be thrown at you**

*Combine first four ingredients in a shaker full of ice and pump
those biceps. Strain into a highball glass with one of them
fancy-ass mega ice cubes. Here's the fun part.*

*Clean and dry your shaker. Take your sprig of rosemary and
lay it down on a piece of foil or other surface that you don't
mind burning. Light the rosemary on fire. As it smokes, invert
the shaker and hold it over the rosemary, catching the smoke in
the process. Once you think it's filled with smoke, quickly close it
over the top of the highball glass. You can carry that thing
around to the other side of the party, and when you take off the
shaker like a cloche over room service food, the smoke will billow
out. It also gives the drink a nice woodsy flavor.*

When my freshman year of college was winding down, there
were a lot of unknowns. Like where was I going to live that
summer? And just exactly how much weight had I gained that

year? But the thing that was weighing heaviest on my mind (and not my thighs) was the housing situation. I could've gone home to live with my mom in my hometown. I could've also lain down in the middle of traffic, but it isn't the preferred thing to do.*

I could've scrambled to stay in Chapel Hill for the summer, but there's something creepy about being in a college town when school is out. The bars that normally have a line at the door are abandoned, tumbleweeds blowing past the foosball table. When you pop in for a quick one, the bartenders' eyes light up as if they haven't had a visitor in decades, like an old man at a nursing home or an employee at Hot Topic. It wasn't ideal.

Luckily for me, those weren't my only two options. Missionary trip to Africa, here I come! Ha—could you imagine? That is *not* what this chapter is about. One day while I was heading to ~~Wendy's~~ class someone stopped me with a flyer. Normally I avoid flyers at all costs, but this time, for whatever reason,† I took one. It was for a camp fair happening on campus, where summer camps would come and recruit new counselors for the summer.

I almost threw away the flyer. I didn't want to be a camp counselor! I'd never even been a camper. The closest I got to singing around a campfire was in my backyard during my pyromaniac phase, if you count doing voodoo chants while holding a Jonathan Taylor Thomas poster as "singing." (Warning: Pine needles ignite pretty fast.)

I had a half hour to waste before my next ~~Frosty~~ class, so I did what I do whenever I pass a boys' locker room: I decided to take a peek, despite the ill-fitting khaki shorts the guy who gave me the flyer was wearing. I walked into that camp fair and was immediately overwhelmed. Table upon table of well-groomed, chipper folks in their respective camp colors and polo shirts lined the rec hall,

*Mom! Obviously this is a drastic comparison. You know it drives me crazy how you pronounce "breakfast" like "breakfrast" and make light sex noises while you eat, but you also know I *adore you*.

†I was probably hoping it was a coupon for a free Wendy's Frosty.

standing behind their small tables decorated to the max for their camp. I felt a little out of place in my Poison Flesh & Blood Tour halter top that I'd made myself, but I sucked up my pride. I did a lap, avoiding any real eye contact, before I talked to my first table.

"Hi! Thinking about being a counselor this summer?" I looked over and saw a smiling woman with a name tag that read LAURIE.

"Thinking about it . . ." I said apprehensively.

Then Laurie sold me. She told me all about this wonderful camp. It was founded in 1919! All the girls wore adorable old-school gray-and-green uniforms! It was tucked into the North Carolina mountains along a gorgeous blue lake and massive rock-faced mountain! But the thing that really got me was the large photo they had printed behind their table.

"That's our Lady of the Lake tradition. It's how we close out every summer." The picture had the entire camp (decked out in all white) gathered on the docks at dusk. Candles floated among the lily pads, and one girl in a canoe in the middle of the lake held up a lit torch. It was a goddamn postcard.

"Where do I apply?" I was hooked.

Driving up to the camp that summer, I was nervous. What if I got camp-catfished? What if this gorgeous mountain camp in pictures was actually the geographic equivalent of a hillbilly meth head with two teeth? What if it was an awful dump and I was stuck there for two months without any friends? My fears were quickly squashed once I hit that camp road. It was pristine. This was no hillbilly. This was the Brad Pitt of summer camps. And not even *Legends of the Fall* Brad Pitt; I'm talking *Meet Joe Black* era.

I spent my summer teaching dance, performing silly shows every night, and basically acting like an idiot while campers laughed. I was good at this, dammit! I loved having a cabin full of girls just on the brink of high school and using those weeks to drill into their heads that boys are idiots and should be treated like white pants: avoid while on your period and after Labor Day.

I felt so at home at camp that I spent my next two summers

there, bursting at the seams every time I made that first drive down
the camp road, making Ariana Grande high notes when I reunited
with my counselor friends.

Especially Hayley. Hayley was my camp BFF. She is literally the
funniest person I know. She says whatever she wants, which is usually hilarious, and has the presence of Chris Farley without being a
three-hundred-pound man. Have you ever met someone and thought,
Gimme some of that? No, not sexually, but just charisma-wise? When
I met Hayley that summer, she made me want to be funnier. If we
were riding in a van of campers and they wanted to hear whatever
bullshit boy band was popular, Hayley would make them listen to
Hall & Oates. If it was '80s day at camp, you'd better believe she was
the first person with a high side pony, painting flames down the side
of a golf cart. We were attached at the hip.

*Here's Hayley and me dressed as a tropical storm, which
made the entire summer rainy.*

When it came time to go back for the third summer, I decided to pass. I was going to miss camp, but I finally had a serious boyfriend, and we were going to road-trip around the southeast and bask in the splendor of our still-metabolized bodies. At least that's what I thought. Two weeks before school ended, boyfriend decided he "wasn't ready for a long-term relationship" and cheated on me. The fact that six months later he and this girl were engaged but it didn't work out is totally irrelevant to this story, but *totally* relevant to my self-esteem.

I. Was. Pissed. My whole summer had been planned around that road trip. I didn't have a summer sublet. I didn't know what to do, and then it hit me.*

I would go back to camp! Obviously I would have free room and board, but more important, I would have a perfect environment to mend my shat-on heart. Trust me, there is no better place to get over a guy than going to an all-girls camp for the summer. Strong female friendships. Zero cell service, so you can't drunk-text your ex. And best of all, a 20:1 female-to-male staff ratio. I immediately drunk-power-walked back to my apartment to e-mail the camp director.†

If this story sounds vaguely familiar, it's because I used it as inspiration for *Camp Takota*. Unlike in the movie, I wasn't engaged and freshly fired from a job, but like the lead character, I did go back up to camp, and it was just what I needed. I quickly fell right into the daily routine of being a counselor, which also includes *living* for your days off.

If you want to know what a day off for a camp counselor is like, just watch *Wet Hot American Summer*. Their version of going into town ends with them mugging old ladies and Michael Showalter shooting heroin in a crack house, which may be a little extreme, but I can tell you firsthand that we camp counselors took our days

---

*An idea and the four whiskey gingers I'd been sipping on.

†This was BS: Before Smartphones.

off seriously. We would go hard on those precious thirty hours a week away from camp.

Rather than throw out my campers' candy that they snuck into camp, I decided to keep it in a large plastic container under my bed. Notice how I sit on it, holding all the power. Mind games are fun.

Don't get me wrong. I loved camp—loved all of it! But there comes a breaking point, usually at day six in a row. You feel like if you have to sing one more song, eat one more smiley face–shaped tater tot, or have one more seven-year-old ask you what a "bagina" is, you're gonna lose it. When the clock struck five p.m. on that day, all you'd see was a cloud of dust behind my Honda Accord (because that's how dirt roads work).

Days off brought a few options. Since our camp was about an hour outside Asheville, most of our days off were spent going to bars in the city and crashing on our friends' couches. Other nights were spent at my friend Chrissie's lake house right outside camp.*

---

*I still go there about once a year to see my old camp friends. In fact, I am writing this chapter from that very lake house right now. Dat shit cray.

Over the course of those three summers, we had some legendary nights off. But the most memorable I ever had was the last one
of that breakup summer. Camp was ending Tuesday but I had that
Saturday night off. It was perfect. Hayley and I decided to keep it
local and spend the night in the small town of Sylva.

Sylva is about twenty minutes from camp. It's the home of
Western Carolina University and not much else. It's the kind of
town that has one bar and whenever a nonlocal walks in a record-
scratch sound effect is cued. The kind of town that could realisti-
cally vote a cat in as mayor because "everybody gets along with
him."

The crew en route was the dream team. First, there was John
from the kitchen staff. John was the best. He was always there
when I needed him—to unlock the kitchen late at night so I could
raid the cheese, or to drunkenly make out with me despite the fact
that I just ate a *lot* of sharp cheddar. Of course, my home girl Hayley was in tow, but her crush, Brian, was joining us. Brian was
and still is a Hagrid of a man, with a huge beard and giant body.
He and Hayley were both on the mountaineering staff. This meant
they were responsible for taking packs of girls on three- or five-
day hikes. They could turn a scrunchie and a stick into a tourni-
quet or calmly scare off a mountain lion. Meanwhile, I taught
dance in the *one* air-conditioned room at camp and was terrified of
squirrels.

As soon as Hayley saw Brian on the first day that summer, she
said, "Mamrie. That man is gonna be my husband." And she had
been laying the tracks all summer. The flirtation was *real*. But this
was the first time they would be off camp property together since
admitting they were into each other. It had to be special.

PRO TIP: Before you make a move on your camp crush, you
have to see him off camp property to make sure your radar isn't
skewed. Sometimes when you are away from society, your standards can drop without you realizing it. He might look like Channing Tatum when he's in a kayak but end up looking like Stockard

Channing when he's in a Burger King. I knew if Hayley needed a special night, I was the person for the job.

I would make them fall in love. I was scheming just like the twins from *The Parent Trap*, except with a lot more "Let's Get It On" and a lot less "Let's Get Together."*

The bell rang, which ended the last activity of the day, and we were free! Thirty hours of freedom! We had the whole night ahead of us and didn't have to be back till midnight the next night, hours after the final campfire had been extinguished and all the campers were fast asleep.

There was no time to waste. We barreled down the mountain and immediately checked in to the first shitty motel we saw. Knowing that part of Western North Carolina, I'm gonna guess it was named the Mosquito Manor. By the looks of our room, one could assume there had been at least five murders in it. But that wasn't gonna ruin our time! A couple Natty Lights in the belly and I revealed our plans for the evening.

"They've got local wrestling at the armory tonight! All we have to do is bring a can of food for their food drive, and five bucks. Local wrestling, you guys! Come on!"

I looked at my crew, their mouths open, just mouth-breathing at me with shocked eyes.

"Mamie, are you serious?" Hayley asked, then chugged the rest of her beer.

"Yeah, I thought . . ."

"FUCK YES! LET'S DO THIS!" she yelled and crushed the beer can with her hand. Everyone was stoked.

Before heading to the armory, we stopped by the podunk grocery store to pick up our canned goods. A can of food and five bucks for a night of entertainment? I knew I had to make my contribution count. It would seem wrong to go up in there with a can

---

*Is it me, or did Hayley Mills with short hair look exactly like Anthony Michael Hall? This is not talked about enough.

of pinto beans or collards—disrespectful, even. Obviously I splurged for a can of artichoke hearts. Classy as fuck!

We paid for our cans, as well as some Funyuns because we had been enjoying *all* the greenery of the mountains that day, and headed to the match. If you haven't eaten Funyuns before, take caution. Those savory rings give new meaning to the phrase "snack attack." 'Cause they literally attack the shit out of your mouth. Half a bag in and your mouth feels like a miniature street fight happened in it, with bite-size tough guys stabbing your cheeks with tiny switchblades. It's like if you went to eat a cone of fluffy pink cotton candy, then halfway through realized it was Pink Panther insulation.

We got to the armory and it was packed—almost a little too packed for a summer day without air-conditioning. The crowd was filled with good ol' boys and sassy grandmas, teenage boys in Dale Earnhardt shirts and girls in camouflage tank tops. I guarantee 85 percent of the people in that room were cousins. And there we were, standing in the doorway, frozen. In any other scenario, *we* would've looked like drunk rednecks, but here? We may as well have been Arcade Fire rolling into that white cinder block room with the amount of stares we got. It wasn't just a record-scratch moment. It was like an entire record store got thrown into an industrial shredder.

We nodded to the locals and quickly found four empty metal folding chairs. The spectacle that I saw in that armory was beyond words. But if I had to use words, I'd say it was a white trash shit show. I loved it. Wrestlers had names like Possum Jones, the Wrath of Tater, and the Sylva Sultan, a.k.a. Earl. The referee had to be at least ninety years old.

It was exactly what I'd hoped it would be! I looked to my right and saw Hayley and Brian not so much holding hands as gripping each other's hands like one of them was about to fall off a cliff. John came back from the snack bar with the massive pickle I'd asked him to get me, and that's when it started. The oh-too-familiar feeling of a panic attack started to creep in. Anxiety with a bunch of weed on top of it while in a roomful of screaming strangers is a doozy, but I tried to brush it off.

This round was between a dude in hunting gear and an old man in a black Speedo who must've been at least sixty-five. I chomped down on that cold pickle and tried to focus on the fun of it. Three bites into the dill and I made eye contact with a teenager across the room. His head was shaved and he looked at me like he had never seen a woman before. I went in for another bite and realized just how phallic that giant pickle was, and stopped myself. It was all too weird. If I'd heard a banjo, I would've passed out.

I slowly put down my pickle like it was a loaded weapon and I was surrounded by cops, eventually breaking eye contact with Captain Creeptastic. I refocused my gaze on the match just as the sixty-five-year-old wrestler pulled a huge chain out of his Speedo to lay down the law. Shit was getting TOO REAL. My paranoid ass had to get the hell out of there. My friends looked entranced by the match, but I pulled them out of it. "Hey, guys. I'm sorry but I gotta get the fuck out of here. Is that okay?" None of them spoke, but they all nodded at me in unison like a row of bobbleheads on a car dashboard.

Back in the car we snapped out of our haze and started using words again. Words like *traumatized* and *scarred for life*. Brian was the first to chime in. "I'm not saying that I didn't enjoy watching people get hit with metal church chairs; I'm just saying we were too high for that." We cruised my Honda down the back roads with the windows down, grateful for our lives. The summer air was hitting our faces, we could see fireflies lighting up in the fields, and the sweet sounds of Justin Timberlake's greatest album, *Justified* blared from the CD player. I was *so* happy to be out of that armory.

When we got back to the motel, the anxiety was totally gone and we were back to our normal, loud selves. We pounded beers, reenacted the wrestling matches, and savored a much-needed night away from homesick kids. John and I chilled outside to give Brian and Hayley more privacy. Normally this is where I would pass the time with a random make-out session, but the Funyun battle scars were still too fresh. After a few beers, I went inside to grab some more from our room, fingers crossed that Hayley and Brian were hitting it off.

Oh, they weren't just hitting it off! They were getting it off. I walked in to see Hayley, butt-ass naked, straddling Brian. She looked directly at me and said, "Ride 'em, cowboy!" with her arm miming a lasso. I burst out laughing, grabbed as many beers as I could, and joined John outside. That image will be *forever* burned into my brain.

Now, as much as I loved having nights off from camp, I equally hated the mornings after. My temples were pounding to their own techno beat, and my breath smelled like a mummy had farted in my mouth. After walking in on the flesh rodeo the night before, I'd gotten straight-up plastered. Luckily, we didn't have to be back at camp till ten p.m. Unluckily, we did have to check out of the roach motel.

We walked into the daylight and it *hurt*. I felt like a miner who had been trapped underground for months and was finally free. The sun burned my eyes, and my brain was half-melted. First stop was to get a big plate of hangover helper:* Waffle House! If you've never been to a Waffle House, you are seriously missing out. They might have "waffle" in their name but they are the Michelangelo of hash browns. They have all these different slang terms to order them. Like:

Scattered: extra crispy
Smothered: with sautéed onions
Covered: melted cheese on top
Lovered: a lil' cigarette ash from the sexiest chef
Glovered: chef takes off glove and uses bare hands for
  extra flavor (not recommended)

---

*How the hell hasn't Hamburger Helper made a line of products called Hangover Helper? That marketing team needs to hire some young, hip newcomer with fresh ideas.

In high school, we would go to our local Waffle House after football games or the morning after parties. I went there so often that I got chummy with the waitresses. In fact, Shirley (my main Waffle Ho) came to my senior school play and I wore a '50s style paper Waffle House hat during curtain call in her honor. Because that's who *I* was in high school.

Looking around, I could tell everyone was feeling as shitty as I was. This was based on the half a hog's worth of bacon the rest of the table ordered. Post–carb fest, my head was still screaming. It was only one o'clock, so we had NINE long hours to burn. We needed a place to go with A/C, so we popped into a movie theater to see the first of the Batman reboots, *Batman Begins*; I remember it as clear as eyes right after Visine. I lasted five minutes before passing the fuck out in the theater, waking up only once to see that my friends were also dead to the world. Brian was snoring so loud that we would've been kicked out if we weren't the only people there. There we were, mouth-breathing and reeking of cheap beer and vodka, paying to sleep in the cushioned seats. A fifteen-year-old usher had to wake us up after the credits ended.

Even that two-hour nap didn't help take the edge off my hangover, and that's when I knew what I had to do: start drinking again.

Like every other tiny-ass town in the South, there were plenty of crappy Mexican restaurants to choose from. Not fancy Mexican like I eat in L.A. When I eat Mexican food in L.A., it's like a kale salad with pepitas and soy beef tacos with fresh pico de gallo. In NC, it's a five-dollar plate of cheese enchiladas with refried beans and a bowl of melted white cheese dip. Essentially you just walk in and ask for a plate of brown with a little iceberg lettuce, and it's fucking delish. So I sidled up to my plate of brown and decided to bite the bullet and get a drink. There was none of this easing-into-it shit either. I'm not one of those people who go down the steps in the pool. I'm a firm believer that you gotta cannonball right in.

"I'll have a margarita the size of my face, please. *Gracias.*"

Four drinks deep and I felt like I hadn't stopped drinking from the night before. I was back, baby! But my hand-eye coordination definitely wasn't. I was still so shaky that every time I picked up my drink, it was like the Jell-O scene in *Jurassic Park*. The front of my shirt was tie-dyed with hot sauce and marg. But the real shaking kicked in when I looked down at my phone.

As my black Motorola flip phone played its Ciara "One, Two Step" ringtone, I saw that the caller ID read "Camp Office." I froze. I felt like someone had punched me in the stomach, but it was probably the eight pounds of queso I'd just housed. I let it go to voice mail and then listened to the voice of the sweetest, most up-beat and wonderful camp director to ever live.

"Mamrie! Give me a call back. I meant to ask you before you left on your day off, but forgot. We would love for you to come back to camp early, if you can make closing campfire. Senior staff got to talking and we would love for you to be this year's Lady of the Lake."

Holy shitballz. Lady of the Lake was that beautiful picture that had gotten me hooked on camp three years prior at the camp fair. They wanted me to be that girl with the torch in the middle of the lake. I was honored. In the world of camp, this was a big deal. This meant that I had been chosen as a representation of all that camp stood for—that I had made this summer memorable for the campers, and thus it was my moment to extinguish the flame, to say good-bye to the summer. I realize this probably sounds like some culty-ass shit, but it was a big deal! And I was beyond touched that they had asked. I knew I had to go, despite being simultaneously drunk and hungover.

We made our way back up to camp. The superwinding, fifteen-mile-per-hour curves didn't help my stomach. Luckily, I didn't spew and got there just in time to put on my camp whites. You see, one of the other traditions for camp is that we wore all white to campfires. While it looked beautiful in pictures, the logic never made sense to me. Why would you put a bunch of girls in all-white clothing to sit in the woods, surrounded by dirt? Not to mention that with that much estrogen floating around, there were a good four to six girls having their first period at any moment. It was a *YM* embarrassing story waiting to happen.

The campfire went off without a hitch, and I was actually keeping myself together despite one camper telling me that I smelled weird.

"It's a new perfume," I said back, hoping that would shut her up.

"Ah. Well, you need to throw it away. It stinks. You smell like my aunt Kathy."

I was not gonna have this sassy little sassafras blow my cover. "Well, I guess your aunt Kathy has very good taste, because this perfume is super expensive."

"So is caviar but it's just eggs out of a fish's butt."

We stared at each other in a total face-off until I was snapped out of it by the voice of our camp director.

"Tonight we have chosen Mamrie as our Lady of the Lake. We think that Mamrie represents the spirit of camp, and the type of girls this place creates. Mamrie, please do us the honor."

I nodded, all charm and innocence. I took the torch, lit it off the fire, then slowly walked out through the woods to meet the canoe. The rest of the camp took their floating candles and began walking out of the woods the opposite direction, all singing the camp song in unison. I carefully got in the canoe and another counselor paddled as I held the torch. As we made it around the bend and out of the woods, the campers were already walking through the clearing, holding their floating candles as they made their way to the docks.

I sat at the front of the canoe, gripping this heavy-ass torch. My hands were quivering, and the stick felt like it was a hundred pounds, but I was determined to keep it steady and lit. But the torch had other plans. Now, normally the torch would be made by the mountaineering staff, but since they were busy humping somewhere, torch-making duty had been given to someone on the theater staff.

But the thespian who'd made the torch had forgotten one crucial element: the wires. Here's how torch-making works. You've got your big stick. The tip is covered in maxi pads, making it look like a giant Q-tip.[*] Once those are stuck on, all you've got to do is wrap metal wires around the pads to keep them in place, then douse that baby in lighter fluid, and you've got yourself a torch worthy of the Summer Olympics! Without the wires, however, the torch will fall apart because the glue from the pads will immediately heat up and not stick anymore. And this is precisely what happened.

As the canoe made its way toward the dock, the pads started falling off the stick one by one.

"Oh my god. They're coming off!" I shrieked to the counselor paddling behind me. Another one dropped off, almost landing in the canoe before I kicked it out.

"Hold it over the water!" she ~~yelled~~ whispered. "It'll be fine."

We paddled on with a trail of flaming pads in our wake. They'd look beautiful for a second, ablaze on the water, then quickly burn out, a trail of crispy black maxi pads nestled among the lily pads. By the time we reached the middle of the lake, with the whole camp watching from the dock, I was left with nothing but a smoking branch. The campers stood in horror as they finished the last round of the camp song. Fellow counselors stood with hands over their wide-open mouths, trying not to laugh. I continued proudly holding this "torch" in front of the canoe, just like in the picture.

The sky was fiery pink. Floating candles surrounded us, and the only noise you could hear was from the crickets and the bullfrogs. I took a moment to lock the image in my memory, then extinguished the bare stick in the lake. There was no sizzle sound,

[*] I like to think the maxi-pad torch was a symbol of femininity, setting fire to the constraints of feminine hygiene products. But really, desperate times called for desperate measures, and there was always a surplus of pads lying around.

just the unsatisfying feeling of a big stick being dipped in a lake. It was like leaning in to blow out your birthday candles and someone does it right before you.* I looked up to see a dock of people shaking their heads as I gave an "oops" shrug. We paddled in as the entire camp slow-clapped at my pathetic display.

Lady of the Lake had been a tradition for eighty-five years. Almost nine decades of women carrying the torch, and I'd fucked it up. Well, maybe not fucked it up, but I definitely put my own spin on it. The image might not have gone in the next summer's pamphlet, but I guarantee it was one of the more memorable ones since 1919. What can I say? I guess I'm bad luck for traditions.

But there is something that I am good luck for! Brian and Hayley have been happily married eight years, and now they have a daughter. What I'm saying is if you want your relationship to last, make sure that I see you have sex for the first time. Maybe even scream, "Ride 'em, cowboy!" at me to be extra safe.

*If you haven't YouTubed that, go forth as soon as you finish this chapter.

Bizarrgarita

2 oz vanilla-infused tequila
1 oz orange liqueur
3 oz orange juice
1 tbsp unsweetened pumpkin puree

For the rim, make a mix of equal parts cinnamon and sugar. If you can find vanilla sugar, amazeballs. If not, throw a vanilla bean into a bag of this stuff for a few hours.

To infuse the tequila, take a regular-size bottle of tequila (trust me, you'll want the whole thing infused; this shit is tasty). Take 2 fresh vanilla beans and slice them lengthwise down the middle. Throw them into the bottle and let them infuse for 3 to 5 days, giving it a little shake each day. When it's to your liking, fish out them vanilla beans or a week later you're going to be drinking Bath & Body Works Vanilla Tequila Body Spray.

Combine all your ingredients into a shaker full of ice. Shake like your life depends on it. Strain into a glass full of ice that is already rimmed with your cinna-sugar. While the ingredients might make you raise an eyebrow, after one of these puppies the only thing you'll be raising is your hand when you say, "Pardon me, bitch, may I have another?"

I love Mexico. Love, love, *lurve* it. I love the food. I love the drinks—Corona and tequila are 87 percent of my bloodstream. (The other 13 percent is a combination of blood, sweat, and pizza-flavored Combos.) But it's not just the partying aspects of Mexico that I love. Sure, if there is a piñata at a party, you'd better grab your two-year-old and get the fuck out of the way because I am going to temporarily lose my mind, and yes, I have been known to throw on a pink taffeta dress and sneak into a quinceañera at the park. But I also highly enjoy the culture.

The first time I ever went to Mexico was in fourth grade. My mom took me, my brother and sister, and my cousin Josh to Cancún. Twenty-four hours and a bad fruit salad later, the bro, sis, and cuz all had a case of what they call Montezuma's revenge. I, however, was free to have a fleeting moment of being an only child. We went to Mayan ruins, we snorkeled, my mom ushered me quickly past Señor Frog's. This was the jumping-off point for my love of all things Mexican.

One thing I'm super obsessed with is Mexican wrestling.* The wrestlers, or *luchadores*, wear crazy masks when they fight. To Americanize it for you, it's Jack Black's potbellied alter ego in the movie *Nacho Libre*. These guys create over-the-top characters who do insane, high-flying moves. They are super famous in Mexico, all while never revealing their true identities. As someone who wants everyone on earth to know my rubber face, I am fascinated by this anonymity. I even started my own *lucha libre* mask collection and break them out at any excuse. Is it cold outside? Better wear a *lucha* mask. Going on a first date and want to make sure the guy likes me for my personality and not just my looks? It's mask time. It works in most scenarios.

There's one time in my masked memories that I was especially happy to not show my face. It was my friend's thirtieth birthday

---

*You might be thinking, *Jesus, Mamez, between the armory story and this, what is your obsession with wrestling?* What can I say? There was a tag team in the '80s called the Hart Foundation that wore hot pink singlets. Having a first name like Mamrie, you get attached to things with at least your last name in common.

party, which happened to fall on Halloween. She is British and super posh—like, as a child she probably referred to Victoria Beckham of the Spice Girls as the poor-level posh. Her even more posh parents were coming in from England to celebrate their daughter's milestone. Since her birthday was on Halloween, I asked if people would be dressing up. "Oh, totally, totally," she said. "It will be a dress-up party."

Cut to me decked out in full *lucha libre* wear. Hologram tights, leopard leotard. I even tied a shower curtain around my neck as a cape. But when I high-kicked into her Brooklyn loft, I saw where the gap between British and American slang came into play. People dressed up, all right. Her dad was practically in a tux. And I was *definitely* the only one dressed up in Halloween gear.

This pic was taken after about the fifth Brit asked me what superhero I was.

But the Mexican tradition I love even more than *lucha libre* is Día de los Muertos. Or for you gringos, Day of the Dead.

If you aren't familiar with this holiday, let me quickly break it down for you. Day of the Dead is a three-day celebration through-out Mexico when family and friends honor the deceased with al-tars, parades, and flowers. You probably have seen Day of the Dead stuff before, be it intricate skeleton face paint on a hipster, or a detailed tattoo of a skull wearing a flower crown (on a hipster's calf). I love how it celebrates the dead and makes something like a skeleton seem not scary. Because I won't pussyfoot around it—I am a total pussy.*

I have tons of Day of the Dead figurines and paraphernalia, but I'd never actually been to Mexico to see it in person until 2008. Maegan and I decided to take the plunge. We scoured the Internet for the cheapest Mexico deal and finally found one for six hundred dollars. It included airfare, transportation to and from the airport, and four nights at an all-inclusive resort. Now, I know what you're thinking. *Six hundred bucks?! Let me guess, they are going to get down there and be sold into white slavery.* Not true! Turns out that some-times when you travel abroad, the only thing you need to worry about is the other Americans.

After a fuck-ton of drinks on the plane, we arrived in Cozumel. Maegan was scared of flying, and y'all know about my fears, so we handled it as we do: by taking down enough vodka to pickle a min-iature pony. By the time we touched down in Cozumel, our tray tables were a wasteland of airplane bottles. It looked like lepre-chaun spring break.

The thirty-minute car ride from the airport to the resort set the perfect tone for the trip. We were crammed into a minivan cab with three sixtysomething retiree couples who passed around a bottle of Drambuie, and everyone (yours truly included) took pulls straight from the bottle. At the time, I figured it was all good be-

---

*If you would like to know the extent of how *not* into scary stuff I am, I once had to turn off Wallace and Gromit's *The Curse of the Were-Rabbit* because I got too scared. Scared of a Claymation rabbit that destroyed peo-ple's gardens. It's that bad.

cause these were seniors. They weren't exactly slutting around and spreading the herp. This, of course, was before knowing that because of medical advancements like Viagra, the STD rates in senior communities are astronomical.

(Also, if you have never drunk Drambuie before, I don't recommend it. Drambuie is one of those liquors that taste so bad, you think they must be good for you. Like, it tastes so bad that there is no way it doesn't also clean your blood or replenish your bone marrow to make the terrible medicinal taste worth it.)

When we got to the resort, we were surprised to see it was gorgeous. Half of it was under construction (hence the extremely cheap rate), and after some boozy pleas, the concierge upgraded us to a nicer room—one with a waterslide from your patio down to the pool, landing you at the swim-up bar. It was like a McDonald's playground for drunks.

The next few days were a total veg fest. Mornings started with us taking our slide down to the pool bar for coffee and Baileys. Afternoons were spent snorkeling and sunbathing. Nights consisted of long dinners and drinks at the resort's bar. And we definitely took advantage of that free room service, by having orders of french fries and beer delivered to our room every night. An American nightcap!

Even though we were having a great time, it was pretty isolating. We would see older couples around, but no one really interacted with each other. We would get showered and go to the resort's bar at night, but it was just us sitting there by ourselves. Just two gals drinking alone as the four men who worked it stood and watched. There was one bartender in particular who would get shy and giggle every time Maegan spoke to him. This was the level of action we were getting—one dude kind of giggling toward us.

But that all changed on the third night. We were sitting on our patio, betting on who would spill the least while going down the slide holding a plate of fries (turns out we tied, each spilling the entire plate), when we heard it. The sounds of youth! We looked over to the bar and saw not one, but *two* couples drinking and laughing. We quickly got on our socializing game faces and made our way over.

And we were pleasantly surprised. They were great! The two guys were best friends, the two gals were best friends, and every year they would take a double-date vacay. They seemed a little Republican for my normal taste, with the guys sporting buzz cuts and boat shoes. But we weren't in America, so I left politics at the door and enjoyed the company.

The next few hours we drank our faces off, played pool, and had some laughs. The bar started closing up around ten p.m., but as the resident young and attractive people at this resort, we wanted the party to keep going. So we invited our new friends up to our room to order (more) french fries and twelve draft Dos Equis.

It didn't take more than a few more brews for us all to agree we should go down the waterslide. Our new friends headed out before us as Maegan and I seized the moment of solitude to dominate those fries. As we stepped out onto the patio, we looked over to see our new friends coupled up. One pair was making out against the pool wall. I looked for the other two, and they were on the slide. Well, the guy was lying on the slide, being straddled by the one who was definitely not his wife but who definitely *was* topless.

That's when it hit me: HOLY FUCK. THEY'RE SWINGERS.

For some reason, I always imagined swingers to be overweight and in their fifties and sixties. They'd all be hanging out in someone's gross living room, paired up and going at it on shag carpeting, and saying things like:

Hey, Gerald, once you're done going down on my wife, I've got to show you my new nine iron.

Linda, how many times do I have to tell you to put your pants on if you are going to taste the fondue? Nobody wants your pubes in the Gouda.

OR:

Ruth, be a dear and turn the TV to NCIS *while you jerk off Terrance.*

But these were the younger generation, the up-and-comers. We stared at them in disbelief for what felt like an eternity, and then the topless wife spoke up. "We were so excited to see y'all at the bar tonight. John kept going on and on about that hot lesbian couple he'd seen around."

Hot lesbian couple? Did they think we were a hot lesbian couple? I got why they would think that we were hot. I had seen a reflective surface, after all—but lesbian? The events of the past few days montaged through my mind. Maegan and me cheersing our champagne as a waiter took a picture. Constantly ordering room service, like we couldn't be bothered to put our clothes on. We swam with *dolphins*, for Chrissakes. This was the most romantic vacation I'd ever been on!

Before I could laugh and clear things up, Maegan took charge. "We came on this trip because we've been having some relationship issues lately."

"Oh, I'm so sorry to hear that," Titties McGee said as someone else's husband played with her belly ring.

"Yeah," Maegan continued as I looked like a deer in headlights. "Actually, do you mind if the two of us have a word in private?" Maegan grabbed my hand and we retreated back to our room.

As soon as she closed the sliding glass doors, we screamed with no volume. The rest of the night we sat quietly, trying to listen to what was happening outside while inhaling french fries. Occasionally we would yell out a line or two as if we were arguing. "No, it's *your* turn to refill the humidifier!" or "I'm tired of always wearing the strap-on!"

Luckily, they were so distracted playing Pick a Husband that they forgot all about us. After taking down the twelve room service beers, we entered a carb coma and both passed out.

The next day came with a massive hangover, the kind where

your body feels like it is vibrating. You crave coffee but you're nervous that the caffeine will push you over the edge and you'll end up crying on the bathroom floor. We started to make our way to the patio to slide down for some hair of the dog but stopped when we realized we didn't know what kind of HBO *Real Sex* stuff had happened on our precious, precious slide the night before. So our last full day in Mexico was instead spent inside, watching a *Sex and the City* marathon in Spanish. The bad news was I felt like a piece of shit for wasting my last day of vacation, but the good news is I can now say *Kegels* in Spanish.

Once the sun started to set, we knew we needed to suck it up and shower. After all, this was the first day of Day of the Dead and we just *had* to experience it. All week, we had seen signs that there was going to be a special show in the resort's theater that night. Bartenders had told us it wasn't to be missed and it was their favorite show all year.

We managed to clean ourselves up, then headed over to the Italian restaurant. I, of course, ordered two entrées for myself and a big ol' glass of wine to keep the hangover at bay. Once the food arrived and I was tagging out my eggplant parm for my lasagna, I looked up to see that Maegan hadn't eaten a bite.

"What's wrong? Do you not like your ravioli? I'd be happy to order a couple pizzas and help you eat those if you like."

She shook her head and stood up. "I'm having a full-on panic attack. I gotta get the fuck out of here."

"Okay, do you want me to have them wrap up your food for later? Maybe we should get an order of puttanesca too . . . just in case."

"I'm not even hungry. I really gotta leave now. I'll meet you outside." She peaced the fuck out as I flagged down the waiter to see if we could just get our meals to go. Before I could stop him, he set down the garlickiest garlic bread I'd ever seen. Fuck. I couldn't just *leave* the food. That would be super rude. Especially since at all-inclusives you don't pay for anything. I would've looked like some asshole who just orders a bunch of shit and doesn't eat it because I can.

To keep my conscience clear, I dove right in. I also didn't want Maegan to be freaking out solo, so I started shoveling it all in fast. There I was, sitting alone with enough food for several people. It was almost as sad as when you order delivery for yourself and they bring you four sets of silverware, just assuming that amount of food *must* be for an entire family. So then you call out to your fake family as you are tipping the delivery guy like, "Madison, I said you can practice cello later. Come eat with Mommy and Daddy." Because if that delivery guy thinks I ordered food for four, you better believe it's four swanky, cello-playing people.

By the time I was halfway through Maegan's ravioli, I looked up and saw the swingers at a table, staring at me with looks of pity. I shrugged my shoulders and pointed outside. "She wasn't feeling well."

They nodded like they were witnessing a lovers' quarrel, a romantic retreat gone wrong. Luckily, they had totally healthy, normal marriages where they fucked each other's best friends. I wanted to yell, "You have no room to judge the state of my fake lesbian relationship!" but I refrained.

After quickly finishing the basket of bread (I wasn't raised to waste), I asked for two shots of tequila to go and booked it straight toward our room. Walking back, I heard, "Maaaaamrie," coming from a couch in the open-air lobby. I looked around and saw no one. I'd almost convinced myself that it was someone's dead Mexican ancestor coming to talk to me, when I spotted Maegan's shoes. Like the witch's in *The Wizard of Oz*, her always-adorable footwear was peeking out from underneath the couch pillows. I pulled one off her face and handed her the shot. I didn't even need to speak. The rules of staving off anxiety between us were known. Like Haley Joel Osment, I was paying that shit forward.

We sat on the couch until her anxiety went from "I'm going to scream my head off and take a dump on the floor" to "This place is weird, right?" Mind you, I was still massively hungover and having to make a conscious effort to string words together to form sentences, but I had to be strong for her.

"Do you want to go back to the room, order beers, and stay away from all the weirdos?" I asked, knowing our night of finally seeing some Mexican culture was going to be a bust.

But she impressed me with her resolve.

"No. We are going to the show, goddammit."

I've said before how when you are having a panic attack everything feels just a little off. Like nothing makes sense. Well, I wasn't even having one and as soon as I walked into this show, I had those symptoms. I can say without a doubt that we were about to witness the weirdest Halloween show of all time.

That's right, not a Day of the Dead show like we had traveled from New York to see. Nope. This resort didn't want its snowbirds to feel homesick for All Hallows' Eve, so it brought the American culture to us. We approached the theater, and all the hotel staff were dressed as very bootleg vampires.

"Watch out!" I warned them. "My purse is full of garlic bread!" No response. This was not my target demo. We entered the theater and it was decked out in fake graves, spiderwebs, fake bats. It looked like someone had given a blank check to a kid at Party City. I *loved* it.

We went to the bar to grab a couple of beers before finding a seat, but the bartender insisted on having us try their signature "scary" cocktail. I kid you not, it was oatmeal with red food coloring and vodka in it, or "Blood Drink," as they called it. The only thing scary about it was that it felt like you were drinking liquid cement that at any point was going to harden in your throat. I asked if I could get a spoon for my drink, and the bartender was not amused. Or maybe he was. It's really hard to tell when someone's face is painted like a skeleton.

We took our seats while chewing our drinks. As the lights came down, a random man's hand tapped my shoulder. I jumped in my seat to find the swinging quartet behind us.

"Hey, hot lesbians. If you get scared during this show and need to hold each other, I won't mind." We forced a laugh through our porridge-tinis and turned back around.

We inched our chairs forward a little and kept spooning down the oatmeal vodka as a guy in a Grim Reaper robe and Jason mask swung a fake sickle at us. I leaned into Maegan.

What followed was quite possibly the greatest thirty-minute show I've ever witnessed, and I've seen that *Full House* episode with two Michelles. If you have never watched a four-foot-ten-inch Mexican man in drag lip-syncing to "Sweet Transvestite," or seen a dude (in whiteface) dressed as Freddie Mercury pretending to play "Bohemian Rhapsody" on the piano while four guys stand behind him with flashlights and rocker wigs acting out the actual music video, *you have not lived*.

Everything was based on Halloween but just a little off, kind of like dollar-store snacks. You'll go to the store craving Cheeze-Its, but settle for Chee Zits. It's close but not quite there. For example, Halloween is all about skeletons. Fact. But when they brought out ten people dressed as glow-in-the-dark skeletons, they danced to Huey Lewis's "Back in Time," from the *Back to the Future* soundtrack. It didn't make sense. Halfway through, Maegan and I had lost it. The hangover mixed with the chunky cocktail on top of sitting in front of people who thought we were a couple sent us over the edge, and we were crying from laughing so hard. Here we had come all the way to Mexico and the closest we were getting to Day of the Dead was a knockoff Beetlejuice dancing to "Simply Irresistible."

Maegan's anxiety had finally calmed and she squeezed my leg to assure me she was all good. That is until ol' Beetlejuice decided to come into the audience to ask for a volunteer. We were practically sitting under our seats to avoid him, when his hand reached out and led Maegan onstage.

Despite the admirable attempt at stage makeup and gunked-up teeth, this BJ was no Michael Keaton. It was actually Captain Giggles, the shy bartender. It was kind of sweet that he needed the safety net of his terrible costume to be able to talk to her. It was like Mrs. Doubtfire without the prosthetic boobs and toying with your children's mental health. And that, my sweet readers, was the day Maegan met her husband.

I kid! That was the day Maegan had sex with her first Mexican bartender.

Still kidding! That was the day Maegan started washing down her Xanax with tequila. This concludes kidding.

The next day we rolled our hungover selves into a cab. This time there weren't any retirees with Drambuie. It was just two shocked women in awe of the night before.

We boarded the plane with our flight must-haves (*Us Weekly* and Doritos) and found our seats. And don'tcha know, when the stewardess came by to grab our drink orders, Maegan ordered a water. A water! On a flight!

She had stared danger (and a knockoff Beetlejuice) right in the face and come out having a great time. I, for one, still needed a margarita. Those swingers were weird, y'all.

Quickshots: Costume Hall of Fame

Y

In the previous chapter I told you guys my *lucha libre* costume disaster. I'm not going to lie; that one was a doozy. But that wasn't my only foray into Halloween costume fuckups. Here are my top low points, in chronological order.

Let us throw back a shot for each!

Halloween 1988 Was Bananas

Most five-year-old little girls want to be princesses, or mermaids, or princess mermaids for Halloween. But not me! I had a very specific vision in mind: I wanted to be Miss Chiquita. Yep, as in the little lady on the blue label on bananas. All I knew about her was that she wore a huge fruit hat, but that's all I needed. I could tell from that quarter-of-a-square-inch sticker that this woman was regal as fuck. Especially her posture.

I told my mom my plans, and her eyes lit up. "Well, Mamrie. Chiquita banana is not a real lady. But she is based on a woman named Carmen Miranda." She went on and on telling me about how Carmen Miranda was an Argentinean actress in the '40s and at one point she was even the highest-paid woman in US cinema. (Looking back, did my mom have a lady boner for Carmen Miranda? Because she sure did know a lot about her.) I was very impressed, and so my decision was made.

There was a costume contest at the local fire department, and I was out for blood. I knew I had to have the best costume, so Mom and I worked together to arrange something fittingly regal. For the dress, I wore a light blue genie costume that I had from a previous dance recital. For the hat, my mom bought a bunch of plastic fruit, which we glued to a cowboy hat. The top even had one of those paper accordion-style pineapples. Pretty brilliant.

I was confident that I was going to win, but I wasn't taking any chances, so I went the extra mile and created a song.

When they called out my age group, I sized up the competition. Cat? Get real. Pirate? Ahoy, idiot! And don't get me started on the toilet paper mummy. I was gonna crush them harder than an Adderall the night before a final. We started walking around in a circle for the judges, and that's when I broke out my secret weapon. I put on my best samba strut and sang, verbatim: "Chiquita Banana puts the mambo in the fiesta! Chiquita Banana puts the mambo in the fiesta!"

It was catchy as hell, and I still get drunk and perform it at parties sometimes. I could tell I was killing it because I looked over to see my mom bragging about me on the sidelines. "Yes, isn't she amazing? Mamrie insisted on being Carmen Miranda to pay homage to the legend. So mature for her age."

We lined up to receive our awards and I could almost feel the Little Caesars gift certificate in my hands. The fireman walked right up to me, extended his arm . . . and handed it to the cat. The *fuckin' cat*. Real imaginative. But, you always learn something from defeat. Especially at a young age.

And that, my dear readers, is when I learned you will get ahead *only* with mediocre, generic bullshit. *I kid!* Seriously, the cat did win but I learned zero lessons whatsoever. I was robbed!

Halloween 1992 Was Out of This World

The first few years I lived in North Carolina, I would still go up to New Jersey to see my childhood bestie, Kara (#Baltimorelayover #neverforget). In fourth grade, I went up over Halloween weekend because she was throwing a party. I prepared a sick martian costume (with all this cool glow-in-the-dark puffy paint on it) and knew I would win her costume contest. Finally, redemption for my Carmen Miranda fiasco!

The only problem was that Delta had lost my luggage and it wasn't going to be delivered in time for the party. After some serious cursing (I had just learned the word *bastard* and loved it, although I still needed help with context. I told the airport employee to find "my bastard luggage"), Kara's mom, Terri, took control. Terri was determined for me to still live my Halloween dreams of being a martian, goddammit.

Terri was the young, cool mom. She smoked Kool cigarettes; had bleached, teased Jersey hair; and would drive us around in her used Jaguar while listening to Rod Stewart. She looked like a rode-hard-and-put-away-wet version of Christina Applegate during her *Married with Children* years. To this day, I think my sister still wants to be Terri Dreyer. Terri obviously had Kara really young, because I have a distinct memory of her turning thirty on one of my visits. She always had a different boyfriend whom she and Kara lived with, which might sound sad, but said boyfriend was always trying to get on Kara's good side and ended up spoiling her. The bitch had a tree house with electricity. *Electricity.* Her tree house was more livable than most of my neighbors' homes in North Carolina.

Being the coolest, Terri let me raid her closet to put the best martian ensemble together. She dressed me up in her wackiest clothes and even had a silver metallic Tina Turner–esque wig to complete the look. I trusted her to make me look good, and felt confident walking into that party. And it was a great Halloween party, full of classic activities: We bobbed for apples, danced to the "Monster

Mash," what have you. Finally, the time came for the costume contest. There was no parading for the judges, although I was prepped with a martian-themed song and dance, obvi. Everyone just wrote down on a sheet of paper who they thought had the best costume.

I was nervous. Maybe I should've performed my original song titled "Outta-This-World Kind of Girl" to seal the deal. I paced back and forth around the party. Which wasn't that easy to do because Terri had put me in these crazy thigh-high boots with toilet paper stuffed in the toes to make them fit. Once the votes were in, Kara announced the winner.

"Listen up, youse guyz, the winner of the costume contest is . . . Mamrie!" I couldn't believe it. I had actually won! I graciously accepted my Halloween gift bag, complete with fake shrunken head, and took a bow.

It was only after the party that I learned just how insane my winning margin was. Apparently I got nine out of the twelve votes. That's right. Seventy-five percent of the entire party agreed that I, the "hocker," should win. Yep. All the boys at the party voted for me, thinking that my martian outfit was actually a hooker's. Hell, a win's a win!

God bless a fourth-grader's spelling, and God bless Terri for helping make that win possible with her slutty, slutty wardrobe.

Halloween 1993 Was More Than I'd Wished For

There were some great moments in 1993. The gang from *Saved by the Bell* finally graduated high school. I choreographed my cheerleading squad's halftime dance to "Whoomp! (There It Is)." And I had the best Treasure Troll collection in my county.[*] I was so obsessed with Trolls, in fact, that I had my heart set on being one that October 31.

---

[*]This is in no way proven, but I stand by it.

My friend Nick was throwing a party and, classic me, I waited till the last minute to get my costume together, but I knew it would be easy. I had seen Troll wigs at the mall and would wear a little belly top and shove a rhinestone into my belly button. Easy peasy.

The day before the party, I asked my aunt, who was watching my siblings and me for the weekend, to take me to the mall to get the wig. She pursed her lips. "Oh, Mame. No can do. I've gotta make dinner for you and your brother and sister."

"Them? Oh, they're fine. Dave will just want to eat frozen pizza and Annie is already stunting her appetite with menthol cigarettes."

"What was that?"

"I said . . . Annie can just make a sandwich."

After a thirty-second stare-down, my aunt still didn't budge. "If you want to be a Troll doll for Halloween, I can help you with your hair. I can tease it to stand straight up and then we'll spray it purple." My own hair, huh? I doubted her at first, but then I remembered that she had been a beauty queen back in the sixties. She could probably work wonders with a can of Aqua Net!

What I didn't know was that when my aunt said she could tease my hair straight up, she didn't mean like a Troll. She meant like a straight-up *beehive*. I had a purple beehive. She didn't want me wearing a belly top in the cold, so I was forced to wear a Troll sweatshirt and leggings. Between the frumpy outfit, purple beehive, and my prescription glasses . . . I didn't so much look like a Troll as I looked like a woman from a *Far Side* comic.

Halloween 2003 Gave Me the Blues

I've never been one to try and pull off the sexy look at Halloween. This may sound surprising considering my aforementioned stint as a "hocker," but it's true. When I went to college at Chapel Hill, every year our main party drag, Franklin Street, would be filled with sexy versions of everything. Sexy librarians. Sexy policewomen. Sexy pediatric heart surgeons. The way I looked at it, why waste your sexy outfit on the drunkest day of the year? At the end of the day, if you wanted to get laid, YOU WOULD GET LAID.

Given how ambivalent I was about trying to slut it up, my junior year my roommates and I decided to go as the Smurfs. I'm talking pre-CGI hanging out with Neil Patrick Harris Smurfs. The classics. I took charge of putting together our costumes. Obviously we would need white sweatpants and royal blue shirts. I broke out my very limited sewing skills and transformed white pillowcases into hats and shoved in pillow stuffing to keep them tall. We obtained some white slippers and *blam*. The only thing left to do was paint ourselves blue from head to toe.

This seemed easy in theory, but shit, to get an even color on our bodies took a lot of coats. Racists who do blackface are the worst of the worst, but I gotta give it up for their endurance. If they only used that stick-to-it attitude to learn about equality, the world would be a better place.

After the paint finally dried, we ended up looking like this:

And we wondered why we didn't get laid. We were fucking terrifying. Please note that we WERE blue. I swear.

We were ready to hit the town, starting at my friend Rachel's party. Rachel lived in the Warehouse, a gorgeous building that I wanted to live in but couldn't afford. It was the only industrial-looking apartments in all of Chapel Hill, and it was all exposed brick and tall ceilings and magic. It was the type of apartment that I imagined I would be living in once I moved to New York. This was before I realized that it costs about eight hundred dollars a month in New York to live in a walk-in closet with a rat for a roommate.

When we showed up at Rachel's, the party was bumping. It was the perfect place to get our pregame on before hitting Franklin Street. And we needed to pregame *hard* because on previous Halloweens, the street was so packed it was difficult to get into a bar. By the time you made it one block, you were already sobered up. I decided to not take any chances, and so I created the "BarBack."

What's the BarBack, you ask? Well, allow me to explain (cracks neck and knuckles, then clears throat for just a little too long). The BarBack is for the drunk on the go. I took a normal backpack and threw in a waterproof cooler lunch bag filled with ice. Next, I tossed in a shaker and disposable shot glasses. Finally, I threw in the elements of a classic shot: the Kamikaze (vodka, Rose's lime juice, and triple sec). And there it was. Now I wouldn't need to worry about finding a drink, though I should have been concerned about *losing my mind*.

And lose my mind I did. I was so proud of my BarBack invention that I showed it to—and took a shot with—everyone I talked to at Rachel's party. I was handing out shots left and right. I thought I was Tom Cruise in *Cocktail*, except I hadn't accidentally gotten Elisabeth Shue pregnant. At least to my knowledge.

Needless to say I got positively blackout drunk that night. I had spent hours on my costume, only to remember wearing it for about an hour. I *do* very clearly remember sitting on the curb on Franklin Street, throwing up on my white slippers. My poor roommate Erika, who was Smurfette for the night, had to deal with me and she was *pissed*, and understandably so. There is nothing worse than looking forward to something, only to have your idiot friend get too drunk so you have to go home early. I felt terrible. But not as terrible as my brain felt the next morning! Just to paint you a visual: Imagine a girl painted blue, asleep on her kitchen floor, with shrapnel from a Totino's pizza feast all around her. Waking up with cheese on your shoulder is bad enough, but throw in a roommate with a chip on her shoulder and it's brutal.

After an extremely hot forty-minute shower (apparently, just because paint is "washable" does not mean it won't stick to every single arm hair like superglue), I worked up the courage to talk to Erika. I sat nervously in the living room and waited for her to come home from the gym or some other place equally productive, only adding to me feeling like shit. When she finally did come home, we talked it out. I probably cried because that is what I do when I am anxious, violently hungover, and fresh out of Totino's. Plus, we were twenty-one-year-old girls. It's a fact that *every* conversation between twenty-one-year-old girls ends with some sort of tears. She was pissed but quickly got over it, because that is what friends do. She went off to study or do something else super-human in my eyes as I settled in for a marathon of *Trading Spaces*. And then my flip phone rang. It was Rachel calling.

"Mame! You were the hit of the party last night with your Kamikaze shots."

"Oh yeah? That's good to know! 'Cause I took a million of them. I am definitely paying for it today."

"Well, that's not all you'll be paying for. . . ."

She went on to tell me that my blue ass was so drunk that I kept losing my balance and walking into walls. Her beautiful, freshly painted walls were now stained with royal blue.

Nowadays the Smurfs are more popular than ever. Every toy store has an aisle filled with Papa Smurf figurines and Brainy Smurf Trapper Keepers. But what you won't find is that discontinued blue creature who only lived for one night. The legendary Hot Mess Smurf.

"But Mamrie! Where are all the pictures of you when you were a kid?" I can hear you screaming into this book. Look, I couldn't find them. My family doesn't keep organized picture albums to reminisce about by the fireplace. To get any old pics, I have to wade through random shoe boxes with photos just thrown in haphazardly. That is who we are! Don't judge us.

But to make it up to you, here are a few more pics from Halloweens past, specifically college.

My sophomore year, my suitemates and I went as the Royal Tenenbaums. I even had Richie's falcon, Mordecai, a fake chicken painted brown and wired to my arm. Seeeeeeexy.

And here is my senior year of college, when we went as Sexy Tetris. Tetris because that game rules. Sexy because we were wearing it.

Alabama Blizzard

**4 regular tea bags (or you could use flavored,
 whatever tickles your pickle)**
8 oz bourbon
3 oz lemon juice
2 tbsp honey or simple syrup
3 cups frozen peaches

*Put the tea bags into the liquor for 1 hour. Think of the tea
bags as someone in a bad marriage. You don't want them staying in there too long or it's going to end up bitter. Then combine everything in a blender and blend! Add ice or water,
depending on the consistency you want. Ideally, this is served
in a leftover mason jar from your perfect cousin's perfect wedding. Extra point if it has a twine bow. This recipe makes
about four servings, 'cause let's face it, making frozen drinks is
annoying. If you asked for one while I was bartending, I would
shoot you a look so evil that you would've thought I'd just been
asked my weight.*

"Sweet Home Alabama," by Lynyrd Skynyrd, is a southern an-
them. As soon as its iconic guitar riff starts, people start hoot-
ing and hollering without a second thought. There's something
about those down-home lyrics that conjures up memories for people,
like riding down the road in a pickup truck with the summer air
blowing in their hair. For others, it's drinking beer with friends at a
summer barbecue. For me, it's forty hours of community service.

This story, like most that end with the cops, begins with a road trip. And just like any good road trip, it's gonna take a while to get there. So, buckle da fuck up!

It was my sophomore year of college, and fall break was coming up. Unlike spring break, no one gives a shit about fall break. It's the Kelly Rowland to spring break's Beyoncé. It's basically a four-day weekend, so most students just stay on campus. At best you go home and see your folks and make out with your high school boyfriend to reaffirm that you "still got it." But I've never been one to half-ass something, so I decided to make the best of my fall break and road-trip it to Alabama to see my friend Virginia. No, that is not a riddle. A lot of girls in the South are named after states. Even more are named after their mothers' maiden names. You roll up onto a college campus in the South and it's all, "Hollingsworth, hurry up!" or "Don't forget the Solo cups, Scarborough!" I'm personally glad I wasn't named after my mom's maiden name, Mayhall. Mayhall is an adorable name said normally, but when people yell it when they're drunk, they sound like donkeys in heat. It's tough enough being named Mamrie. I never got to have those personalized stickers and pencils that kids coveted. I've never rolled up on a beach souvenir shop and found a tiny surfboard key chain with my name on it. The closest I got was a spoon with Mamie Eisenhower's name on it that my mom added an *R* to. But it wasn't the same as a key chain, not that I needed a key chain as an eight-year-old. I did, however, need a key chain ten years later, when I drove eleven hours south to Tuscaloosa, Alabama. (Go ahead and put on a helmet, 'cause I just busted out a beautiful Segway.)

Yes, I did say eleven hours. Some people might be too intimidated to do a drive this long by themselves, but not me! I love a good road trip . . . and even a bad one like the movie *Road Trip*. I spend half of the drive pretending I'm a VH1 diva and the other half talking out loud to myself. This usually involves telling someone off from days earlier whom I didn't have the balls to tell off in the moment. It's cathartic, and I do it constantly. Why, driving in the car the very morning I wrote this chapter, I told off the wait-ress who'd rolled her eyes at me at Olive Garden last week.

"B'scuuuuse me! Don't put 'unlimited breadsticks' on the menu if you don't mean it! You need to change it to 'five free orders of breadsticks with a side of attitude on the sixth.' Also, bravo on the slogan 'When you're here, you're family,' because I haven't felt this judged since Thanksgiving 1997."

Driving alone also means there is no one to judge the amount of snacks you consume, with the convenient follow-up of no one being able to judge the amount of farts you rip. There are times when I let my farts go so hard in the car that it makes me go the speed limit. Not because I am worried I'll get a speeding ticket. I do it because I am worried I'll be pulled over, roll down the window, and accidentally kill the cop via fart suffocation.

So knowing that I could entertain/exhaust myself in the car, I headed on my one-woman road trip. Eleven hours and five days' worth of sodium later, I rolled into Tuscaloosa completely ex-hausted. I got to Virginia's house and it was a sea of cowboy hats, cutoff jean shorts, and pink plaid shirts tied at the waist. Had I taken a wrong turn and landed in a Daisy Duke cosplay conven-tion? Before I could ask someone where Jessica Simpson was sign-ing head shots, Virginia ran over to me, squealing, and hugged my neck. She was definitely a few games of beer pong deep. Appar-ently, all these people were at her place pregaming for the night's activities.

"Are we going to a Barbie rodeo?"

"No, dude. We're going to a fuckin' Lynyrd Skynyrd concert! They're playing on campus."

"Are you fucking serious?"

"No, I'm fucking Dalton, but I am telling the truth."

She nodded, grinning ear to ear. This was followed by one of those hug-and-jumps in unison while screaming. Virginia had been after Dalton for years. *And* I was about to hear "Sweet Home Alabama" played *in* Alabama. It was perfect timing, like randomly walking up on Jay-Z and Alicia Keys performing "Empire State of Mind" in Central Park. Or going to Venice Beach for the day only to find David Lee Roth busting out a toe-touch and singing "California Girls."* Or being in Rome and saying "When in Rome" after you do anything! I was *all* about hearing "Sweet Home Alabama" in its rightful place. After all, I was raised in North Carolina. Ninety-five percent of radio stations were classic rock.

The news perked me right up, and I joined in the pregame festivities. The show was exactly as expected: a perfect mix of drunk college kids knowing only "Sweet Home Alabama" and older locals calling out for B sides that Skynyrd has never played live. Everyone in the crowd drank enough whiskey to numb the pain of knowing it wasn't the original singer. Granted, the guy has been with them since 1987, but you still always know in the back of your mind it's not the original. Sarah Chalke did a bang-up job as Becky on *Roseanne*, but she was always the replacement Becky.

I proceed to get ripped on whiskey and might've cried a little during "Tuesday's Gone." Once all the lighters were extinguished in the crowd and everyone felt how badly they had burned their fingertips on them, we stopped by a food cart. I was ready to go right to bed after finishing my late-night snack, but Virginia had other plans.

"My sorority is having a mixer! You have to come."

A mixer? *Oof.* For those of you who aren't in college, or the closest you've come to partying in the Greek system is being late-night wasted at a falafel shop, a mixer is a party between a sorority and a fraternity. I had been to one with a friend before, and it felt like fifty arranged marriages meeting for their first dates. The last thing I wanted was to be a cock block between Beauregard and Georgia, or whoever the fuck I would inevitably offend later in the night.

*Katy Perry, you know I love you, girl, and you know I have a special place in my heart for cupcake bras, but Diamond Dave will always be the master of songs about ladies from Cali.

"Come on! The Delta Chi guys are super fun!" she pleaded, seeing the disinterest in my face despite it being currently stuffed with cheese fries.

"The only Delta I want to associate with is Delta Burke."

I knew for a fact that *Designing Women* reruns were coming on at midnight on Lifetime. As much as I wanted to curl up to some quips from Annie Potts, Virginia had a pouty face. She really wanted to go, and I didn't want to be a boring guest, so I caved.

"It'll be fun! We don't have to stay long. And it's not even being held at their house; it's at this random bar a few blocks away."

We got to the mixer and it was just what I'd suspected. Everyone looked exactly the same as a Carolina frat/sorority scene except the accents were slightly thicker. The same clothes, the same jewelry, the same drunk guy named Harrison Edwards IV who was threatening to take his pants off. The only thing that felt foreign was the surroundings. This "bar" felt more like a church's rec building. It was painted-white cinder blocks, wood paneling, and folding tables set up with beer pong. People were playing darts in the corner.*
The bar was already barely stocked, and when I ordered a whiskey ginger, the ginger ale was served out of a two-liter.

I quickly realized that this wasn't a real bar. This was a makeshift bar set up in a random building. They didn't want everyone to have to trek back to the frat house and lose steam, but they also wanted all the underage members to be able to drink without an ID. This was the modern equivalent of a speakeasy. Except instead of the password being "piccadilly saxophone" it would've been a Dave Matthews Band lyric.

And like any good speakeasy, it got busted by the cops. These

---

*Whoever decided that darts are a good game to play in a bar is a goddamn crazy person. If I see there are people playing darts in the same bar as me, I don't care if they are forty yards away—I savor my beer like it's my last, 'cause all I can picture is a dart going straight into my jugular like I'm a lion being tranquilized.

cops were hip to this fake bar game and wanted nothing more than to make a few Delta Whatevers shit their pants in fear their parents might find out about their college-y ways.

"Okay, everybody. When we come around, I want everyone to have their IDs ready!" Officer Okra exclaimed with way too much pride. It's like, dude, you are busting up a beer pong party. There is no need to act like this is *The Wire*.

The officer went through the lineup, examining each Alabama license like it was the Da Vinci Code. When he came to me, I had a slight moment of panic. Did I use my fake ID? Did I even have my real ID? Back at Chapel Hill, I was so used to whipping out my ID that made me a graduate student named Emily who was twenty-four, but here, for once in my college life, I didn't use a fake ID to get into a place. There had been no doorman. I'd never claimed to be twenty-one. There was no drink in my hand when they busted the joint. I was in the clear! So, I confidently handed over my actual North Carolina driver's license showing my real age of nineteen.

The officer scrutinized it and I started to sweat. He looked up at me. "Ma'am, it's obvious you've tampered with this ID."

"That's my real ID, and it says my actual birth date. What's the problem?"

All confidence I'd had two seconds earlier vanished. Had I given him my fake?! All the blood rushed from my face and I turned white as a ghost. Luckily, I naturally have the complexion of a ghost, so I hoped he didn't notice.

Normally in telling this story I might call this cop an asshole and breeze past the embarrassing details, but since I am trying to write an actual truthful book, I will be honest despite the following being more embarrassing than the time I waited in line for seven hours to get lottery *NSync tickets my senior year of high school. This "tampering" that Colonel Mustard Greens was referring to? It was real. And it was born from a desperate moment in college.

You see, during my first two months of college, I was still seventeen and it *sucked*. I really wanted to ~~vote~~ go out dancing at the eighteen-and-older clubs with my roommates and get older boys to buy us fishbowls of blue alcohol. So, one night, in my under-eighteen frustration, I took a thumbtack and tried to scratch out my birthday to say 1981 instead of 1983. As someone who was a bartender for *many* years, I now realize that this is a laughable act, but desperate times call for desperate measures. After a few good scratches, I knew I'd made a mistake and stopped. The license still said my real birth date—it just looked like someone had gone off on it with some sandpaper or stuck it in a rock tumbler. It looked so amateur. It was like rolling into a bank with a novelty check forged by Mickey Mouse and saying you'd just inherited Disney World—pure, stupid desperation.

I couldn't deny it. I was scared when the officer pulled out his little book. I didn't even like to drink Alabama Slammers; now I was going to be thrown in one! I held my breath as he wrote on his little pad. When he was done, he handed me over a ticket for underage drinking. Not that bad! Until I looked and saw there was a court date on it for thirty days after the issue. But that's not all! The officer didn't only serve me a court date and a massive pain in my ass; he took my license.

I begged him not to.

"I'm driving back to North Carolina by myself. Can I please just have my license back?"

"No, ma'am, it's been tampered with."

"But what if I get pulled over and then I'm driving without a license?"

"Don't get pulled over," he told me. Great advice from a so-called enforcer of the law. That was right up there with "Be sure to pull out."

I was bummed. I tried to shake it, but that was the truth. I left Tuscaloosa the next day with a pit in my stomach. And that wasn't from all the consolation biscuits I'd eaten to suffocate my feelings. I drove back to North Carolina carefully, trying my best to not get pulled over, which meant actually doing the speed limit. That eleven-hour drive turns out to be more of a fourteen-hour one when you actually adhere to the law.

Back in my dorm room, my roommates and I all sat around telling each other about our fall breaks.

I vegged out on the couch and had a Gilmore Girls *marathon!*

My sister and I went to the beach for a few days!

My town had the cutest pumpkin festival!

I got a court date!

Their heads all turned to me.

"Who's Court? Court Calhoun from the third floor?"

"No," I corrected them. "Court, like actual court. With a judge and stuff. It's not a big deal," I said, laughing, while pulling out my briefcase-size laptop to look up how strict Alabama laws were. "It'll probably get dropped."

Four weeks later, I convinced my friend Laura to take this weekend trip down to Alabama with me. This was not an easy feat. Unlike my 2.5-GPA ass, Laura had her shit together. Of course, I didn't mind missing class to drive down for my Friday court date. I went to class about as often as an Olympic gymnast gets her period, but I wanted to have a copilot this time. I convinced Laura that we should leave early as fuck on Thursday, then we'd be to Alabama by dinner. That way I could make my Friday court date and we'd have a couple of nights to party in Tuscaloosa before making the trek back for Monday classes.

This is what friends do for each other, guys. In her heart of hearts, Laura probably didn't want to drive twenty-two hours in one weekend so her friend could go to court. But in her Hart that was her friend Mamrie, she knew I'd bug her till she caved. I have family members who wouldn't do that! But she was like, "Adventure! Let's do this."

Of course, I did entice her a little with the prospect of us making it a truly ridiculous time, as I was going to buy a bunch of weed for the road. I know what you're thinking. *Real brilliant, Mamrie. Your plan is to travel with an illegal substance to make a trip to an out-of-state court date more fun. . . .* To that I say, thank you. I thought it was pretty brilliant myself.

We hit the road on a mission. I needed to get down to Tuscaloosa and clear my name, also hopefully not serve any jail time. At this point in the chapter you might be wondering, *Mamrie? Why the hell is this chapter called Alabama Blizzard? Did you seriously miss your court date because there was a fluke blizzard in October in the Deep South?*

Close! We almost missed my court date because Laura and I hit many blizzards on our way down. . . . Dairy Queen Blizzards.

If you aren't familiar with this American classic, the Blizzard is the original McFlurry. It's ice cream blended with toppings, and it is *beautiful*. It takes away the pressure of having to make the perfect ice-cream bite by incorporating the toppings into the soft serve. I do realize that is the most privileged sentence I have ever written.

We hit the road with a vengeance and a quarter ounce of weed. Weed—spoiler alert—gives you the munchies, and my friend Laura has the biggest sweet tooth of anyone I've ever met in my life. When we went to the dining hall, she would make it a point to show us how many desserts she could eat, stacking up the small white Styrofoam containers like they were plates at those sushi places with the conveyor belts. When we went to see the remake of *Charlie and the Chocolate Factory* and Augustus Gloop fell into the choc river, Laura screamed out, "Amateur!" Way too loudly, I might add.

With Laura's and my sweet teeth in tow, we made it all of forty miles before we were stopping for a treat. First place we saw was a Dairy Queen—no-brainer. We walked in, both trying not to look stoned, which was basically impossible. When the sweet-faced high school girl said, "Hi, what can I get y'all today?" I fell out laughing like I'd just heard the world's funniest joke.

"Sorry," I said, still cranking out some Mamrie mumbles, which is basically me laughing without opening my mouth, "thought of something from earlier."

Luckily, Laura took over. "We'll just take one large Oreo Blizzard."

We'd decided before going in—so intensely that you would think we were politicians in a war room—that we would just split one. There was a long road ahead of us and we didn't need to be gluttonous.

"Y'all want this to go, right?" the sweet-faced high school girl said to us, sticking two spoons in our Blizzard.

"Yes, ma'am," we said, visions of Oreos dancing in our heads.

"Okay, then," she said, walking toward us. That's when the unthinkable happened: She flipped our Blizzard, our precious, precious Oreo Blizzz, upside down. Laura gasped. What was she *doing* with our dessert? My instincts kicked in and I started to put my hands underneath it to catch it. I just stood there with my hands out like a firefighter who's about to catch a baby from a burning building. But to our ~~horror~~ delight, the Blizzard was staying in place. We looked on at this cherub-faced fifteen-year-old holding our ice cream upside down, monotonously counting out loud to three before flipping it back upright.

"There y'all go. Enjoy," she said, handing it to us like it was no big deal. I slowly reached out and took the Blizzard, not knowing how to respond. Once back in the car, Laura spoke first.

"Da *fuck* was that?"

"I have *no* idea!" I said, shoveling Blizzard into my mouth. I knew I needed to get as much in as possible before handing it to Laura, as we were both superfast eaters. Our other friends refused to split apps with us because they knew we would be licking the ramekin of marinara from the mozzarella sticks clean before they were finished putting their napkins on their laps.

She motioned for me to hand back the Blizzard, then said with a mouthful of Oreos, "I don't know what just happened, but I do know I'm gonna want another one of these in a hundred miles."

And she wasn't lying. Halfway into South Carolina, we stopped for another Blizzard. Sure enough, the girl flipped it upside down with a completely blank expression, counting out loud to three.

Once back in my Accord, we ate our Blizzard in silence. We sat there dumbfounded, passing the Blizzard back and forth. Mind you, this was before smartphones. We couldn't just google "What the fuck kind of Blizzard mantra does Dairy Queen do" to calm our stoned-as-a-goat brains down. No, no. We didn't know what was happening, we needed to know, and we were too high to ask.

The only thing we could do was cross another state line and get another Blizzard. By God, this mystery would be solved! At this point, though, we weren't very hungry. We'd already split two Blizzards. Cut to us smoking some more weed.

By the time we spotted our first DQ in Georgia, I was so high that I was laughing at the local radio commercials like it was a Dave Chappelle album. Inside, I thought a fat kid eating a banana split was funny. I thought I was going to pee my pants because of a woman's shirt that read I'VE GOT CATTITUDE. We walked up to order our Blizzard, our eyes looking like albino rabbits'.

"Hey there, ma'am. We will take one large Oreo Blizzard," Laura told the teenage boy who was so pissed he was working at the DQ instead of at the skate park.

I was standing behind Laura laughing so hard that zero volume was coming out of my mouth. I looked like I was screaming with the mute button on. "Mamrie, you have to get it together or they'll call the po-po," Laura whispered loudly at me.

"You called him 'ma'am,'" I said, wiping tears from my eyes.

"I did not. . . . I did? Son of a biscuit," she said, laughing with me at this point. Unamused, our DQ employee told us that our Blizzard was ready. "Moment of truth."

"Here you go." He handed us our Blizzard. We stopped our giggling immediately. Our faces went blank as we stared at him, waiting for him to do the flip. "Are you going to take it?" he asked us, completely confused. Laura reached out slowly, taking the Blizzard from him like candy from a stranger.

Back in the car, we ate our Blizzard in silence. The only noise was our stomachs. After eating one and a half Blizzards each, they sounded like whales giving birth. So much for that whole "not being gluttonous on this trip" idea. I was so full, I was literally short of breath. I went to unbutton my pants and they were already undone. Then came the paranoia.

"We weren't imagining the first two flips, right?" I said, genuinely concerned.

"We couldn't have. There's no way."

"Did we get *Training Day*ed? Did we imagine it?"

"Mamrie. We did not get *Training Day*ed. We are stoned."

We continued down the road for a while, bellies aching from the amount of dairy coursing through our guts. These days if I ate three *bites* of a Blizzard, that Blizzard would turn into a tornado of farts.

Three more hours down the road and we were finally crossing the Alabama state line. I couldn't let go of what we had witnessed, though. The truth was out there and I needed to find it.*

"We gotta get one more Blizzard."

"Are you crazy?!" Laura asked me, already knowing the answer.

"Maybe I am. But we gotta crack the mystery of the Blizzard. A Blizzard in every state." She looked at me like she might puke. After a deep inhale, she held her hand out like Thelma reaching for Louise before they drive over the cliff. I placed the freshly packed bowl in her hand, cranked up the music, and went in for our last round.

I felt like I had just given the pep talk in *Rudy*, but instead of the outcome being a hardworking kid getting a shot, it was two girls getting stoned and eating way too much ice cream. We walked into that Dairy Queen like we owned the place. In my mind there were wind machines and AC/DC playing, but in reality it was just fluorescent lighting and easy listening. I'm pretty sure I palmed a small child's face to get him out of my way as we headed directly to the register.

---

*For those keeping track, you can also add *The X-Files* to the list of Things Mamrie Is Irrationally Terrified Of.

Laura took the lead. "Hiiii."

"Yes, you are," the judgy teenager behind the counter said, too proud of his joke. I stood a few feet back from the register with my arms folded across my chest like I was the bouncer at Marquee (or a really pouty Michelle Tanner). We wanted answers, and nobody was getting in the way of it.

"We will take one large Oreo Blizzard, please," Laura said, looking over her shoulder as we nodded at each other slowly. From a distance it must've looked like we were about to rob the DQ and were just *verrrrry* bad at it. The snarky teenager rolled his eyes and headed to make our treat. Laura joined me a few feet back from the register and also folded her arms. Nothing to see here. Just two extremely high college girls who think they are in the Secret Service.

After what seemed like a lifetime, he came to the counter holding a freshly whipped Blizzard. We approached the counter like it was a roulette table and we had just put all our money on red.

"Here you go, one Oreo Blizzard," he said, holding it out to us. Then, right before we could grab the cup, he flipped it over. It felt like it was in slow motion, but again, I had smoked more weed and eaten more sugar in the past eight hours than I had in my entire life. He started counting. "One Mississippi . . . two Mississippi . . . thr—"

Splat!

We looked down in horror, mouths agape. The teenager looked back and forth between the dumped Blizzard and us, until his manager walked up, a scowl on his face.

"Chad, that's five this week. Go get some rags and clean up this mess." Chad skirted away as the DQ manager reached out and shook our hands. "Well, looks like that Blizzard wasn't thick enough for you. I'll be right back with your prize."

Prize? We were still totally fuckin' baked and thus extremely confused. But who cares? Prizes are always fun! I don't care if it's a temporary tattoo out of a cereal box or *The Price Is Right*'s showcase showdown that's only a tacky dining room set, a year's worth of Woolite, and a portable outdoor sauna. Laura and I held hands, awaiting our inevitable diamond tiaras that read THE DAIRY QUEENS or keys to the franchise à la Willy Wonka.

"Sorry for the wait, ladies. I wanted to pick you out a good one."

A good one? You mean, you had trouble deciding between the pink and yellow Jeeps? Determining if we got the trip to Lake Havasu or Miami? Writing us a million-dollar novelty-size check or a regular-size check to keep it classy?

We looked up to see this man, the hope for our new life, with a shit-eatin' grin, holding a massive Oreo ice-cream cake.

"Here's your Oreo Blizzard ice-cream cake! Enjoy!"

What the actual fuck. We would soon learn that DQ was running a promotion that said if your Blizzard wasn't thick enough, the customer could win a free cake. So that flipping and weird counting? Some boss's idea of being a real showboat to the customers. Benihana has their onion volcano, and I guess Dairy Queen wanted a little flare too. *However*, it was up to the franchise owner's discretion, which explained the one in Georgia not doing it. What was never explained, and what I'll always wonder, is how after driving through three states and having eaten a bucket of Blizzard each . . . Laura and I ate the majority of that ice-cream cake as we rolled into Tuscaloosa.

The rest of the trip was full of surprises. We got to Tuscaloosa and were so sick that we couldn't go out drinking or have any fun. Laura and I stayed in and watched *Friday* as Virginia and all her friends went out. When I got to court, I was terrified. I felt like I was going to shit my pants but knew it was just an aftereffect of consuming two gallons of ice cream the day before.

I ended up getting forty hours of community service for my charge, which I spent picking up trash and cleaning up elementary schools in my home county over Thanksgiving break. It was embarrassing, sure—but not as embarrassing as explaining how I managed to gain seven pounds on a three-day road trip.

Up in Smoke

2 oz dark crème de cacao
2 oz Baileys Irish Cream
3 oz vanilla vodka

For the rim: Freeze an extra-dark chocolate bar, then grate it very finely. Mix half chocolate dust, half smoked sea salt. Dip the rim in chocolate syrup, then dip it in the choco-salt mixture.

Combine all your booze into a shaker full of ice. Shake as hard as you can to attempt to burn a few of the many calories you are about to consume with this decadent drink. Strain into a chilled martini glass. Calmly proceed to have mind blown.

Don't worry. This chapter is not three thousand words about my undying love for Cheech & Chong. The courts told me that would be a violation of the restraining order. Instead this is a celebratory drink in honor of quitting a bad habit. Cheech, I wish I knew how to quit you.

The summer before I moved to New York was spent on the Outer Banks with Melissa, my Topless Tuesday cofounder and overall hell partner in crime. Her mom was nice enough to let me crash in the guest room of their beautiful beach house. It was situated right on a golf course, which I couldn't imagine growing up on. The closest hole to my childhood home was the one my next-door neighbors dug in their yard, filled with a hose, and called an inground pool.

I waited tables all summer at a seafood joint. Little did I know that this would actually be helpful training for when I would work at that seafood place in New York. And thank God I didn't know, because that would've killed my postcollege optimism! While I was making customers believe that our tuna was to die for (never tasted tuna in my life), Melissa worked in the costume department for a historical play called *The Lost Colony*.

But when I had actually had a night off and Melissa was free from hemming loincloths, we were throwing parties. That is, when her mom went out of town. Lucky for us, Melissa's mom, Marie, is a complete hoot (it's where Melissa gets it from) and went on trips with her girlfriends often. True story: One time we threw a massive mojito party at her place and the next day Marie decided to come home early. It was basically that scene from *Weird Science* where the place is trashed and gets cleaned up in a rewind, fast-motion tornado. I'm almost positive the classic '80s "pick up a pizza box off the floor to find a passed-out partygoer underneath" move happened. By the time Mama Marie walked through the door, the place was *sparkling*. We totally got away with it! That is, until Marie noticed that her entire *huge* mint bush in the yard was mysteriously missing and she went all Italian mother on me.* And when Italians get mad, it's on a whole different level. The first time I saw Melissa lose her temper I basically ran a tornado drill.

I digress (also, I just had to google "I digress" to make sure I've been using that phrase right for the past ten years). The point of this chapter is not to tell you about what a *horrible* houseguest I was in the mid-2000s. The point is . . . going to happen at some point in this chapter. Back off.

So, these were the months leading up to my big transition to New York. Now, a rational person would spend the summer hitting the gym before hitting the audition scene. But I am *not* a ra-

---

*I adore you, Marie, and I'm sorry about that one time I bought your teenage son beer.

tional person. I'm a rash of a person, at best. I decided to take a different route. In my head, I was about to be too broke to afford food. As soon as I got to the city, the pounds were just going to slide off me. I was going to be a *starving artist*. I was preparing for a total bohemian lifestyle. It was going to be just like *Rent* but with slightly less AIDS. So, I decided to consciously spend the summer packing on some extra pounds.

That's right. I gained weight—on purpose. I prepared for that move like a bear prepares for hibernation, just getting a good ol' basecoat of blubber that would, no doubt, melt off as I ran to catch subway trains and 20-percent-off Bed Bath & Beyond coupons blowing in the wind.

In my head, I was gonna be a goddamn waif by Christmas. You know how in the movie *Se7en* Brad Pitt finds that guy who's starved to death in bed and then he just pops up and scares the shit out of you? That was *goal* weight.

When I was really stoned that summer, which was most of it, and stuffing my face with mozzarella sticks, I'd turn to Melissa and declare, "I'm about to be a starving artist, dammit. I'm doing this for my health!" This, of course, was met with her rolling her eyes so hard that you'd expect one of her eyeballs to pop out like a pug's.

Summer came to a close and I quit the waitressing job that I'd gotten by promising I would stick around after the summer. I didn't have time to explain the catch-of-the-day specials to tourists anymore—I was off to make my NYC dreams come true!

There was one part of my big-city fantasy that was true: I was poor. Besides a duffel bag of clothes, the only possessions I moved to New York with were an air mattress with a hole in it and two cartons of cigarettes. And as we all remember, three hundred bucks and an out-of-control roommate.

For my first few weeks in New York I slept on that deflated air mattress, folded in half, with a sheet over me. That is about as comfortable as sleeping on a pool float that has been ripped to shreds by a pit bull. I would lie on the uneven hardwood floors of my room and say to myself, "I bet this is exactly what female comedy icon Julia Louis-Dreyfus had to do when she first moved to New York." I'd smile to myself before remembering that JLD actually came from a family of billionaires.

Then I'd go take my fifth hot bath of the night because our landlord refused to fix the heat and I didn't want my tears to turn to ice.

The saddest part about this visual is that I would actually bring guys back to this pathetic scene. (*Rutabaga!*) I don't just mean someone I hit it off with from a bar down the street. I'm talking about someone I met in the East Village and would allow to take a thirty-dollar cab or hour-long subway all the way into Brooklyn, only to see that the charming girl in the cute vintage dress lived in squalor. Lord knows for that trek these guys must've thought I lived in an expansive Dumbo Loft that my daddy had bought me. That, or that they were gonna get laid. Either way, they would be left sorely disappointed (sore because sleeping on hardwood will do a number on your back).

There was one particular post–drunk hookup morning when I realized I might want to rein it in a little bit. After a typical night of sweaty dancing on Avenue A, I brought a hot guy back to my place, another sad notch on my make-out belt—a belt that was getting long enough to fit pre–Subway Jared. The next morning, he rode the subway into Manhattan with me. A risky move, but I had to go to work and he insisted on escorting me in.

He was way into me, saying things like:

Mamrie, we should totally go to the MoMA this weekend.

So, Mamrie, where do you want me to take you to dinner Friday?

I nodded and listened to him, all the while thinking to myself, *I have no idea what your name is. Is it Joseph? Naw. Josephs don't have lip piercings. Oh good God, did you have a lip piercing last night? UGH. Maybe it's Joe. Joe seems like a common New York name.*

I took a break from my inner monologue to see that Dude was looking at me, concerned. The train climbed the Manhattan Bridge as the morning sun glistened on his lip ring. I decided to come clean.

"Look, I think you are great. You are super cute and I'd love to hang out with you again, but I need to admit something. I have no idea what your name is."

He looked hurt. Fuck, it was Joe. I should've just called him Joe. Before I could apologize to Joe, he spoke.

"My name is Scorpion."

. . .

. . .

I waited for him to laugh at his own joke. He sat there deadpan. Who was this comedy genius keeping a straight face after that? What kind of a nightmare would it be if I had actually brought a dude home who goes by Scorpion? That is when I realized that he wasn't joking, and I needed to pump the brakes on hooking up out of boredom.

After all, I was in New York! There were plenty of other things I could do for fun. The *Friends* gang never watched TV, but they loved watching Ugly Naked Guy through his window. Could voyeurism be my new entertainment? Ya damn right it could.

And that is when my smoking really turned up a notch. Instead of going out, I would sit in the bay window of my empty living room, chain-smoking and drinking ten-dollar magnums of Yellow Tail chardonnay. I'd watch the "A Bum Talking to Pigeons" show. If the bum decided to pull his wiener out, I would change the channel and watch the "Old Lady in the Adjacent Apartment Yelling at Her Husband" hour. After a month of this, my tobacco well ran dry. So, I quit cold turkey.

But, here's the deal, guys. I was a *smoker*. I wasn't a smoker for a long time, but for that brief moment in time, it was hard-core. Like Romeo and Juliet's love. The romance between me and Parliament Lights was so intense that it quickly burned out. But who could blame me? I grew up outside of Winston-Salem, North Carolina. And if you know nothing about that town, you still know that's two brands of cigarettes with a hyphen in between them. Cigarettes are, like, free there.

In fact, no shit, I went to the R.J. Reynolds cigarette factory as my fifth-grade field trip. Picture a group of thirty ten-year-olds shuffling through a cigarette factory. *Look, children, this is where they make the menthols.* And the kids go, *Ohhhhhh.* Everyone smoked. And everywhere. You could smoke while picking out a new hose at Walmart or let your ashes fall into your scattered, covered, and smothered hash browns at Waffle House. It didn't matter. What did matter is cigs were eleven bucks a pack in NYC.

The week of quitting also happened to be the same week I landed a job. Things were looking up! Maegan was still managing the recording studio and had an open receptionist spot. It was a revolving door of celebrities and also had an air hockey table. You know the type. I loved the people there and the prestige of saying, "Yeah, I work at a recording studio. It's like, okay, or whatever."

All the glamour aside, truth be told, the pay was shit. I was making eight bucks an hour. That's before taxes and with an eight-hundred-dollar rent. Needless to say, I worked every possible second of overtime I could eke out and still barely broke even.

Luckily for me, my responsibilities weren't exclusive to answering the phone and ordering celebs' lunch. (Hello? Have you ever ordered *American Idol* Season 2 winner Ruben Studdard a *Reuben* sandwich? The man stays on brand.) No, no. There was one other line in my job description that really changed the game for me.

And that, my friends, was being in charge of the candy dish. Pardon me, the two candy dishes. First, there was the classic old-school dish. You had your butterscotches, your peppermints, those strawberry candies that have the splooge in the middle. It was a senior-center panty dropper of a candy dish. But then we had the chocolate dish to class up the place. I'm talking Hershey's Miniatures, mothafuckas. Tiny Kit Kats, tiny Reese's cups. Hershey's

Nuggets Special Dark. *All* the top names. Of course, there was also a constant stream of the classic miniatures like Mr. Goodbar and Krackel.*

It was my responsibility to keep these dishes stocked. I had the coveted key to the snack closet that held the arsenal of treats. Now, before we start judging, please know that it started off so innocently. I would have a couple of pieces of chocolate here and there.

Oh, I better grab a mini–York Pattie; I've got coffee breath!

It's only three o'clock? I'll just take one Hershey's Dark to curb my appetite for a healthy dinner.

Hi, Sharon! Have you lost weight? I'm gonna eat a 3 Musketeers in your honor! HAHAHAHAHAHAHA . . . Sharon?

And that's when shit derailed. I quickly learned that I could survive solely off this candy during the day and not have to spend money on groceries. Which helped, since I was more broke than Owen Wilson's nose. But what kind of person wants to eat chocolate all damn day? I'll tell you who. A person who just quit smoking a pack of cigs a day, cold turkey.

My intake of candy went off the charts. I was eating so many miniature candy bars that I would actually stick my hand deeper in the trash can to hide the wrappers. I didn't want the shiny evidence sitting there on top.

I remember being in a client-services meeting and my boss saying, "Guys, seriously, we are going through, like, four hundred percent more chocolate than we normally do. What's the deal?" That's when I sheepishly raised my hand and admitted that the FedEx guy helped himself to two handfuls a day.†

This terrible diet lasted through the entire winter. Whatever

---

*Krackel bars come only in those bags of miniature candy, right? There aren't normal-size Krackel bars sold on candy shelves. So, riddle me this, how the hell is it a miniature? If it's the only kind, wouldn't a miniature be the size of a Tic Tac? Boom. In your fucking face, Milton S. Hershey.

†*Not true.* Sorry, FedEx Gary.

money I saved on food was being spent on larger pants, but I couldn't help myself. At this point, I was addicted. I've always scoffed at those stupid magnets and aprons about "chocoholism." You know the ones. They've got a doodled grandma in sunglasses saying, "Hand over the chocolate, and no one gets hurt!" But there I was, slowly turning into the live-action version of a *Cathy* comic. ACK!

Winter in New York finally let up, and it was spring. Melissa was graduating from college, and I thought it would be super fun to surprise her. So, I hopped on a Greyhound bus to Chapel Hill.

Now, if you've never had the pleasure of riding on a Greyhound bus before, oh man, you've got to try it. The sights (people fighting), the smells (someone trying to smoke weed in the bathroom mixed with undertones of Chinese food) . . . it's unlike any experience you've ever had. For some reason people assume that being on a Greyhound is like being on international waters, and common laws don't apply. If you're extra lucky you can even have your cell phone stolen out of your lap while you're sleeping, which is precisely what happened to me!

After thirteen hours of breathing through my nose, the bus finally pulled into the station. My friend Chrissie picked me up knowing that Melissa would soon be coming over to retrieve the graduation gift that I'd "sent" to Chrissie's. An hour later, I was crouched in a wrapped box waiting to pop out. I'm gonna be brutally honest with you guys—*I live for this shit.* I love surprising people! Specifically, with *myself* as the prize. I would totally be one of those strippers who pops out of cakes if I trusted myself not to eat said cake. Before I knew it, I was jumping out of the box, screaming, "Surprise!" And let me tell you, Melissa was *shocked.* She immediately started crying and hugging me, jumping up and down. Finally, she pulled away, ready to speak.

Wiping away a tear, she looked me in the eyes and said, "You got fat!" And you know what, guys? I couldn't even blame her. I had. I had gained twenty-five pounds in five months of tiny chocolate bars. *Twenty-five pounds.* I still looked like myself. But I also looked like I had a bee allergy and had just been stung by a bee eighty times. All that "starving artist" talk from the summer before was laughable.

There I was, back in my home state, with all its incredible southern cuisine, feeling like the Michelin Man. In true NC style, Melissa was throwing a pig pickin' for her graduation party. For you folks who didn't grow up in a town that takes cigarette factory field trips, a "pig pickin'" is when you bring in a pitmaster to roast an entire pig in your backyard.

You know how when you are packing a little extra padding you get self-conscious about pigging out in front of people? For someone who was feeling fat and hadn't eaten meat in thirteen years, obviously I . . . *ate seven pounds of pork that day.* Yep! I had some vegetarian mental break and said, "Fuck it. I'm gonna eat some fuckin' pork." I was like the Tasmanian Devil with BBQ flying everywhere. I literally *pigged* out.

The rest of the weekend was amazing! I made plenty of jokes about my weight and how it was all from candy, and how that made me one step closer to my dream of being John Candy. I knew that when I got back to NYC, I was going to have to cut off the rampant choco-addiction cold turkey. And guess what? I did. And then I gained thirty pounds solely off Fritos. I kid! It was only five pounds.

In the end, I learned a lot about myself that first winter in New York—a lot about my addictive personality, my perseverance, and my ability to cut things off. But probably the most important thing I learned was . . . Don't eat a shit-ton of pork for the first time in a decade right before a fourteen-hour bus ride home.

Flaming Sips

1 oz gin
1 oz grapefruit juice
½ oz chili simple syrup
Champagne

To make the chili syrup, simply take one red Fresno chili and slice it in half lengthwise, removing the seeds. Throw that into a saucepan on the stovetop with 1 cup of water and 1 cup of sugar until the sugar is totally dissolved. Let it simmer for 5 minutes or so, until the spice level is to your liking.

Add the gin, grapefruit juice, and chili syrup to a champagne flute. Top with bubbly, then take that flute to the face like an overeager band geek.

You can't ring in the New Year without a big glass of brut. Or fourteen glasses of bubbly. This champ of champagnes gives your taste buds a little kick and might even help you slow down on the drinking.

Oh wait, we add extra booze to the bubbly. Never mind!

Y

Throughout my life there have been lots of things that I've set the bar really high for, only to end up being disappointed. Like losing my virginity, or the end of every episode of *House Hunters*. But the number one fail is always New Year's Eve.

When I was a little girl and would try my hardest to stay up till midnight, sipping my sparkling apple juice, I used to fantasize about what New Year's Eve would be like once I was a grown-up. I had visions of looking fabulous in a cute new dress, holding a glass of champagne as all my closest friends count down: three . . . two . . . one. Then the handsome gentleman I've been talking to all night dips me, planting the hottest kiss ever on my lips as fireworks explode in the air. We come up from the dip, and I say, "What's that for?" He strokes my cheek and says, "Because I still can't believe you're my wife."

Boom! See, you thought he was a stranger but he was my husband. You just got Shyamalaned.

Alas, there is no magical kiss. No fireworks. Hell, there ain't even a cute dress. Most New Year's Eves in adulthood you end up getting into a random fight with a friend and leaving the party barefoot, then wake up with a week-old Chipotle burrito in your bed and the super-embarrassing apology texts you sent said friend opened on your phone. It always struck me as odd that on NYE you make resolutions for the coming year and everyone gets all excited that *next* year will be *the* year. Then you spend the first day of the new, exciting year hungover and eating food so greasy you can't snap your fingers for a week.

New Year's Eve celebrations in college are no good, either. You want to spend the holiday with all your new best friends at school, but it's winter break, so you have to go home. This usually means trying to plan a big NYE with the high school friends you haven't seen since that week you were home over summer break. There's too much pressure to have fun! And too much pressure to laugh at your old friends' new stories about puking in some quad that you've never heard of.

New Year's Eve my freshman year kicked off the streak. My high school girlfriends and I wore matching denim catsuits, so you know we meant business. In my defense, I was eighteen years old and "Love Don't Cost a Thing" was at the top of the charts.*

---

*I never understood the lyrics "If I wanna floss, I got my own." I get that *floss* means "to flaunt," but to me it always just sounded like J.Lo was dating a neglectful orthodontist.

With our blue-jean camel toes in tow, we headed down to Charlotte, North Carolina, the nearest big city to our little town, Boonville. But truth be told, any town with a handful of stoplights (and
a Melting Pot. Hellooo!) felt like Gotham compared to my little
hometown speck on the map. We had a perfect party-hopping itin-
erary, but there was one tiny detail we didn't plan: where we were
going to sleep. Charlotte is a good hour and a half from Boonville.

So! We did what any modern, independent women would do.
We called our mildly attractive guy friends who lived in Charlotte
and paired off. Now, before you go judging (leave that to Judy—
hey, Judy!), it's not as terrible as it sounds. We didn't dole out hand
jobs to crash on a dirty futon.* It was all innocent make-out stuff,
and truth be told, we had all already kissed our respective pairings
at some point or another in high school. This was just a victory lap
of sorts. Necking down memory lane, if you will.

Now, readers, let me take this moment to offer you a bit of advice. Do *not*, under any circumstances, kiss someone at midnight
you don't like, unless you are *certain* he doesn't like you either.
'Cause if you think you are having a random tongue war and he
actually has a crush on you, that motherfucker will look at you
with such sadness the next day, you'd think you had just taken his
virginity. But that's what happens on New Year's Eve. There is a
different romantic pressure put on your inaugural kiss of the year.
It's not just a regular ol' smooch. It's an honor. So if it's going to be
meaningless for you, double-check that the lack of feeling is mu-
tual.

That year I made the mistake of not asking, and woke up to my
friend Chris *watching me sleep. Awwwww, that's so sweet!* you might
say. No! Watching someone sleep is not sweet; it's creepy. The only
reason for watching someone sleep is if you are a first-time parent
making sure your newborn is still breathing, or if you're a hospice

---

*Everyone knows a New Year's Eve hand job should be rewarded with
at least lunch at Fuddruckers or a Bath & Body Works gift card.

nurse—that is, unless death is involved, don't be creepin' on my sleepin'.

I opened my eyes to Chris staring at me, which was bad enough, but then he followed it up by asking me, "Want some gummy bears?" The man was eating gummy bears and watching me sleep.

From there, the New Year's Eves only got worse. Sophomore year we ended up sleeping in a car after getting lost looking for a field party for four hours. Junior year my friend took one bong rip at a party and thought her anus had turned into a tail. She refused to leave the bathroom because she thought people would see said "ass tail." Then I held her hair back while she puked up cupcakes as everyone else outside the bathroom watched the ball drop.

By the time it got to be my senior year, I was determined to break the cycle. I told my high school friends that I would have to sit out Charlotte that year. Instead, I was going to head to the New Year's Eve capital of the world: New York City. Not only that, but I was going to bring crazy ass Melissa. Not only *that*, I had also gotten tickets to see the Flaming Lips at Madison Square Garden. And *not only that*, but I had hired a limo to drive us! That last part isn't true; I just got caught up in trying to top myself. There was a plan, and goddammit, it was going to be a trip for the ages! Little did I know just how much of a trip it would be.*

Melissa was the ideal travel partner for this epic New Year's Eve. She was the type of friend who picks you up to go buy craft supplies at Michaels and drops you off with a tiger tattoo and a new boyfriend named Roscoe. The only problem was that it was the day after Christmas when I came up with this plan. I gave her a ring, praying she could do it.

At this point, in the mid-2000s, people had these things called ringback tones. You'd call your friend and instead of having to lis-

---

*Foreshadowing, kids. And I ain't talking about a kind of makeup technique.

ten to the same boring ringing sound that's been playing since the Alexander Graham Bell days, you got to hear a song! And Melissa always had the best songs.

I was breaking it down to "2 Legit 2 Quit" when she finally answered. "What up, bitch!"

"Hey . . . so . . . I have an idea for New Year's. It's totally cool if you aren't up for it but I got tickets for the Flaming Lips at MSG. Want to make the trek? . . . Melissa? Melissa, did you hang up on me?" I was offended for a minute until she let me know she had dropped the phone and was doing her end zone dance in celebration. The plan was set. We were going to meet in Chapel Hill super early on New Year's Eve day and drive up together. I also got my camp counselor friend Hayley (a.k.a. Ride 'em Cowboy) to grab a ticket and join our adventure.

With the top down on her Volvo convertible—big mistake, it was December—we hit the road. According to the map (this is pre–Google Maps! How ancient!), it was going to take us around eleven hours to get there. It probably could've taken nine, but I went ahead and factored in stopping at three or four Sonics for Texas Toast grilled cheese, since Melissa was bringing weed.

Where we were actually going to sleep when we got to New York, we had no idea. I called up Hayley to see if she had any suggestions. Her "Push It" ringback blasted in my ear.

"Hey, girl, it's Mame."

"Mamie. Get your tight ass over here." Hayley was already there with friends.

"We just got on the road, dude. But I wanted to see where y'all were staying. Meltdown and I don't have a sleeping plan yet."

"Stay here with us, ya dumbass. There's a bunch of us crashing."

"I don't want to intrude. . . ."

"You won't be intrudin'. You'll be rudin' if you *don't* get your ass here. They gave us this huge weird room. Someone must've been murdered in here or something. Anyway, you and Melissa can sleep on the floor."

A weird massive room crammed with a ton of people and a possible history of homicide? *I was in.* It might sound like sketch central as an adult, but to a broke college student with nowhere to stay in Manhattan, I felt like Pretty Woman. Except I *would* be kissing on the mouth.

When we got there, everyone was so happy to see us—and not just because we came with four grocery bags filled with shitty champagne. Everyone was so happy to see us because they were all on drugs. I forgot to mention that these were my hippie friends, and their drug of choice was mushrooms.

Hayley swung open the door with, "Mamie! I'm tripping ballzzzz," then planted a huge kiss on me.

"Of course you are, crazy!" I hugged her neck as she led us into the *Dateline NBC* suite.

"I want some mushrooms!" Melissa said, going right to the guy in the room who had them like a heat-seeking missile. Oh Lord, if everyone else was going to be on drugs, I figured I might as well get drunk, so I cracked open a bottle of champagne and didn't bother putting it in a cup. I had always wanted to try mushrooms before. I'd been around my friends when they'd eaten them, and I knew it wasn't that crazy. They would just draw in coloring books and stare at a neon Natty Light sign for four hours.

But I get really nervous about trying new things like that. I've never even taken a Vicodin for pain. I double-check the label every time I take Advil for cramps, for God's sake. Even though I was intrigued, I wasn't ready to dive in, so instead I sipped my five-dollar bottle of pink André and watched Melissa as she ate them.

If this had been a roomful of people on acid instead of mushrooms, I would've booked it the hell out of there. People recount acid stories like Vietnam vets recount flashbacks. It's rarely pretty. You never hear:

And then the flowers looked super huge and all the pinks were so *pink and I realized my face hurt 'cause I had been smiling for seven hours.*

It's always:

So then the fire started crawling out of the fireplace toward me but luckily the walls were covered in blood so I knew it wouldn't burn the house down and so I just wrapped myself up in a giant omelet and counted the ghosts in the room.

I wasn't going anywhere near that stuff! To this day I am terrified that someone is going to slip me acid "as a joke." I don't even eat those dissolving breath-freshening sheets.

But mushrooms? I was intrigued. Everyone looked so smiley and like they were having the *best* time.

And this is where I'm gonna throw a big ol' *rutabaga* on the field!

I caved. This was the New Year's Eve when I tried mushrooms.

I probably wouldn't have done it if they were the gross, dried-out-looking 'shrooms I'd seen before. These mushrooms, though? They were chopped up into tiny pieces and put into homemade Reese's cups. They were even wrapped up in gold foil. It was like a Pinterest board for hallucinogens come to life.

Before I tell you just how amazing it was, let me take this moment as a quick PSA about drug use. I do not condone it. I do not promote it. And I do not suggest it. Seriously. I don't think drugs are cool. I saw that episode of *Saved by the Bell* where Jessie gets addicted to caffeine pills. I am always *so excited*, I don't need pills for it! However, as a twenty-one-year-old adult, I felt like experimenting and felt safe in this group of friends. Did I mention that two of them were almost through nursing school? Hayley actually worked the freak-out tents at music festivals, so if there was anyone to try a drug around, it was her.

As I sat there rationalizing in my head why this was a totally cool idea and how it was going to set this New Year's Eve apart from all the shit ones before, someone grabbed my wrist. "Take it easy, Mamie," Hayley said, lowering my hand, which was full of mushroom chocolates. I'd been inhaling them as I was lost in thought. What can I say? I'm a sucker for the chocolate and peanut butter combo. I had forgotten there were even drugs in them and was just satiating my sweet tooth.

If I'd eaten to my heart's content, it would've been bad. I would've been walking down Broadway three hours later, eating lasagna with my hands and thinking I was the Garfield Thanksgiving Day Parade balloon. Luckily, Hayley had stopped me, and I waited anxiously for the effects to kick in. By the time we were ready to head out, I had housed the champagne and couldn't tell if I was just a lil' drunk or feeling the mushrooms yet.

According to my pupils, I *was* feeling it.

Everyone except Melissa, Hayley, and I was going to see their favorite third-tier jam band, the Disco Biscuits. While I give the band kudos for the great name, the actual show was highly lacking in both disco and biscuits and so it wasn't for me. Plus, we three troublemakers were seeing the mo'fu'in' *Flaming Lips*!

As soon as we left the room, I immediately felt a tingling sensation throughout my body. The walls of the hotel looked like they were pulsating a little. They looked like how a didgeridoo sounds, if that makes sense, but I know it doesn't, so fuck it. The floral-print carpet that I hadn't even noticed coming into the hotel became *so* vibrant. The designs in it were ever-so-slightly moving. It was literally a magic carpet. I could've stayed in that hotel hallway and watched the carpet dance for hours, but there was no time to spare. There were Flaming Lips to be watched.

The hotel lobby was packed full of people, and I did my best to act natural, which was next to impossible. The only thing I can compare it to is being an extra in a movie. A few years later, in my early twenties, I would pick up work as a background actor to make a little cash, and I was consistently horrible at it. Let's say the scene was at Starbucks and I was supposed to put sugar in my coffee. A totally normal action that I do every day, right? Well, as soon as that director would yell, "Action!" I would forget how to act like a human. I would pick up the sugar and look at it like a caveman seeing fire for the first time. Super casual.

This is how I was acting in the lobby, *trying* to remember how to walk normally—a function I have performed since I was eight months old (#talentedbaby #dontbejealous). At one point I said out loud, "I am walking through the lobby right now." Awkward or not, I strutted all the way through that lobby in my floor-length tan suede coat. You see, this was the winter that I decided to dress exclusively like Kate Hudson in *Almost Famous*. I'm talking bohemian blouses, long skirts, and those long suede coats with the fur trim. That was my uniform. I felt super Penny Lane, except that my fur was faux and I hadn't nabbed it from a rock star boyfriend. Mine was from T.J.Maxx. Ain't no shame in my money-saving game.

We miraculously got to the Garden and regrouped our brains before heading in. Tickets? Check. ID? Check. Possible oncoming stroke? Check. Wait, what? Am I having a stroke? I definitely smell something burning, which is a known sign of an oncoming stroke.

"Does anyone else smell burning?" They just laughed and pointed at me. *Oh my god. I'm having a stroke. I have an allergy to mushrooms and the side effect is strokes.* Just as I was about to call 9-1-1, Melissa brought me back to reality. "Mametown, chill. You aren't having a stroke. You just lit yourself on fire." *Phew, I just— what the fuck!* I looked down and from the way I was holding my cigarette, I'd just straight-up set my fur trim on fire. Cut to me rolling around on the corner of Thirty-third and Eighth. So much for keeping a low profile.

We made it to the show with a few minutes to spare, taking that time to buy beers the size of our heads. And thank God they were huge, because we basically all had to take out second mortgages to buy them. Just as we were about to head to our seats, Hayley stopped us.

"Shall we?" she asked, pulling out three shiny chocolates from her coat pocket. You would've thought they were the last Willy Wonka golden tickets, judging from the squeals we let out. We jumped up and down as our sacred Bud Lights spilled all over us. But in a moment of clarity, we decided it was necessary to play it cool and eat them in the bathroom, as if anyone could tell what they were. Obviously the smartest choice for us was to wait in line, then all go into the handicap stall together. Not at all suspicious.

Now, I had never been to a Flaming Lips show before, but I had seen one on TV. Massive balloons bounce around the audience. Beautiful projections are displayed in time with the music. Wayne, the front man, even walks over the audience in a giant bubble ball like a hamster. It's a sight to see even if you're stone-cold sober. And at this point (let's be honest) I was, in fact, "tripping ballz."

So, there we were. The entire spectacle was happening all around us. They played "Do You Realize??" with a huge time-lapsed sunset projected behind them. The three of us had our arms around each other and swayed to the music. I looked to my right at Hayley and saw a single tear running down her cheek.

They played a few more songs as we danced awkwardly, and then it was time for the big New Year's Eve countdown. The entire arena shouted together—a little too early, if you ask me.

Twenty! Nineteen! Eighteen!

Who starts counting down at twenty? It's like being at a surprise party and hiding when the birthday boy leaves the office five miles away. My knees are way too fucked up to be crouching that long. Just as we were rounding single digits in the countdown, a random teenage boy approached us.

"Excuse me. I know this is super dumb but I'm here with my sister and have no one to kiss at midnight. I was wondering if—"

Before Hayley and Melissa had the chance to tell him to fuck off, I screamed, "Get on in this chick gumbo!" then grabbed all of their faces for an ~~awkward~~ epic four-way kiss as the clock struck midnight.

The cutie, taken back, mumbled thank you and walked away with a smile from ear to ear. It was magical. We listened to a few more songs while repeatedly being yelled at by ushers to not dance in the aisles, then decided to peace out before it ended.

We stopped outside, as I lit a cigarette. "Chick gumbo? Mamie, what the hell is chick gumbo?" Hayley asked.

I shrugged. "No idea. But we gave that kid a story. And hopefully he didn't give us herpes." I took a long drag off my cigarette, celebrating the fact that I could still crack a joke despite having crazy brain.

"Umm, Mametown?" Melissa said. "Hate to interrupt but you are on fire again."

I wasn't falling for it. "Yeah, right. Like that would ever happen twice."

She went on. "If you aren't on fire, what's that smell, then?" Sonofabitch. I smelled it too. Sure enough, I looked down to see my fur trim blazing again, and I proceeded to stop, drop, and roll. My signature move of the night.

Once I was completely extinguished, we embarked on our journey back to the hotel. Yes, it was only one block away. But seriously, when you are on mushrooms, tying your shoe can turn into a two-hour adventure. I distinctly remember asking a horse cop what breed his ride was, to which he replied, "Horse." To which I replied, "A little, but only because I was screaming at the concert 'cause of all the mushrooms."

As we entered the lobby, I reminded my friends, "Be cool." Meanwhile, my jacket was still lightly smoking. (Ahh! A smoking jacket! I wish I would've made that pun that night. Guess I'll have to wait till the next time I set myself on fire.) We made it through the sea of bitches in sequins and squeezed into the elevator as it was closing.

There were three guys already in the elevator, and we lined up in front of them. It was dead silent. Now, elevators are always awkward. That's a given. Whenever I am in an elevator with one other person, it doesn't matter if it's a hot UPS deliveryman or an old lady with three poodles, I always picture us making out as the doors close. This is the kind of fucked-up mentality you develop when you watch too many romantic comedies. I also think that most women meet their dream man by being clumsy, and anything can be solved with a dance montage. Thanks a lot, Cameron Diaz!

As soon as I heard the ding of the elevator doors closing, I visualized a three-on-three make-out session and couldn't stop giggling.

The rest of the elevator was completely silent, which made me giggle even more. I briefly considered asking the guys if they wanted some chick gumbo, but I decided against it (thank *gawd*). Even imagining asking them made me laugh even harder, but with my mouth closed. I felt like a kid in church who has heard someone fart. You want to crack up but you know your mom will slap you. My cheeks went flush.

"I am burning the fuck up in here—anybody else?" I asked, hoping to break the awkwardness.

"Maybe you're on fire again," Hayley replied matter-of-factly.

I looked down earnestly to make sure. "Nope. I'm good." This elicited zero reaction from the guys behind us. Nada.

Finally we reached our floor, and immediately fell out of the elevator and lost our shit. I'm talking, on the floor, army-crawling while laughing. I was laughing so hard that I started to pee my pants, which made me laugh even harder.

"I just peed my fucking paaaaants!" I exclaimed.

"Then take them off!" one of the girls yelled.

Take them off? Brilliant. The girls started chanting, "Take it off! Take it off!" as I got down to my bra and panties. That's when I noticed the carpet again.

"It really does look like it's dancing," I said in awe.

"It's fucking beautiful," Melissa added. Then, as if on cue, we began singing "Do You Realize??" to the carpet, swaying back and forth as I stood in my skivvies. By the time we got to the second verse and Hayley's single tear started making its encore appearance, someone cleared his throat.

We looked behind us to see the three dudes from the elevator. "Ummm, excuse us." They had seen the entire thing, and they were not at all amused. Which, calm down, three dudes, it's NYE in NYC. Like, don't go to New Orleans on Fat Tuesday to check out the ironwork. They scooted past us, hugging the wall like they were on the edge of a building. Granted, we looked like rejects from a Hunter S. Thompson–themed strip club.

I picked up my pants and we booked it down the hall and into our room. "*Guyz*, I have a brilliant idea," I said as Melissa and Hayley lay on the bed plotting how to get food to the room without having to leave the bed. "Why don't we fill up the tub with all that shitty champagne we brought? We can ring in the New Year bathing in champagne. That's gotta be good luck or some shit."

I didn't even wait for their reaction before I began unwrapping the foil off the bottles. I was ready to get *fancy*. Bathing in champagne sounded like something Marie Antoinette would do. That, and have crazy hair, and insist people eat cake. I could get on board with that.

One by one, I dumped the champagne bottles, excited for such a lavish nightcap. I called to the girls to come in. "You ready for luxury?" I asked as the last of the bubbly poured into the tub. They looked at my masterpiece for a few seconds, then Melissa spoke.

"That's, like, four inches deep." And she was right. All that champagne, all those bottles combined, only added up to a few yellowish inches. A few *unimpressive* yellowish inches. It looked like a toddler's bath after he'd taken a whiz in it. Hayley and Melissa went back to the bedroom to continue their mission for snacks. I'm telling you, when you are on mushrooms even the simplest tasks feel like an adventure. Them talking about how to get pizza sounded like a plot to take down the Soviet Army.

"Y'all are missing out!" I shouted as I peeled off my panties and lowered myself into the cold tub. I'm going to be honest with you, dear readers. It wasn't the most comfortable experience. I wouldn't recommend it at all, actually. It was cold as shit, and the bubbles didn't so much tickle my skin as they made my crotch burn. But in that moment, I didn't care. I wanted to remember this New Year's Eve, with its music and its adventure. All that setting myself on fire had turned me into a phoenix rising from the ashes. I sat in that shallow champagne birdbath and thought to myself, *This year is going to be good. I can feel it. . . . Or maybe that's the mushrooms talking.*

ACKNOWLEDGMENTS

I have so many people to thank, or "give props to," as the kids say, for helping this book become a real thing.

First and foremost I want to thank my Internet peoples. You know who you are. The views, the gifs, the comments, the seats at live shows, and the general positive energy you throw my way daily is so very appreciated. Y'all are the raddest group to have backing me up, and I want you to raise both hands right now and high-five yourself. . . . Do it. . . . I'll wait. . . .

My friends. Maegan, Melissa, Hayley, Ashleigh, Erika, Joselyn, and Kirby for letting me share stories about them and also making sure that I survived those moments in real life! Everyone thinks their friends are the shit, but mine really are, and I am forever grateful to them for accepting and even encouraging my crazy.

A special friends shout-out to Hannah and Grace. You guys are as supportive as you are inspiring. I really won the ultimate scratch off of friendship, and I am going to stop because I know how Grace feels about sincerity. Y'all are my bras to the titties of life. #ohhohhhpartygirl

My family for allowing me to share a peek into the unique freakness that is us. Mom, Dad, Anne, Dave, and Annie. Although I can't remember if I actually got permission, so I am going to keep things moving. . . .

ACKNOWLEDGMENTS

Extra huge thank-you to Keal for being my number one across the board in all categories. BFF, BF, BB (Beanz Butler). Thank you for always having my back when I need you, and refilling my wine when I REALLY need you. xo

My team. Vincent, CC, Cait, for putting so much time and trust into a woman who makes the majority of her living off taint jokes.

My editor, Kate Napolitano, for always being on the same wave length and for not only letting me let it all hang out in this first book, but always telling me to "Mamrie-ify" it.

And finally, BEANZ HART. Yes, I am thanking my dog. You might say dogs can't read and this is pointless and I say, FUCK OFF. Beanz, thank you for accompanying me on all my writing retreats to Palm Springs and always being super stoked when you see me even if I've only been gone for five minutes.